D0500064

Ethical Practice in Psychology

"This important book chronicles the development of the 2007 APS Code of Ethics, analyses key aspects of the extensive developmental process that underlies the Code, and explores the principles that have fashioned its content. It will substantially enhance both ethical understanding of the contemporary practice of psychology and the basis for ongoing regulation of psychologists."

Dr Ian Freckelton, SC, Professor of Law, Forensic Psychology and Forensic Medicine, Monash University, Australia

Ethical Practice in Psychology

Reflections from the creators of the APS Code of Ethics

Edited by Alfred Allan and Anthony Love

A John Wiley & Sons, Ltd., Publication

This edition first published 2010
© 2010 John Wiley & Sons Ltd.

Code of Ethics in Appendix
© The Australian Psychological Society Limited

Wiley-Blackwell is an imprint of John Wiley & Sons, formed by the merger of Wiley's global
Scientific, Technical, and Medical business with Blackwell Publishing.

Registered Office
John Wiley & Sons Ltd, The Atrium, Southern Gate, Chichester, West Sussex, PO19 8SQ, UK

Editorial Offices
The Atrium, Southern Gate, Chichester, West Sussex, PO19 8SQ, UK
9600 Garsington Road, Oxford, OX4 2DQ, UK

350 Main Street, Malden, MA 02148-5020, USA

For details of our global editorial offices, for customer services, and for information about how
to apply for permission to reuse the copyright material in this book please see our website at
www.wiley.com/wiley-blackwell.

Library of Congress Cataloging-in-Publication Data

Ethical practice in psychology : reflections from the creators of the APS Code of Ethics / edited
by Alfred Allan and Anthony Love.
     p. cm.
   Includes bibliographical references and index.
   ISBN 978-0-470-68365-1 (pbk.)
   1. Psychologists–Professional ethics.   2. Professional ethics.   I. Allan, Alfred.   II. Love, A.
(Anthony), 1950–
    BF76.4.E818 2010
    174′.915–dc22

                                   2009043697

A catalogue record for this book is available from the British Library.

Set in 10 on 12 pt Minion by Toppan Best-set Premedia Limited
Printed and bound in Singapore by Fabulous Printers Pte Ltd

1   2010

Contents

List of Tables

Notes on Contributors

Alfred Allan, LLB PhD, is Professor of Psychology at Edith Cowan University, Australia. He is a member of the inaugural Psychology Board of Australia, the former Chair of the Ethics Committee of the Australian Psychological Society (APS), a former member of the Ethical Guidelines Committee of the APS and a former Chair of the Ethics Committee of the Psychological Society of South Africa. He is a member of a number of Institutional Ethics and Disciplinary Committees. He is the author of two books on ethics and law in psychological practice.

David Collier is currently the Chief Executive Officer of the Australian Institute of Radiography and is the former Chief Executive Officer of the Psychologists Registration Board of Victoria, a position he held for five years. In this role he was intimately involved in the registration of psychologists and the investigation and adjudication of complaints. He is also a former chair of the Council of Psychologists Registration Boards of Australasia.

Graham R. Davidson, PhD, is an Emeritus Professor of Central Queensland University, where he was Foundation Professor of Psychology from 1997–2004, writing and teaching in the areas of research and professional ethics. He is a Fellow of the Australian Psychological Society and has served as Chair of the APS Ethics Committee, a Member of the APS Ethical Guidelines Advisory Group, Editor of the *Australian Psychologist*, and as APS Director of Communications and APS Director of Social Issues. He has also served on the Northern Territory Psychologists Registration Board and the Queensland Psychologists Board.

Anthony W. Love, BA (Hons), MA (Clin Psych), Dip Ed (Tert), PhD, is Professor of Psychology at the University of Ballarat. He is deeply interested in the ethics of psychological practice and has been a member of a number of Institutional research ethics committees as well as the Ethics Committee of the Australian Psychological Society. He teaches ethics and has done so to students at all levels, from first year through to professional doctorate, as he is a firm supporter of the value of integrating ethics across all areas of psychological curricula.

Sabine Hammond, PhD, is Associate Professor and Head of the national School of Psychology at the Australian Catholic University. She is a former member of the Ethics Committee of the Australian Psychological Society and has served as a member of the Psychologists Registration Board of Victoria since 2004.

Marie R. Joyce, PhD, is a Visiting Senior Research Fellow in the Quality of Life and Social Justice Flagship at Australian Catholic University in Melbourne, Australia. She is a practising Clinical Psychologist in the State of Victoria, a Fellow of the Australian Psychological Society (APS) and is the current Chair of the Ethical Guidelines Committee of the APS. She is a former Chair of the APS Ethics Committee and has served as Chair of her university institutional research ethics committee.

Mick Symons, BA (Hons), BEd (Counselling), MA, joined the National Office of the Australian Psychological Society (APS) 10 years ago and is currently the Manager Member Services. In this capacity he is intimately involved in the administration of ethics by the APS and plays a pivotal role in the functioning of the Ethical Guidelines Committee of the APS, which creates and revises ethical guidelines, and the Ethics Committee. He is also the author of a number of publications on professional issues and ethics in publications of the APS.

Donald M. Thomson, BA, LLB, MA, PhD, is Honorary Professor, Centre for the Mind, The University of Sydney, and Adjunct Professor, Sellinger Centre, School of Law and Justice, Edith Cowan University. He was Foundation Professor of Psychology at Charles Sturt University and Edith Cowan University, and was a barrister at the Victorian Bar. He is a former Chairman of the Victorian Psychological Council and a former President of the Victorian Psychologists Registration Board and a Fellow of the Australian Psychological Society.

William Warren, BA (Hons), MA, M Psych (Clin), PhD, Dip Law (LPAB), is a Conjoint Associate Professor in the University of Newcastle, Australia. He is a Fellow of the Australian Psychological Society, a member of the Clinical and Forensic Colleges and is presently Chair of the Ethics Committee. A member of the NSW Psychologists Registration Board since 1998, he has been in part-time private practice and held an honorary appointment at the HNEAHS Centre for Psychotherapy since 1980.

Foreword

A hallmark of any profession is its ability to be self-regulating. Members of a profession agree on standards of practice that can be expected of them all and resolve to adhere to those standards in their everyday professional activities. As a result, the clients, the public, the government, and other members can be assured of the quality of services provided by individual members of that profession. The standards of a particular profession are usually encapsulated in documents such as codes of ethics. The Australian Psychological Society (APS), since its inception, has prided itself in the standards of excellence its members set themselves and their demonstrated capacity to be a self-governing, socially responsible profession. Its practice standards are captured in the APS Code of Ethics and the accompanying Ethical Guidelines, both of which are updated and revised on a regular basis. The previous update of the Code of Ethics took place in 1997 and several minor amendments have been incorporated since then, culminating in the version published in 2003.

We live in a time of rapid change, however, and the Code can become outdated. Every decade or so, it becomes necessary to revisit the Code and scrutinize it thoroughly. Developments in practice, in community standards, in the legal context, in the scope of psychological practice and in the profile of the Society's members are some of the changes that necessitate a close examination of the assumptions, the form, and the content of the Code, to ensure it can reflect the standards and aspirations of the Society into the foreseeable future. In 2006, major shifts in the Australian cultural context had occurred or were appearing on the horizon, particularly in relation to health care and the role that psychologists play in health care delivery. The APS recognized that it was time for another careful examination, from first principles, of the existing Code to establish what changes, if any, would be required. It initiated the arduous process of drafting, consulting with constituents, and careful revision required to produce a new Code befitting the APS, its members and the community.

The APS Board charged a small Working Group, appointing Professor Alfred Allan as Convenor, to undertake this extremely important task. Professor Allan was ably suited to the task. He was the then Chair of the Ethics Committee of the APS, bringing a wealth of relevant experience to its deliberations; he had outstanding credentials as both a psychologist and a lawyer, providing the scholarly and professional leadership needed to guide its activities; and, most importantly, he had the personal attributes, the consultative skills and the collegiate relationships with other members to ensure its processes were both open and inclusive, yet focused on task completion within the tight time frame imposed on the Working Group.

Under Professor Allan's guidance, the expert Working Group members, Dr Elizabeth Allworth, Professor Graham Davidson, Associate Professor Sabine Hammond, Dr Marie Joyce, Professor Anthony Love, Mr Malcolm MacKenzie, Professor Donald Thomson, Associate Professor William Warren and Dr Jack White, together with Mr Mick Symons, Manager of Member Services of the APS, toiled long and hard to discharge their collective task. They were joined by David Collier, who was then the Chief Executive Officer and Registrar of the Psychologists Registration Board of Victoria, who was the representative of the Council of Psychologists Registration Boards of Australasia.

Many others were consulted and they contributed on an ad hoc basis. The Working Party spent many hours debating, discussing, researching and drafting the initial version before distributing it to APS members for consultation and comment. After several rounds of consultation with key informants and bodies within the Society and with other stakeholders in the profession, they then carefully redrafted the document, ensuring at all times that the new version would perform in real life as well as it promised to do on paper. It was with great satisfaction that they witnessed the endorsement and adoption of the new Code of Ethics by members of the APS in August 2007 and the release of the eighth edition of the Ethical Guidelines, revised to reflect the new Code's contents, in August 2008.

This book documents the complex and demanding process undertaken by the Working Party. The separate chapters are written by various members, highlighting the breadth of knowledge and depth of experience they brought to their collective task, and capturing the thinking and reflection that was undertaken to produce the final version of the new Code. It provides insight into the basis of ethical reasoning, judgement and decision-making of some of the leading lights in the field of psychology and ethics in the Australian context.

Their diversity and heterogeneity reflects the membership of that community. Their ability to reconcile and integrate these diverse views is a testament to their respect for, and acceptance of, each others' views. The text is an invaluable document of this enterprise. It will be of interest and benefit to anyone seeking a deeper understanding of the ethical framework that guides members of the APS as we head towards the second decade of the twenty-first century.

Professor Lyn Littlefield, OAM
Executive Director, Australian Psychological Society.
Melbourne, May 2009

Preface

This book has its origins in a project to create a new Code of Ethics for the Australian Psychological Society (APS). The chapters are written by members of the Working Group (Group) that reviewed the 1997 Code of Ethics, and they reflect the research that the authors undertook in preparation for, during and after the review. As the members of the Group found the review process very stimulating and felt that their knowledge of ethics in general, and ethical codes in particular, had grown during the process, they decided to share their research findings and insights with a broader audience.

The authors' aim is to capture aspects of the review process as well as we can, describe problems we experienced, provide explanations for some of our decisions and engage in an examination of the final product. We trust that this book will serve as a valuable resource on professional ethics and a chronicle of an important event in the history of the APS. We believe that as a historical document, this book can serve as a guide to the members of future committees who review the APS, and other, ethics codes.

The contributions have been peer reviewed. The opinions stated by the respective authors do not necessarily represent the official view of the APS or that of other contributors to this book.

We acknowledge the insights of members of the Group who did not write chapters yet contributed to the work. Elizabeth Allworth, for instance, made noteworthy contributions in respect of organizations and systems; Jack White contributed in relation to forensic psychology and Lyn Littlefield in respect of international trends in professional ethics. We in particular acknowledge the invaluable support we received from Graham Davidson, Lyn Littlefield, Nicholas Voudouris and Vicky Mrowinski. We also thank the staff of the publishers, Wiley-Blackwell, who were involved in the production of the book, in particular Darren Reed.

Alfred Allan and Anthony W. Love

Chapter 1
Introduction

Alfred Allan

The historical roots of professional codes of ethics can be traced back to the Hippocratic Code nearly 2,500 years ago. The first known ethics code for psychologists was adopted by the Consulting Psychologists Association in America in 1933 (Dunbar, 1990 cited by Louw, 1997a). The atrocities committed by Nazi and Japanese health professions during the Second World War and the emergence of psychology as a profession after the War provided impetus to national professional psychological bodies to prepare ethical codes of their own. In Australia, the Australian Branch of the British Psychological Society (BPS) adopted the Code of Professional Ethics (British Psychological Society [Australian Branch], 1949) that was based on a code from Minnesota, in 1949 (Cooke, 2000). At the time, this placed the precursor of the Australian Psychological Society (APS), which was formed in 1944, ahead of other national professional psychological bodies. For example, the American Psychological Association's (APA) first ethics code was published in 1953 and, according to Louw (1997a), this code was adopted with few changes by professional associations in other countries such as South Africa (1955), the Netherlands (1960) and Canada (1962). The BPS only published its ethical principles in 1983.

In the nearly 60 years since 1949 the Australian Code (which at times was called the Code of Professional Conduct) has evolved but retained certain unique features (discussed below) that made it distinctive when compared with other codes. Most of the changes to the Code were made during major reviews in 1960, 1968, 1986 and 1997, but amendments were also made periodically between these reviews.

The first Code of Professional Ethics was a relatively short document with an emphasis on the responsibilities of psychologists to act in the interests of their clients, other interested parties, members of the profession, colleagues, and the community. Although the authors of the 1949 Code did not explicitly use the word *principle,* the Responsibility principle was clearly visible, as was the Nonmaleficence principle, for instance, when the authors reminded psychologists that they were "responsible for a high degree of professional competence" (Cooke, 2000, p. 112). The tone of the document was generally descriptive rather than prescriptive and the term *psychologist* was consistently used in it.

At the Annual General Meeting in 1956 the members instructed the Executive to "enquire into the working of the Code" (British Psychological Society [Australian Branch], 1960, p. 1). This group for the first time referred to general principles in the 1960 Code of Professional Conduct but the general principles were not clearly articulated. The authors of the 1960 Code also used the word *principle,* but in the sense that the authors of later codes used the word *standard.* For instance, principle 13 of section B provided that "[I]t is unethical practice to give or receive any form of commission or other remuneration for referral of clients for professional services". Compared to the 1949 Code, provisions regarding research and teaching were more prominent in the 1960 Code. The 1960 Code was a comprehensive document of 35 pages consisting of an introduction, 10 sections of principles, and two appendices. An addendum and a circular explaining the procedures to be followed in cases of complaints or criticism were later added to the 1960 Code. The authors of the 1960 Code used the word *psychologist* and prescriptive language, which they explained in the following fashion:

> *The principles contained in this Code are formulated in terms which denote varying degrees of obligation. Members will find that the most vital principles are the most strongly expressed, in terms such as "must", "it is obligatory", etc., indicating that strict observance of such principles is binding on members.* (p. 1)

On 21 August 1968 the APS, then a professional body in its own right, adopted a Code of Professional Conduct that was published in the *Australian Psychologist* two years later (Australian Psychological Society, 1970). The authors of the 1968 Code continued using prescriptive language and replaced the word *psychologist* with *member,* except in the general principles section. This Code has the structure that was used until 2007, namely a statement of general principles followed by sections of standards. The 1968 Code had eight sections of standards and also three appendices that, for instance, dealt with issues such as the employment of unqualified persons in psychological practice. It also had an *Advice to members* section, which contained advice such as:

> *Members should strive to attain the highest degree of professional competency and integrity in the application of psychological knowledge and techniques.*

In 1976 the Annual General Meeting appointed a working party to inquire into the ethics of psychological practice and research (Cooke, 2000). This working group tried to improve the face validity of the Code by "asking psychologists to give examples of the kinds of things they thought were unethical" (Cooke, 2000, p. 190). The authors of the 1986 Code of Professional Conduct (Australian Psychological Society, 1986) formulated the three general principles that are also found in the 1997 Code of Ethics (Australian Psychological Society, 1997), namely, Responsibility, Competence and Propriety. The 1986 Code further consisted of seven sections of standards and five appendices. Appendix D, for instance, provided guidelines for the ethical use of aversive therapeutic procedures. The word *psychologist* is consistently used in this Code.

A major reorganization of the APS took place in the mid-nineties and in this process the Code was also reviewed. The new Code was adopted on 4 October 1997 and had the same structure (three general principles and eight sections of standards) and, to a large extent, the same content as the 1986 Code. There were, however, important changes, such as the insertion of standard B.10, which proscribes sexual relationships between psychologists and their former clients for two years. In standard B.11 the authors provided the criteria that would be applied to determine whether sexual relationships between a psychologist and clients that they engage in after two years are unethical. One notable omission from the 1997 Code were the appendices of the 1986 Code, with the exception of the procedure for persons considering involving any section of the Code. Most of the material in the omitted appendices was incorporated in the Guidelines the APS started formulating and eventually published in 1994. In the preface the authors of the 1997 Code referred users to these Guidelines and explained that they were meant to clarify and amplify the application of the principles established in the Code and to facilitate their interpretation. The first collection of the Guidelines was published in 1998. The original version of the 1997 Code used the word *psychologist* throughout, but it was replaced with the word *member* on 2 October 1999. This amendment was made in response to a concern expressed at the meeting of the Trans Tasman Council of Psychologist Registration Boards held in Canberra on 28–29 September 1998 regarding the use (and definition) of the word *psychologist* in the 1997 Code as originally adopted by the APS. This concern stemmed from the fact that the use of the title psychologist is regulated in all the States and Territories.

It is a function of the APS Ethics Committee to reassess regularly the APS Code to ensure that it maintains face validity and remains relevant (Garton, 2004; Sinclair, Poizner, Gilmour-Barrett, & Randall, 1987) and functional (Louw, 1997a, 1997b). The process of calibration is necessary because of the continued evolution of the APS and changes in community standards, the law, and professional structures and practices in Australia and internationally. These routine reassessments led to minor amendments to the 1997 Code in 1999, 2002 and 2003. At its first meeting on 24 November 2004, the 2004–2005 Ethics Committee, however, identified a range of factors that indicated the need for a more comprehensive review of the Code. The most important of these factors will be discussed next.

As the historical overview above demonstrates, a feature of the APS Code had been its evolutionary development which, especially since 1986, had mostly involved piecemeal amendments without a major review. An advantage of this approach was that the Code was familiar to members of the APS and that the standards had face value. As will, nevertheless, be discussed in greater detail by Allan and Symons in Chapter 2, some users of the 1997 Code did note aspects of the Code that were affecting its functionality. There had also been developments in the theory and practice of applied ethics that were not necessarily reflected in the extant Code.

As an organization the APS had also evolved considerably, especially since the mid-nineties, and though the Code was revised at the same time, some of the ramifications of these organizational changes manifested only later and were therefore not considered when the revision took place. Whilst these deliberations were taking place the APS was also embarking on a governance review that led to the restructuring of the Board of Directors and a revising of the functions of the directors.

Nationally, the turn of the century saw important changes to legislation that impacted on professional practice of Australian psychologists, such as the amendments to privacy legislation (Privacy Act, 1988) in 2001. Despite the differences between law and ethics, there is a close relationship between legislation and the content of codes (Tomaszewski, 1979), and codes are a vehicle to educate psychologists about the law. It is therefore essential that ethical codes should be updated regularly to ensure that they reflect the law of the jurisdiction in which they apply.

Whilst the APS Code will always have a national identity because it reflects the law, community attitudes and culture of Australia, the APS must also be cognizant of professional developments at an international level because psychologists across the world face common ethical problems and share common ethical principles (Tomaszewski, 1979). An important development at a geopolitical level in recent times has been globalization, and specifically the closer collaboration of countries at regional levels, as demonstrated by the expansion and consolidation of the European Union and the signing of the North American Free Trade Agreement. One corollary of these accords is that national professional bodies in countries that are signatories are encouraged, if not compelled, to develop common standards. In Europe this had led to the acceptance of a meta-code of ethics by the European Federation of Psychologists Associations (EFPA[1], 1995) at its general assembly in 1995 and the Trilateral Forum on Psychology, Education, Practice, and Credentialing (Bailey, 2004) is working on a meta-code for North America (Edwards, 2000). Australia has likewise entered into a free trade agreement with Singapore (2003), Thailand (2005) the United States of America (2005) and was, at the time the Ethics Committee was considering the review, negotiating such agreements with other countries.

Psychologists themselves have also realized that they should consider identifying and, if necessary, developing international ethical standards. One aspect is that careers are now very portable and working overseas for at least a short period of one's career is more likely to become typical of psychologists in the twenty-first century. Another factor that drives this idea is technological developments, where the Internet and other forms of telecommunication for instance, are changing the way in which psychologists provide services to clients and make it possible for them to provide services across national boundaries (Allan, 2008). An ad hoc joint committee of the International Union of Psychological Science and the International Association of Applied Psychology have therefore commenced formulating a Universal Declaration of Ethical Principles for psychologists (Ad Hoc Joint Committee, 2005; Gauthier, 2004). Meta-codes are unlikely to replace national codes of ethics, but no professional body that is reviewing a code can ignore them.

Members of the Ethics Committee also noted that a number of codes, and in particular the New Zealand Code (New Zealand Psychological Society, 2002) and the Code of the South African Professional Board for Psychology (Professional Board for Psychology, 2002) explicitly referred to the human rights of people. The advantage of doing this is that it would provide the APS and its members with a broader norm system that could guide their ethical decision-making in areas not covered by the Code. The importance of having such a broader referral system became apparent during the debate in and around the American Psychological Association's handling of criticism against their members' activities during the Gulf War and after it in military prisons such as the one on Guantanamo Bay (Behnke, 2006; Miles, 2007; Olson, Soldz, & Davis, 2008).

A set of issues that led to much discussion amongst Ethics Committee members was the relationship between the APS and the Registration Boards[2],

---

[1] The body has since been renamed the European Federation of Psychological Associations. The EFPA adopted a revised code in Granada, Spain in 2005 (European Federation of Psychologists Associations, 2005).

[2] At the time of these discussions there were rumours that the registration of health professionals in Australia was about to be reviewed. In December 2005 the Productivity Commission (2005) in its Australia's Health Workplace report recommended the

the role of the APS and therefore the Ethics Committee, in the regulation of APS members, and the use of the APS Code by Registration Boards, tribunals and courts. The regulation of psychology as a profession consists of three functions, namely the accreditation of training programs, the registration of psychologists and the disciplining of errant psychologists. Whilst the APS has never played a role in the registration of psychologists, it has played a major role in the accreditation of psychological training programs and the disciplining of its members. The APS's influence in both these areas has, however, been eroded since the establishment of the State and Territory Registration Boards (Registrations Boards) starting with Victoria in 1966 (Cooke, 2000).

In the case of accreditation, the establishment of the Australian Branch was in part driven to ensure that psychologists in Australia conformed to high academic standards (Cooke, 2000). In 1972 the APS established two accreditation committees, one for courses leading to associate membership and the other for post-graduate courses leading to full membership. These two committees were later consolidated as the Course Development and Accreditation Committee (CDAC) to decide which courses would be recognized by the APS as sufficient for membership. In subsequent years the Registration Boards have entered the field and this led to the formation of the Australian Psychological Accreditation Council (APAC) in 2003, consisting of representatives of the APS, the Registration Boards and the Heads of Departments and Schools of Psychology Association (HODSPA).

The erosion of the APS's regulatory role can also be seen in the case of the disciplinary function. Until the formation of the Registration Boards, starting in the middle 1960s, the APS's disciplinary functions took place at two levels. At an internal level it governed the interaction between its members to ensure order and solidarity amongst them. This internal disciplinary function of the APS is still intact and is unlikely to change. At an external level the APS acted against members whose negligent or unscrupulous behaviour could harm members of the public and tarnish the public image of the society and psychologists. This external disciplinary role of the APS has to a large extent, but not totally, been taken over by the Registration Boards.

The APS, to start with, retains an external disciplinary role because the National Competition Policy that was implemented in the 1990s requires the

formation of a Registration Board covering all health professions that would take over the accreditation of education programs and the registration and regulation of practitioners at a national level. This was put on the agenda of the Council of Australian Governments (COAG), but in 2007 the proposal was changed to nine separate national boards, including one for psychologists. At the time of writing it appears as if this national registration board will become a reality on 1 July 2010 (Council of Australian Governments [COAG], 2008) and will consist of 10 national boards.

Registration Boards to primarily focus on the protection of the public and the fostering of professional competition (Crook, 2004). An implication of this narrow focus on the protection of the public is that Registration Boards formulate and enforce minimum *standards of conduct* for psychologists. Therefore, behaviour that many psychologists would consider to be unacceptable will not incur the sanction of Registration Boards because it does not raise a significant issue of public health or safety. Professional bodies like the APS, in contrast, are obliged to articulate and enforce higher *ethical standards* for the profession. For example, a Registration Board recently refused to consider a matter where a psychologist had, in a forensic report, commented about the psychological characteristics of a person who the psychologist had not assessed because it ruled that the behaviour did not raise a significant issue of public health or safety. This decision may be correct from the perspective of a Registration Board; however, this is behaviour many psychologists will consider to be unethical and is proscribed in principle VI(H) of the speciality guidelines for forensic psychologists of the American Psychology-Law Society (Committee on Ethical Guidelines for Forensic Psychologists, 1991) and clause 7.3 of the South African Code (Professional Board for Psychology, 2002).

The Ethics Committee must, furthermore, discipline members whose negligent or unscrupulous behaviour could harm members of the public and tarnish its public image or that of psychologists, even though the matter may already have been dealt with by the relevant Registration Board. There are three reasons for this. Firstly, no professional organization can be perceived to condone the behaviour of a member who is seen as a danger to the public. The APS, secondly, provides a referral service to members of the public seeking the services of a psychologist and it could be argued that by providing the names of members to potential clients the APS implicitly represents the members as competent and ethical practitioners. There is therefore a high likelihood that referred clients who believe that they may have been wrongfully harmed by members could sue the APS. The APS must therefore have a system of monitoring and regulating the professional behaviour of its members. The APS, thirdly, uses its group purchasing power to negotiate group professional indemnity insurance for participating members. As the premiums members pay are influenced by the insurance claims made against members, it is important for the APS and its members to ensure that the professional behaviour of all members is of such a standard that it will not attract claims from aggrieved clients.

Nevertheless, the disciplining of psychologists is the primary responsibility of the Registration Boards and therefore the Council of Psychologist Registration Boards (CPRB) and the APS have agreed that the Ethics Committee will refer all complaints against members to the applicable Registration Board, with the exceptions of complaints by members against each other that do not involve the public. When they refer complainants to Registration Boards, the APS invites them to resubmit complaints to the APS once they have been dealt with by the relevant Registration Board or if it refuses to deal with the matter. The Registration Boards also occasionally refer matters to the APS out of their own accord.

Despite the decline of the APS's role as a disciplinary body, its Code has maintained a prominent position and is seen by the Registration Boards and Courts (*Psychologist Registration Board v Robinson*, 2004) as the primary indicator of acceptable professional conduct among Australian psychologists. It is also very likely that civil courts may, if they have not yet done so, use the APS Code to determine the standard of conduct that is expected of psychologists. The Ethics Committee welcomed this general acceptance of the APS Code because it is clearly not in the interest of the profession to have a proliferation of ethical codes for psychologists which are expensive to draft and could lead to disparate, or apparently disparate, standards. This may confuse both psychologists and members of the public. The Ethics Committee further noted that the legislation in some states and territories currently requires some Registration Boards to refer serious disciplinary matters to administrative tribunals where they will be adjudicated by lawyers. This has two important implications. To start with, the experience in Canada demonstrated that a code will maintain its status as a regulatory document in such a forum only if its provisions are enforceable (Dobson & Breault, 1998). Furthermore, the code must make a clear distinction between enforceable minimum behavioural standards and aspirational standards on the one hand, and practice guidelines on the other hand.

After considering all these factors, the Ethics Committee decided on 21 January 2005 to recommend to the Board of Directors that the Code should be reviewed. In response the Board of Directors appointed a Code Review Working Group (Group) in April 2005 which engaged in a process of research, in-depth deliberation, and consultations with members, other stakeholders and other knowledgeable people that are described more fully by Allan and Symons in Chapter 2. The first face-to-face meeting of the Group was a roundtable discussion on 16 and 17 February 2006 and many of the chapters in this book evolved from working papers presented on this occasion.

A glimpse of the research that preceded the review of the 1997 Code can be found in Chapter 3, where Alfred Allan firstly recorded the material he presented at the roundtable in which he explored the function of codes of ethics and the functionality of the 1997 Code. In the latter part of the chapter he indicates how the Group in response tried to improve the functionality of the 2007 Code. Chapter 4 by William Warren is also based on material he presented at the roundtable in which he critically and provocatively examined the multiplicity of codes that regulate the behaviour of psychologists and questioned whether a comprehensive review of the 1997 Code was required. In Chapter 4 he examines how the Group tried to address some of the matters he raised in his presentation and also reflects on some of the philosophical issues that emerged during the deliberations of the Group.

A major stakeholder that was directly involved in the review process was the CPRB; its representative, David Collier, is therefore ideally suited to comment on the review process as an observer. He does this in Chapter 5 and also provides a broader perspective on the work of the Group and the 2007 Code.

The Group decided at its round table meeting that it would use a principle approach in drafting the 2007 Code and in Chapter 6 Alfred Allan discusses the principles that underlie the Code and explains how these principles were identified. In the next chapter Graham Davidson, Alfred Allan and Anthony Love discuss the practical implications of some of these principles with reference to issues of consent, privacy and confidentiality. In Chapter 8 Anthony Love considers how educators can use this explicit framework of the 2007 Code to teach trainee psychologists and practising psychologists about ethics. He also considers the role that the Code can play in educators' replanning of ethics education for psychology students and make suggestions for improving ongoing professional development of psychologists.

Another explicit goal of the Group was to bring a greater emphasis on social psychology into the Code and in Chapter 9 Graham Davidson reflects on the efforts the Group undertook to do this and the obstacles it encountered and explains the social impact of the provisions of the 2007 Code.

The Group's deliberate decision to exclude practical guidelines from the 2007 Code meant that there are no specific provisions in it regarding, for instance, working with older and younger people. The 2007 Code, however, provides ample guidance to psychologists working with these populations as Marie Joyce demonstrates in Chapter 10, where she considers some core ethical issues for psychologists working with children, in particular informed consent and confidentiality, with reference to United Nations' Convention on the Rights of the Child. Marie also considers the inherent limitation of the principled approach used by the Group by examining the virtue ethics approach of the philosopher Emmanuel Levinas.

In Chapter 11 Sabine Hammond considers the important issues of management of boundaries and multiple relationships. Complaints about inappropriate mixing of roles, conflict of interest and boundary violations accounted for a high percentage of complaints received by Registration Boards and these issues evoked many vigorous debates amongst the members of the Group. As this was particularly true in respect of the sexual activities by psychologists in relation to their clients and former clients, Alfred Allan and Donald Thomson discuss and explain the relevant standards in the 2007 Code in greater detail in Chapter 12. In the final chapter of the book, Anthony Love and Alfred Allan consider the ethical challenges that face the profession in the foreseeable future.

The purpose of the authors of this book was primarily to share the insights they gained during the review process, record the issues they grappled with during the process and, in some cases, critically consider some of the standards in the 2007 Code. As such, the book provides valuable insights in the review process of a code of ethics, the problems that confront people who undertake such a task and is also a valuable source of data about professional ethics. The authors trust that the book will encourage readers to become immersed in the issues that are covered so they are informed and can contribute to the ongoing evolution of the APS's Code of Ethics.

References

Allan, A. (2008). *An international perspective of law and ethics in psychology.* Somerset West, South Africa: Inter-ed.

Ad Hoc Joint Committee. (2005). *Draft: Universal declaration of ethical principles of psychologists.* Unpublished manuscript.

Australian Psychological Society. (1970). Code of professional conduct and advice to members. *Australian Psychologist, 5,* 75–95.

Australian Psychological Society. (1986). *Code of professional conduct.* Melbourne, Australia.

Australian Psychological Society. (1997). *Code of ethics.* Melbourne, Australia: Author.

Bailey, D. S. (2004). Beyond our borders. *Monitor on Psychology, 35,* 58.

Behnke, S. (2006). Ethics and interrogations: Comparing and contrasting the American Psychological, American Medical and American Psychiatric Association positions. *Monitor on Psychology, 37,* 6.

British Psychological Society [Australian Branch]. (1949). *Code of professional ethics.*

British Psychological Society [Australian Branch]. (1960). *Code of professional conduct.*

Committee on Ethical Guidelines for Forensic Psychologists. (1991). Speciality guidelines for forensic psychologists. *Law and Human Behavior, 15,* 655–65.

Cooke, J. S. (2000). *A meeting of minds: The Australian Psychological Society and Australian psychologists 1944–1994.* Melbourne: Australian Psychological Society.

Council of Australian Governments (COAG). (2008). Comminiqué [Electronic Version]. Retrieved 26 March 2008 from www.coag.gov.au/meetings/260308/index.htm#health.

Crook, A. (2004). Movement on acts: Psychologist and the state psychologists registration boards. *InPsych,* 10–11.

Dobson, K. S., & Breault, L. (1998). The Canadian Code of ethics and the regulation of psychology. *Canadian Psychology, 39,* 212–18.

Edwards, H. P. (2000). Trilateral forum on professional psychology working notes of the year 2000 meeting [Electronic Version]. Retrieved 2 December 2005 from www.fitpsy.org/cached/trilateral/trilat2000.pdf.

European Federation of Professional Psychologists Associations (EFPA). (1995). Meta-code of ethics. Retrieved from 12 February 2000 from www.cop.es/efppa/metacode.htm.

European Federation of Psychologists Associations. (2005). Meta-code of ethics. Retrieved 12 February 2006 from www.efpa.be/ethics.php.

Garton, A. F. (2004). Psychology in Australia. In M. J. Stevens & D. Wedding (Eds.), *Handbook of international psychology* (pp. 437–52). New York: Brunner-Routledge.

Gauthier, J. (2004). Toward a universal declaration of ethical principles of psychologists: A progress report. Retrieved 10 May 2007 from www.am.org/iupsys/ethprog1.pdf.

Louw, J. (1997a). Regulating professional conduct Part I: Codes of ethics of national psychology associations in South Africa. *South African Journal of Psychology, 27*, 183–8.

Louw, J. (1997b). Regulating professional conduct Part II: The Professional Board for Psychology in South Africa. *South African Journal of Psychology, 27*, 189–95.

Miles, S. (2007). Medical ethics and the interrogation of Guantanamo 063. *The American Journal of Bioethics, 7*, W3.

New Zealand Psychological Society. (2002). *Code of ethics.* Retrieved 17 September 2003 from www.psychology.org.nz/.

Olson, B., Soldz, S., & Davis, M. (2008). The ethics of interrogation and the American Psychological Association: A critique of policy and process. *Philosophy, Ethics, and Humanities in Medicine, 3.*

Privacy Act 119 of 1988. (Commonwealth).

Productivity Commission. (2005). Australia's health workforce: Research report [Electronic Version]. Retrieved 19 January 2006 from www.pc.gov.au/study/healthworkforce/docs/finalreport.

Professional Board for Psychology. (2002). Ethical code of professional conduct. Retrieved 17 September 2003 from www.psyssa.com/aboutus/codeofconduct.asp.

Psychologist Registration Board v Robinson. (2004). QCA 405.

Sinclair, C., Poizner, S., Gilmour-Barrett, K., & Randall, D. (1987). The development of a code of ethics for Canadian psychologists. *Canadian Psychology, 28*, 1–11.

Tomaszewski, T. (1979). Ethical issues from an international perspective. *International Journal of Psychology, 14*, 131–5.

Chapter 2
The Development of the 2007 Code

Alfred Allan and Mick Symons

Whilst the Australian Psychological Society's (APS) Code of Ethics is a dynamic document that is continually evolving, the changes are normally fairly minor and of an editorial nature. One reason for this conservative approach is to give members certainty about the ethical aspirations of the APS and the minimum behavioural standards expected of them. Substantial changes must, nevertheless, be considered when circumstances dictate this. At its meeting on 24 November 2004 the 2004–2005 Ethics Committee of the APS commenced discussing whether a comprehensive review of the 1997 Code was indicated. At its following meeting on 21 January 2005 the Ethics Committee agreed:

> That given the changes within thinking about ethical codes nationally and internationally, and principles being drawn up internationally, the Committee considered it an opportune time for the Board of Directors to form a Working Group to review the current APS Code of Ethics.

The Ethics Committee then unanimously passed a resolution moved from the Chair recommending, "to the Board of Directors that a Working Group be established to review the APS Code of Ethics" (Resolution 7).

In response, at its meeting in April 2005, the Board of Directors established a Working Group (Group) to review the Code. The members of the Group were Alfred Allan (Convenor), Elizabeth Allworth, Graham Davidson, Sabine Hammond, Marie Joyce, Anthony Love, Malcolm MacKenzie, Donald Thomson, William Warren and Jack White. Lyn Littlefield in her capacity as Executive Director and Mick Symons in his capacity as Manager of Member

Services represented the National Office of the APS and Julia Brown served as secretary. The Terms of Reference were:

- *To review the APS Code of Ethics in the context of the international principles currently being developed under the International Union of Psychological Science, and advise the Board.*
- *To ensure the APS Code of Ethics applies across the diversity of settings in which psychologists work.*

The members of the Group were selected on the basis of their knowledge of ethics, involvement with the Ethics Committee of the APS and capacity to represent a range of areas of practice within the APS. Planning for the review commenced during 2005 but was delayed when Julia Brown resigned from the APS. Her position was later filled by Christine Simpson.

Whilst the Ethics Committee appreciated that Psychologist Registration Boards will always have discretion regarding whether, and how, they want to use the APS Code, it decided that it would be to the mutual benefit of all parties to inform the Council of Psychologists Registration Boards (CPRB) of the review process and offer it an opportunity to give input when and if it chose to do so. The Executive Director of the APS raised this issue with the CPRB at its meeting in Wellington in New Zealand in 2005. During the meeting the CPRB nominated Ann Stark (the chair of the Tasmanian Board) and David Collier (the Registrar of the Psychologist Registration Board of Victoria) to attend the proceedings of the Group.

To structure the planning stage, the Chair requested Group members to research and prepare papers on various topics of importance. Research undertaken during this stage included the doing of literature reviews and interviews of peers. The first Group meeting took place in Melbourne on 16 and 17 February 2006 and was also attended by David Collier (Ann Stark was unfortunately not able to participate in the review process), who indicated that he "was present as a participating observer" who took as his "brief from the CPRB the need to maintain a degree of separation from the APS view of the world psychological" (Collier, 2006, p.1).

The meeting was structured as a Roundtable where Group members presented a series of papers pertinent to the topic of the code of ethics (see Table 2.1). Each paper, with the exception of that of Elizabeth Allworth who was not able to attend, was presented by its author.

After the presentation of the papers the Group debated issues arising from the papers, including the question of whether the APS needed a code at all. There was consensus in the Group that ethics is about people's awareness of the right and wrong of the moral judgements they make, and that it is the duty of the APS to encourage members to engage in the highest level of ethical

Table 2.1 Papers presented at Roundtable meeting

Presenter	Title of paper
Alfred Allan	The functions of a code of ethics.
Elizabeth Allworth	The APS Code from the perspective of a person working as an organisational psychologist.
Graham Davidson	The APS Code and social ethics.
Sabine Hammond	The APS Code compared to the codes in Europe
Marie Joyce	The APS Code from the perspective of a psychologist working with children and in education.
Anthony Love	The APS Code from the perspective of a person who teaches ethics to students.
Malcolm MacKenzie	The APS Code from the perspective of a person working as a therapist or counselling psychologist.
Mick Symons	The APS Code compared to the Universal Declaration of Ethical Principles for Psychologists.
William Warren	Does the APS need a new code of ethics?
Jack White	The APS Code from the perspective of a psychologist working in the courts and corrections facilities.

thinking. Some members argued that the APS could do without a code of conduct, which could actually be seen as an attempt by the APS to impose rules on its members about what to think and do. In the ensuing debate there was agreement amongst the Group members that a code of conduct could encourage lower order (rule-based) moral decision-making (see Kohlberg, 1976) and that ethical behaviour is more than the following of rules. The majority of the Group, nevertheless, believed that there was a place for standards of conduct, provided that they are grounded in ethical principles that Australian psychologists and psychologists in other parts of the world agree with. They further believed that lower-order reasoning could, to some degree, be countered by making explicit the principles on which the code is based, and how they relate to the different standards (rules). A further issue debated was that if the APS published a code of this nature, it should be honest and refer to it as a code of conduct rather than a code of ethics. The majority argued that a code which is explicit about the principles it is based on is more than a code of conduct, as the aspirational part does in fact promote ethical decision-making at a higher level. Whilst a code of this nature technically could be described as both a code of ethics and a code of conduct, the Group resolved to refer to it as a code of ethics because the document clearly enunciates a set of ethical precepts that underscore the minimum ethical standards that the profession expects of its members. This nomenclature was consistent with the nomenclature used in the preceding code.

The Group therefore decided to structure the new Code around ethical principles which were clearly identified and which reflected the ideals to which psychologists aspire, and then to use these principles to underpin the particular minimum basic standard to which psychologists should adhere. The Group further agreed that more specific indicators of acceptable behaviours which serve to facilitate ethical decision-making should be incorporated in the set of Guidelines already published by the APS.

The Group debated the perception of some psychologists, for instance in rural areas, that certain aspects of the 1997 Code, such as the standards aimed at governing multiple relationships, did not apply to them. After considering several scenarios the majority of the Group decided that many of the perceived ethical differences experienced by, for instance, forensic, organizational and rural psychologists were imagined rather than real (also see Weier & Davidson, 1999). The Group, however, agreed that the new Code should provide a conceptual framework that groups of psychologists could use to develop ethical and practice guidelines for the practice needs of the group, preferably in collaboration with the APS's Ethical Guidelines Committee. There was strong support within the Group for clear statements regarding the social responsibility of psychologists, but some members warned that it may be difficult to formulate enforceable standards in these regards and several aspects relating to social responsibility may have to be clearly identified as aspirational statements. There was unanimous agreement that the Group should consult broadly with the membership regarding the form and content of the new Code.

Before the conclusion of the meeting David Collier offered some comments as a participating observer. During his commentary he confirmed his opinion that there was, and there would continue to be, a healthy tension between the Boards as entities within their states and territories, and the APS as a national professional society which reflected the different roles of these bodies in the Australian psychological community. He strongly supported a principle-based approach and indicated that he would suggest to the CPRB that it accept four over-arching principles as the general principles for ethical professional behaviour: *respect for a person's rights and dignity, competence, responsibility and integrity*. With slight modifications, noted below, these general principles were adopted as the framework for conceptualizing the new Code.

The Group thereafter decided on a modus operandi and set itself timelines. As a first step Alfred Allan and Mick Symons were instructed to prepare an initial draft of the proposed new Code and submit it to the rest of the Group for further discussion.

The First draft (Draft) had the same components as the 1997 Code; namely, an Introduction (which was called a Preface), a Preamble, and an expanded Definition section. The Draft itself used descriptive rather than prescriptive terminology and was constructed around four principles: *respect, propriety, integrity and responsibility*. The authors tried to make a clear distinction between principles, aspirational statements and minimum ethical standards in the Draft, and to formulate a document that would provide support and guidance to psychologists working in a broad range of settings.

The First Draft had three tiers. Each general principle was accompanied by an explanatory statement to help psychologists and others understand how the principle should be applied and spelled out specific standards of professional conduct. The ethical standards derived from each general principle provided the minimum expectations with regard to psychologists' professional conduct. As would be expected given the work that had gone into creating earlier versions of the APS Code, much of the substantive content of the 1997 Code was retained and incorporated in the revised structure of the Draft. Some provisions were, however, reformulated. For instance, the authors were mindful of the criticism that has been expressed by regulators in Canada that the Canadian Code is not enforceable in all respects because its provisions are not tightly written and because constructs are not properly defined (Dobson & Breault, 1998). The authors therefore tried to ensure that the standards were distinct, formulated in terms of specific behaviours and could be interpreted independently of supporting material.

The Draft was circulated to Group members on 24 June 2006 and the Group then commenced a series of face-to-face and telephone meetings to prepare a Consultation Draft. These meetings took place in August, November and December 2006, and February and March 2007. During this period there were also numerous email, telephone and in-person consultations between the Chair and various members of the Group. They also spoke to people in other spheres who were proficient in the area of professional ethics, such as Dr Ian Freckelton regarding the regulation of professions in general and Professor Michael Perlin from the New York Law School regarding the role of human rights in professional ethics. At each face-to-face meeting the Executive Director briefed the Group regarding APS matters and external developments that had a bearing on the Consultation Draft, for instance the federal government's plans to introduce a single national registration body as was recommended by the Productivity Commission in its 2005 report *Australia's Health Workforce* (Productivity Commission, 2005).

Ultimately the Consultation Draft code was built on three general ethical principles: *justice and respect for the rights and dignity of people and peoples, propriety and integrity*. The responsibility principle was deleted when it became apparent that it overlapped extensively with the other principles.

The Consultation Draft Code was published on the APS website in April 2007 and through notices in the April 2007 edition of *InPsych* and *APSMatters*, the APS' fortnightly electronic newsletter, members were invited to comment. Invitations were also circulated to all Member Groups of the APS – Branches,

Colleges and Interest Groups. The Consultation draft was also circulated for comment to the Psychologists Registration Boards in Australia, the Board of Directors, Heads of Departments/Schools of Psychology, and to postgraduate and fourth-year psychology programme co-ordinators. The opinions of selected members who are knowledgeable about ethics were specifically sought.

During April and May of 2007 members of the APS responded in high numbers to the opportunity to give feedback about the draft revised Code. The Society received more than 65 formal submissions, several of which were from branches, colleges and interest groups on behalf of their members, meaning that even more members had offered their comments and improvements to the document than the number of submissions would imply. A number of Registration Boards also responded and several members provided informal feedback.

The Group was deeply appreciative of the way in which members engaged with the Consultation Draft and found the comments very useful. The Group felt confident that it was not acting in isolation when compiling this significant document that will greatly affect the field of psychology in Australia. Comments ranged from brief general feedback to an almost line-by-line critique of the Consultation Draft. They were predominantly positive. A small selection of the positive comments[1] is:

> *Generally the Code seems sensible and should be easily understood.*

> *I think the code reads very well.*

> *Generally I am of the view that it is a job "well done".*

> *Praise – the new format of opening each section with the general principles, explanatory statements and ethical standards followed by the numbered items makes for easy reading. This is a welcome improvement.*

> *Thank you for the opportunity of reviewing the draft of the new Code of Ethics. It has clearly been a very big task, and it seems you have been very comprehensive in your work.*

> *I have reviewed the draft code of ethics and I don't have any suggestions other than the minor grammatical issue of not having a comma after the word "and". They are excellent.*

> *I have read the Review of the APS Code of Ethics several times. Feedback: – well written, easy to read, and very definitive and clear. I am a supervisor and appreciate the efforts of APS Board of Directors to review these important documents. Many thanks for this opportunity.*

---

[1]The names of the respondents are withheld to protect their privacy.

I like the new structure of the code with the three general principles underpinned by specific ethical standard: each standard acts as a facet of a principle (Costa and McCrae would approve!). The new structure seems more user-friendly to me and less wordy than the current code.

It is very pleasing to see a revision of the Code of Ethics at this time, and particularly one written in Plain English. … In general the new code is unambiguous and easy to interpret.

We really have no feedback … it seems fine and wonderful, and the wheel really couldn't be any rounder.

Congratulations on an excellent draft Code. I particularly liked the emphasis on respecting clients' cultures and dignity and on research authorship.

I downloaded the revision of the code and congratulate the author(s) on good work. Plain English that Is Not Peremptory Even When Prescriptive might be another title!

Some feedback was more critical.

Our preference remains that the prescriptive form of language be used throughout the code.

The Code has high expectations of psychologists and that is as it should be. It did lead one of our reviewers to remark though: 'Do we also walk on water?' You will get her gist.

Overall I think they read well, but I'm a bit disappointed, and I think my organisational and community psych colleagues might be as well, that they are still very focussed on individual service delivery contexts, with the assumption that our duty of care is primarily/only towards clients themselves (and perhaps this comes through less strongly than when the emphasis was on client welfare as the top priority?).

The revision of this document is indeed timely. However, the revision reflects quite a radical change. In the first instance, I am curious as to the motivation behind the significant change in the format of the document?

I suppose my main thought is that if you articulate the overarching principles clearly enough they should operationalise easily without endless explanation and examples. Heaven help us if APS members don't already know that Respect automatically means no coercion, boundary transgressions, multiple relationships etc.

Our only reservation was that ethics as related to the teaching of psychology is not adequately covered in the document.

The recommendation for amendments mostly focused on specific subsections of the Consultation Draft. To the surprise of the Group a notable number of points of criticism were aimed at changing standards that had been taken from the 1997 Code without any, or only minor, changes. Members also expressed divergent opinions regarding the same issues. For instance, as was indicated in the excerpts above, some members supported the use of descriptive language, whilst others preferred prescriptive language.

The Group discussed the comments and new insights of Group members at its final face-to-face meeting in May 2007 and additional subsequent audio meetings. The Group accepted the bulk of suggestions which it received and incorporated them into the Penultimate Draft. Where suggestions from different members or groups of members differed, the Group followed the suggestion that was in accordance with the general approach it followed. Where comments were based on a misunderstanding of the Consultation Draft, the Group tried to reformulate the specific standard. In some cases the incorporation of changes prompted related changes elsewhere in the Draft.

The changes made included making a clearer distinction between the first General Principles in the Preamble and providing a very brief explanation of each. The General Principles were re-labelled A, B and C (instead of 1, 2 and 3) to emphasise that their order did not imply a hierarchy. In response to the feedback received that the name of General Principle A was cumbersome, the Group removed the word *Justice* from it in the Penultimate Draft.

The application of the Code was expanded to include the conduct of psychologists in their capacity as members of the Society to make it clear that members were subject to the Code whilst acting as office-bearers or members of APS Committees. The term *psychologist(s)* was defined to refer to all members of the Society irrespective of their grade of membership, and was moved from the Preamble and incorporated in the Code proper. The definition of *moral rights* was tightened to make it clear that it referred to universal human rights as defined in the Declaration of Human Rights by the United Nations.

Several standards under all three General Principles were reformulated or reorganized in response to members' comments. Standard A.1.1, for instance, had to be reformulated because it implied that psychologists should take political or social action. This concerned members who commented:

> As written this may imply an advocacy role for psychologists which may not be intended.

> It seems it could be a little too broad and people may complain that the psychologist did not do this where the discrimination or prejudice had nothing to do with the psychological service – could an expression such as "where appropriate" be used?

A.2.4 was amended on the recommendation of a member to make it clear that psychologists who review the work of colleagues should do so in a respectful manner.

Most of the members' suggestions regarding the Propriety general principle was of an editorial nature, but on the recommendation of a member, standard B.3(g), which provides that psychologists should maintain proper professional boundaries with clients, was expanded to include colleagues. Some members were concerned that the Consultation Draft did not make it clear that there was an obligation on psychologists to refer clients where it is appropriate.

> *It may be useful to mention that responsibility for appropriate referrals is included as part of a psychologist's professional responsibility.*

> *There ought to be the addition of another clause:*
> *(c) Approach other professionals when a client's benefit is at stake.*

This prompted the Group to make standard B.8, which deals with professional collaboration, a stand-alone standard and to reformulate it.

In respect of the standards associated with the General Principle Integrity, most discussions of the Group centred on standard C.4.3, and specifically what psychologists should do if they wish to engage in sexual activity with former clients after a period of two years from the termination of the service. The suggested provision attracted many comments, mostly suggesting minor editorial changes, but some focussing specifically on the two-year period.

> *We argue that the two year time period is arbitrary (unless the APS could provide some evidence that this is an appropriate time period) and that the appropriate time period will vary across different types of professional services. We would also argue that in the case of clients who are being treated for a mental health problem, there should never be a sexual relationship.*

> *Also, is there some rationale for the 2 year time frame and beginning sexual relationships with former clients – I may be hardnosed here but why is this area just not treated as a "never", instead of setting up a supposed time frame of acceptability – i.e. is 729 days really such a crime but 731 is not??? Otherwise, nice job.*

As will be discussed in Chapter 12, the Group decided that the total prohibition of sexual activities between psychologists and their former clients was not acceptable, but tried to find a workable compromise that accounted for the competing ethical principles. The Group did, however, incorporate C.4.3(d), that provides that psychologists do "not accept as a client a person with whom they have engaged in sexual activity", on the recommendation of a member.

The Penultimate Draft was then reviewed by Jeanette Jifkins, the APS's in-house lawyer; the APS's general manager Barry Whitmore; and the APS Board of Directors, who all provided valuable input. The Penultimate Draft was then referred to the APS's external lawyers, who made a range of minor suggestions which mostly required amendments to the definitions and text. The Final Draft was approved by the Board in June 2007 and adopted by the members at the APS's 41st Annual General Meeting held in Brisbane on 27 September 2007.

The Preface of the 2007 Code provides information regarding its adoption and the manner in which it should be cited. In the Preamble the authors provide a short history of the APS Code, the review process it undergoes and its ambit and information regarding the General Principles. Mention is made of the fact that the 2007 Code is complemented by a series of Ethical Guidelines (the Guidelines) which clarify and amplify the application of the General Principles and specific standards contained in the Code, and facilitate their interpretation in contemporary areas of professional practice. Members' attention is drawn to the fact that they should act in accordance with the laws of the jurisdictions in which they practice and, in so far as it is appropriate, organizational rules they may be subject to. (See Table 2.2 for an outline of the 2007 Code.)

To help users understand the 2007 Code, Definition and Interpretation sections are provided. In the Application section the authors make it clear that the Code applies to all members of the APS and remind members that there are legislative requirements that apply to the use of the professional title *psychologist* and they must abide by such requirements. The Code consists of three General Principles, each of which is introduced with an explanatory statement to assist members to understand the context of the ethical standards set out under that General Principle. This is followed by the Ethical Standards derived from each General Principle, which provide the minimum expecta-

Table 2.2   Structure of the 2007 Code of Ethics

Preface	
Preamble	
Code of Ethics	
	Definitions
	Interpretations
	Application of the Code
A	Respect for the rights and dignity of people and peoples
	Explanatory statement
	Standards A.1–A.7
B	Propriety
	Explanatory statement
	Standards B.1–B.14
C	Integrity
	Explanatory statement
	Standards C.1–C.7

tions with regard to psychologists' professional conduct and conduct as members associated with activities of the APS.

The General Principle of *Respect for the rights and dignity of people and peoples* requires psychologists to regard people as intrinsically valuable and to respect their rights, including the right to justice, autonomy and privacy, to engage in conduct which promotes equity and the protection of people's human, legal and moral rights and to respect the dignity of all people. Compared to the 1997 Code, the most significant changes incorporated under General Principle A in the 2007 Code are contained in standards A.2, A.3 and A.5. Standard A.2 reflects societal expectations in regard to the appropriate behaviour of professional people in respect of clients and other people and groups they interact with. Standards A.2 and A.3 provide information that is aimed at educating members regarding the legal-ethical requirements about how to obtain fully informed consent for the provision of services and the requirements of confidentiality in practice, respectively.

The General Principle of *Propriety* requires psychologists to ensure that they are competent to deliver the psychological services they provide, to provide services to benefit and not to harm, to protect the interests of the people with whom they work, to protect the welfare of clients and the public and to maintain a positive image of the profession. The most significant change incorporated under General Principle B is the alignment of research guidelines with the National Health and Medical Research Council guidelines in Section B.14.

The General Principle of *Integrity* reflects the need for psychologists to have good character, acknowledges the high level of trust intrinsic to their professional relationships and acknowledges the impact of their conduct on the reputation of the profession. The most significant change incorporated under General Principle C is in regard to the express provision for ethical standards relating to conflicts of interest in section C.3. The circumstances giving rise to a conflict of interest have been clearly identified and the proposed Code addresses conflicts of interest in a broader manner than the 1997 Code.

We trust that this chapter demonstrates the rigour of the review process and that it was guided by research, deliberation and consultation. No code is perfect, but the Group believes that the 2007 Code reflects the ethical views of the majority of psychologists in Australia at this moment.

References

Collier, D. (2006). *Ethics Code Review Committee: A report to the Council of Psychologists Registration Boards on attendance at the meeting of the Australian Psychological Society National Ethics Committee Code Review Committee*. Melbourne, Australia: Council of Psychologists Registration Boards.

Dobson, K. S., & Breault, L. (1998). The Canadian Code of ethics and the regulation of psychology. *Canadian Psychology, 39*, 212–18.

Kohlberg, L. A. (1976). Moral stages and moralization: The cognitive developmental approach. In T. Lickona (Ed.), *Moral development and behavior: Theory, research and social issues* (pp. 31–53). New York: Holt.

Productivity Commission. (2005). Australia's Health Workforce: Research Report [Electronic Version]. Retrieved 19 January 2006, from www.pc.gov.au/projects/study/healthworkforce/docs/finalreport.

Weier, J., & Davidson, G. (1999). Remote rural community perceptions of ethical psychological practice. *South Pacific Journal of Psychology, 11*, 24–47.

Chapter 3
The Functionality of the Australian Psychological Society's 1997 and 2007 Codes of Ethics

Alfred Allan

As discussed in the Introduction, the APS and the environment in which it operates have undergone many changes since 1997 and this raised questions about the functionality of the 1997 Code. A review of the work of authors such as Keith-Spiegel (1994), Louw (1997a, 1997b) and Sinclair, Poizner, Gilmour-Barrett and Randall (1987) suggested that codes have four major functions.

The first function of a code is to assist in the *professionalization of a discipline.* Historically, a profession is seen to represent a cohesive group of people who earn their living by undertaking a common activity and publicly claim that they are competent (i.e., proficient in a discipline, unimpaired and ethical), and who are therefore allowed by society to regulate most aspects of their professional activities. It is therefore no coincidence that national professional psychological associations first started developing and publishing their ethical codes at the time that psychology was engaged in establishing itself as a profession (Louw, 1990, 1997a, 1997b).

Internally within the profession, codes were used to professionalize practitioner psychologists by unifying them through the regulation and management of their professional relations to ensure that they remained dedicated to the profession and to the professional welfare of other psychologists (Dunbar, 1992). Externally within the community, codes were used to protect the public by regulating psychologists' professional behaviour, to market psychology and to shape the public's perception of the social identity of psychologists as a competent and regulated body of professionals fit to deal with certain mental health issues, thus paving the way for statutory registration of professional psychologists (Dunbar, 1992; Keith-Spiegel, 1994).

Since 1949, when the Australian Branch of the British Psychology Society adopted its first code of ethics, two changes have taken place that raise questions regarding whether codes still have a professionalization function. Louw (1997b), firstly, points out that psychology is now well established as a profession. Whilst this is true, this does not mean that codes cannot serve an internal function by unifying members through stating the common standards that they share. It can also serve to distinguish psychology from similar professional groups. The second change is that the Registration Boards have taken over from the Australian Psychological Society the regulatory and disciplinary responsibilities for practising psychologists. The fundamental question this raises is whether psychology is still a profession in the sense that it is no longer fully self-regulating. A full exploration of this question is beyond the ambit of this chapter, but it does appear that the definition of what a profession is has been evolving as the status of professions has diminished in society. Nevertheless, as discussed in Chapter 1, professional bodies still have a disciplinary role to play vis à vis the conduct of their members, and they are best placed to articulate the highest ethical standards rather than merely the minimum standards of conduct for the profession. Furthermore, as public sentiment towards the professions has diminished, it has become more important for professional bodies to shape their profession's public image and corporate identity. Codes, as public documents which are freely available to the public, can send a powerful message about the profession to society and can therefore be used to create and maintain the public image of the profession. Codes therefore seem to have retained a role they had initially in maintaining the status as a profession.

The second function of codes flows from the first in that they serve as *public expressions of the ethical principles*[1] *of the profession* (Sinclair et al., 1987). Such an expression informs society, and reminds members about these principles. The ethical principles must therefore be clearly and precisely formulated, even though the authors of codes for pragmatic reasons often collapse them into three or four general principles[2].

Codes also must *guide and support psychologists in their ethical decision-making*. Codes should ideally provide guidance for all psychologists when they are confronted by ethical problems, irrespective of their approach, speciality, and type of work or settings in which they work. Most users of codes would prefer this guidance to be given in the form of explicit ethical rules, but it is impossible to produce a code consisting of a list of invariable rules that will accommodate all circumstances encountered by psychologists (see Gordley,

---

[1] My definition of an ethical principle in this context is that it is an overriding moral obligation that people use to guide their behaviour, provided that it is not overridden by a higher-ranking obligation.
[2] Note that in this chapter I distinguish between eight principles which have been collapsed into three superordinate or *general* principles in the 2007 Code.

1984). Such an approach furthermore encourages a rule-bound approach to ethics. A better strategy for authors of codes is to state clearly the principles underlying the code and then to formulate ethical standards that flow from these principles. This approach encourages users to utilize a higher-order principle-based approach to ethical decision-making. The ability to make ethical decisions at this level gives psychologists a mechanism that they can use when they are confronted with novel situations where the standards do not provide an answer to a problem, because the standards will by necessity be limited to those covering the most common situations psychologists may encounter. Authors such as Sinclair (1998) suggest that a code should also provide a model of ethical decision-making that psychologists can use to guide them when dealing with complicated ethical issues. Many such models have been developed by authors (for a review of models prior to 1997, see Allan, 2008; Cottone & Claus, 2000) and all involve a systematic, linear, rational decision-making process. The Canadian, New Zealand and 2006 British codes provide such models. It is equally important that codes should provide support to psychologists who perceive what they consider to be unethical behaviour or feel coerced into doing something that they feel would be unethical. For instance, psychologists may feel that employers' expectations will give rise to unethical behaviour on their own part (see, for example, Weinberger & Sreenivasan, 1994). In this case, a code can be helpful to such psychologists by giving them explicit guidance on how to approach the situation. A code can also be used by psychologists to illustrate the common standards of psychological practice, because it represents the collective authority of psychologists working in a specific jurisdiction (Garton, 2004).

The final function of codes is to *help the profession meet its responsibilities to society* (Keith-Spiegel, 1994). Parsons (1968) submits that a core criterion of a full-fledged profession is that it "must have some institutional means of making sure that … [members' competence] … will be put to socially responsible use" (p. 536). This clearly requires professions to ensure that their members are well educated and regulated so that they obey the laws of the land and act to the benefit, and not detriment, of society and its members. Some psychologists, however, believe that because many mental health problems have their origins in the social circumstances of people, psychologists independently and collectively also have a responsibility to bring about change within society. The nature and ambit of this aspect of the social responsibility of psychologists are controversial and difficult issues as the longstanding debate about psychology's social responsibilities demonstrates (see, for example, Davidson & Sanson, 1995; Kendler, 1993, 1994, 1999; Pellegrin & Frueh, 1994; Plaud & Vogeltanz, 1994; Prilleltensky, 1991, 1994; Stroud, 1994; Tomaszewski, 1979). The social responsibilities of psychologists are addressed by Davidson in Chapter 9.

The use of codes to educate and regulate the members of a profession is not controversial and the two functions are compatible. To be functional in both cases, it is important that a code should have a cohesive and coherent conceptual framework. Sinclair (1998), with reference to Kohlberg's theory of moral development, submit that a code must therefore be built around clearly and precisely formulated *ethical principles*. The ethical implications of each of these principles should be clearly *explained* further to assist with the interpretation of the principles, especially if there appears to be inconsistencies between the principles. Authors can also use these explanations to set aspirational standards which users of the code should strive to achieve. Nevertheless, because "fine aspirations alone are unlikely to exercise significant effect on the behaviour of professionals" (Freckelton, 1996, p. 164), the authors of a code should, finally, formulate specific *ethical standards* that state the minimum standard of behaviour that will be tolerated from users of the code. These standards must be in a form that will enable users to understand and internalize them, and to enhance this process they must have face validity and be logically derived from the relevant principles (Sinclair, 1998). The standards must, however, also be in a format that will enable disciplinary committees and tribunals to enforce them; that is, it must be possible to demonstrate convincingly that a psychologist's behaviour has fallen below a clearly stated minimum behavioural standard. The Canadian code, for instance, has been criticized for not being specific enough in describing unacceptable conduct in behavioural terms in that it uses relative or evaluative terms such as "too much" and "as completely and objectively as possible" (Dobson & Breault, 1998, p. 213). Standards must therefore be formulated in language that is clear and unambiguous and refer to specific and concrete behaviour (Dobson & Breault, 1998). Enforceable provisions, furthermore, must be clearly distinguished from aspirational statements that reflect attitudinal and behaviour expectations (Sinclair, 1998), etiquette rules and practice guidelines.

There may occasionally be a conflict between the educational and regulatory functions of a code. For instance, whilst it may be better for educational purposes to provide greater detail about the informed consent process, good drafting for regulatory purposes requires a precise definition of informed consent without unnecessary details. When faced with such contradictory interests, the authors of codes must make a policy decision regarding which function to favour by taking into account their understanding of the current needs of the profession.

1997 Code

The founders of the Australian Branch of the British Psychological Society (BPS), as the APS was known until 1965, saw the development of a code of ethics as an integral part of the evolution of psychology as a profession (Cooke, 2000). Although the degree to which the APS Codes actually contributed to the *professionalization* of psychology in Australia is impossible to determine empirically, Cooke (2000) nevertheless believes that the APS Codes played a major role in unifying psychologists in Australia. He cites in support of his conclusion a letter written by Frank Naylor in 1992 which says that the APS's "… ethical position has been the cornerstone of its existence" (Cooke, 2000, p. 189).

The external role of the Code can be gauged from the fact that it was used by most state and territorial registration boards and also by the courts. Section 21 of the Western Australian Psychologists Registration Act (1976), for instance, explicitly instructed the Board to have due regard to the Code when it formulated rules of professional conduct for psychologists. The Psychologists Board of Queensland adopted the Code as a statement of professional standards for psychologists practising in that jurisdiction and made legislative provision for its adoption in the Regulation. In a test case in Queensland, the Queensland Court of Appeal accepted in *Psychologist Registration Board v Robinson* (2004) that the APS Code is considered by "psychologists of good repute and standing … as setting forth standards to which they, as professionals, should adhere" (par. 24). A criticism by some users[3] of the 1997 Code was that the word *member*, rather than *psychologist*, was used, and that this usage diluted the impact of the Code by excluding those psychologists who were not members of the APS. (See Chapter 1 for a discussion of this issue.)

Since 1960, the APS Code has contained general principles; and the three general principles of Responsibility, Competency and Propriety first appeared explicitly in the 1986 Code of Professional Conduct (Australian Psychological Society, 1986). Provisions that were in accordance with the Responsibility and Competency general principles, however, were present in the 1949 Code. Nevertheless, despite their long history, some users of the 1997 Code found that these general principles were conceptually unclear, incoherent and poorly articulated. Users questioned whether these general principles, particularly principle III (Propriety), could in fact be called general principles because they did not appear to have a specific focus. Collectively, the general principles also appeared to be very narrow when compared with the general principles of the American Psychological Association (APA), Canadian Psychological Society (CPS) and New Zealand Psychological Society (NZPS) codes. A close analysis

---

[3] Since 1998 I have every year asked groups of postgraduate psychology students, and occasionally workshop attendees, to compare the 1997 Code with other codes, such as the American Psychological Association (APA), Canadian Psychological Society (CPS) and the New Zealand Psychological Society (NZPS) codes. The information from users that I refer to in this chapter was collected at these occasions.

of all the provisions of the 1997 Code, however, reveals that the ethical principles found in the literature and other codes can be found in it. (See Chapter 6; Allan, 2008.)

As a tool to assist psychologists in meeting their *social, regulatory and educatory responsibilities*, the 1997 Code had weaknesses and strengths. For instance, the utility of the APS Code as an aid to psychologists, both individually and collectively, trying to meet their responsibilities to society has been debated since at least the 1970s (see for example Viney, 1973) and remains a concern (D'Arcy, Gridley, Sampson, & Beckwith, 2005; Davidson & Sanson, 1995). Users also commented on the dearth of provisions in the 1997 Code regarding social responsibility and compared it negatively to the Canadian and New Zealand codes. From a regulatory and educatory perspective a positive aspect of the 1997 Code, compared to some other codes, was that it defined the three key constructs *client, member* and *research*. Nevertheless, the lack of explicit distinctions in the 1997 Code among general principles, enforceable ethical standards, practice guidelines, aspirational goals and rules of etiquette reduced its utility as a regulatory and educational tool.

Users, nevertheless, thought that the specific ethical standards were well presented. They, firstly, made conceptual sense and were easy to access. Like the APA (American Psychological Association, 2002) and South African Psychologists Board (Professional Board for Psychology, 2002) Codes, the specific standards in the 1997 Code were grouped together under areas of practice. For example, all the provisions relevant to the practice of psychological assessment were in section A, making it easy for students and practitioners to find and refer to them. The specific standards, secondly, were usually in the form of explicit, specific, concrete standards of behaviour that had face validity. Finally, the specific standards had good face validity; for example, B.6 provided very clear instructions regarding the use of information about criminal acts disclosed by clients. This good face validity may be due to the procedure used by the authors of the 1986 Code who asked "psychologists to give examples of the kinds of thing they thought were unethical" (Cooke, 2000, p. 190). The Canadian Psychological Association used a similar procedure to formulate its current and previous Code.

Whilst the organization of the standards under areas of practice had benefits, the method nevertheless made it difficult to establish the link between the specific standards and the general principles and meant that not all the provisions which fitted together logically were arranged together. For example, the confidentiality rule received specific attention in General Principle III(a) and in sections B.1, B.3, B.6, B.21, C.7, E.11, E.16, E.17, F.7 and G.8(i). This meant that there were large numbers of duplications; for example, consent was dealt with in General Principle III(a) and in sections B (Relationships with clients) and E (Research) with some associated provisions in A (Psychological assessment procedures), C (Teaching) and D (Supervision and teaching). Whilst users found the clear statement of the ethical standards and the manner in which they were presented helpful, others also found them confusing. For instance, they pointed out that whilst Section E on research required informed consent as a prerequisite for research, there was no such provision in Sections A (Psychological assessment procedures) and B on relationships with clients. Test takers, therapeutic clients, students and research participants, all of whom the 1997 Code defined as clients, thus were at risk of receiving differential treatment in respect to their right to make informed, autonomous decisions in the context of the services of which they were recipients. Users also questioned the appropriateness of having ethical standards about research, as most psychological research is currently governed by guidelines and other directives developed by the National Health and Medical Research Council (NHMRC), the Australian Research Council or Universities Australia.

Members of the APS Ethics Committee who were required to apply the 1997 Code when dealing with complaints about APS members also concluded that although the 1997 Code had numerous provisions that regulated the behaviour of members towards clients and each other, there were gaps in the 1997 Code in respect of situations where members in their capacity as APS office bearers or members of APS committees acted inappropriately towards other APS members or APS office staff members. These perceived limitations were causes for questioning whether the 1997 Code's construal of professional conduct was sufficiently broad enough to encompass all aspects of members' conduct *qua* APS members.

Users also criticized the utility of the 1997 Code as a *guide* to appropriate ethical behaviour. They expressed the view that the language used in it did not guide but, on the contrary, was rigidly prescriptive when compared with the language used in some other Codes, particularly the APA Code. This was because it consisted of prescriptions and proscriptions and exhortations such as *must* and *must not* (Garton, 2004). The 1997 Code was silent in that regard about how members should understand and differentiate between terms such as *must, should, may, shall, will* and so on. Some users also held the view that the provisions of the 1997 Code were of limited assistance to them because its focus was on psychologists who teach, do research or do therapy and counselling within private practice settings with individual adult clients. They explained that the 1997 Code did not give guidance to psychologists working in the community or non-clinical settings such as education, corrections or business organizations. Other users pointed out that the 1997 Code, when compared with most of the other Codes, had little to say about culture other than in general principle III(b) where members were exhorted to be sensitive to cultural differences. They contrasted this unfavourably to the New Zealand Psychological Society (NZPS) Code that emphasizes sensitivity to diversity, especially culture, and to relationships between Maori and non-Maori people.

The 1997 Code, on the other hand, was unique amongst modern codes in that, through section H.6 and the *Procedures for persons considering invoking any section of the code* (Invoking procedure section) appended to the 1997 Code, it gave guidance to members regarding the steps they should take when confronted by what they considered to be unethical behaviour by a colleague. Many users of the 1997 Code, however, did not consider it to be a document that *supported* them when they perceived what they considered to be unethical behaviour or when they felt they were being coerced to do something that they considered to be either ethically questionable or clearly unethical. This is not necessarily a fault of the Code, but could reflect the lack of understanding that users of codes have about the functions of codes and therefore an issue that the Review Working Group (Group) needed to consider in its deliberations.

2007 Code

The Group noted that psychology has become well-accepted as a profession in Australia and that provisions purely aimed at enhancing the *professionalization* of psychology were therefore redundant. Since the inception of the 1949 Code for psychologists practising in Australia, society has, however, become more critical and demanding of professions. These demands include expecting professions to act in a socially responsible manner and to be transparent and accountable for their actions and those of their members. The Code, as a corporate document that is freely and easily accessed through the APS website from virtually anywhere in the world, can and should be used, therefore, to address and direct societal expectations of psychology. Promulgation of the Code as a public document is also a means of enhancing the image of psychology in Australia in general, and the APS specifically. To do this the Code must be a document that reflects the status of the APS as a well-organized, peak professional body that represents a competent and regulated group of professionals who are fit to deal with mental health, behavioural and emotional issues in their various roles as educators, researchers, consultants and clinicians. In doing so, the Code should reflect ethical principles shared by psychologists across the world and articulate clearly the APS's (and Australian psychologists') acceptance of their responsibilities to society and support for the human rights of all people.

As a public document that binds the APS and its members, the Code should be accurate, reasonable and not susceptible to misinterpretation. The Group therefore restricted the number of aspirational statements in the 2007 Code to a minimum and clearly identified them as such to minimize the risk that readers of the 2007 Code may be misled into thinking that standards psychologists strive to achieve are, in fact, minimum ethical standards.

As will be discussed in greater detail in Chapter 6, the Group decided to continue to use a *principled approach* in the preparation of the 2007 Code. The eight principles that underlie the 2007 Code are explicitly mentioned in the Preamble and the document is structured around them. The *justice* and *autonomy and rights and dignity of people* principles were collapsed into the Respect for the Rights and Dignity of People and Peoples general principle[4] which has a strong deontological character. The Propriety general principle consists of the nonmaleficence and beneficence principles and aspects of the responsibility principle and has a consequentialist nature. Other aspects of the responsibility principle and the veracity and fidelity principles have been collapsed into the Integrity general principle. The Group refrained from assigning weight to the different general principles as they are all conditional and consequently their relative weight will differ from situation to situation.

The Group attempted to address some of the user criticisms of the 1997 Code described above. For instance, after obtaining legal advice, the Group defined and used the word *psychologist* in the 2007 Code but, in doing so, drew APS members' attention to the fact that the title of psychologist is regulated by legislation and should be used only by persons who are registered as psychologists. The definition of the word *conduct* was formulated in such a way as to clarify that the provisions regulate all behaviour of members as members of the APS, including behaviour towards other members and APS office staff. To address the perception of some psychologists that the language used in the 1997 Code was too prescriptive and rigid, the Group tried to use descriptive language rather than words such as *must* or *should* in the 2007 Code.

The Group also considered comments by some psychologists who saw themselves as being excluded by the 1997 Code. The Group concluded that some of the criticism, for instance, that the proscription of sexual activity with clients should be restricted only to therapeutic and counselling clients, was not sound. (This is discussed further in Chapter 12.) The Group nevertheless tried to draft the 2007 Code in a form that would give guidance to all psychologists irrespective of their professional activities, how they define their clients, or the settings in which they work. The Group, for example, defined the concepts such as *client*, *conduct* and *psychological service*, and formulated general principles and explanatory statements in such a way that those sections of the new Code would provide a broad conceptual framework for all psychologists. At the same

---

[4] To avoid confusion I will spell general principles with capital letters.

time the Group formulated the standards in a way that would not exclude specific groups of psychologists, or make it difficult for them to adhere to the Code. The Code was further shaped by the comments of members on the Consultation Draft. As the majority of registered psychologists and members of the APS are involved in psychological assessment, therapy and counselling, it is therefore possible that the focus of the 2007 Code remains somewhat aligned towards these prevalent professional activities. In this regard the 2007 Code is not unique because the range of activities psychologists are engaged in is so broad that it is virtually impossible to satisfy the wishes of every group of psychologists. The Group considered the approach that was followed by the drafters of the 1960 APS Code (British Psychological Society [Australian Branch], 1960) and the South African Code (Professional Board for Psychology, 2002) which provides specific guidance to psychologists working in forensic settings in sections J and 7, respectively. The Group, nevertheless, believed that the conceptual framework of the 2007 Code will make it possible for the APS and groups of psychologists to develop specific ethical and practice guidelines that cater to the needs of psychologists who believe that the 2007 Code offers insufficient guidance on how it might apply in their practice settings. The Group, therefore, envisage that psychologists who, for example, teach or work in specialities such as community, forensic and organizational psychology, will work with the APS Guidelines Committee to develop ethical guidelines that apply to their specific practice needs.

The Group refrained from formulating specific standards where the activities of psychologists are already specifically governed by another generally accepted, reputable authority. For instance, in the case of research by psychologists, most is governed by the research codes, statements, guidelines and other directives developed by the National Health and Medical Research Council (NHMRC), the Australian Research Council, or Universities Australia. The Group also tried to avoid including provisions that could be regarded as practice guidelines, that is, rules about generally acceptable practice where there is a degree of discretion. Elevating practice guidelines to the status of ethical standards may lead to them being inflexibly applied by non-psychologist users of the 2007 Code without regard to the practical realities of situations.

The Group expressed the hope that the clear conceptual framework of the 2007 Code will encourage psychologists thus to use it as a support in finding constructive resolutions when the demands of an organization or other people require them to behave in a manner they believe is unethical. In negotiations with employers it is important for psychologists to appreciate that because the 2007 Code reflects the standard of practice of the majority of psychologists in Australia, it is very likely that civil courts will use it should clients sue the employers of psychologists.

The Group considered whether to incorporate a decision-making model into the 2007 Code that psychologists could use to guide their decision-making. The research regarding decision-making is very wide ranging and sophisticated; and there is a large number of ethical decision-making models available in the literature that generally utilize a systematic, linear, rational process (for review, see Allan, 2008; Cottone & Claus, 2000). These models have been criticized on the basis that there is evidence that most ethical decision-making does not involve a proactive or linear process (Sinclair, 1998; Williams, 2004). The availability of such a model in a code may, however, encourage psychologists to use an explicit and systematic rational evaluative approach, taking into account the principles of the relevant code (Seymour, Nairn, & Austin, 2004). Seymour and his colleagues furthermore point out that such a model will assist psychologists when they have to demonstrate that they had made an ethical decision in a responsible manner. Whilst the Group believed that it is important for psychologists to make use of a decision-making model, or models, it did not consider that prescribing a specific model was within its competency. The Group also decided that the Invoking procedure section in the 1997 Code dealing with procedural matters should not form part of the 2007 Code but could be incorporated into the APS's rules and procedures for dealing with complaints and with members' professional conduct. This document is available to all members of the APS.

The Group considered it important that the 2007 Code should be an instrument that would assist the APS and psychologists to meet their responsibilities towards society. The specific scope of social responsibility and the level and type of active participation in relation to issues of public interest that could be expected from psychologists, however, turned out to be problematic. This issue is discussed by Davidson in Chapter 9. It is sufficient to say here that this is one area where the Group felt that it was not entirely successful in achieving its own goals.

The Group reasoned that key constructs in the 2007 Code should be clearly defined and that it should have a clear conceptual framework based on well articulated principles, in order to enhance its utility for educational and regulatory purposes. The Group therefore expanded the definition section of the 2007 Code considerably and used a three-tier structure (general principles, explanatory statements and ethical standards) to construct the 2007 Code. The principles underlying the 2007 Code are clearly articulated in the Preamble and for practical reasons collapsed into three general principles. To improve the utility of the 2007 Code as an education tool[5] and encourage a higher conceptual level of ethical decision-making, the general principles were tightly

---

[5] For a more comprehensive discussion of this aspect see Chapter 8 by Love.

defined and the relationship between general principles and ethical standards made evident. This required a radical change to the format of the 2007 Code compared with previous versions of the Code where specific ethical standards were presented under headings reflecting areas of practice. In the 2007 Code each general principle is accompanied by an aspirational explanatory statement that elaborates on its impact on professional conduct. The Group limited the use of aspirational statements in these explanatory statements and the standards that follow them to avoid misleading the public or creating a situation in which psychologists are held answerable to unrealistically high standards. The ethical standards (standards) derived from each general principle constitute the third tier and provide the minimum expectations with regard to psychologists' professional conduct and in their capacity as members of the APS. These standards were drafted with great care to constitute a clear statement of the minimum behavioural requirements that will be tolerated by the profession, and to ensure that they contain no ambiguities and inconsistencies that could impede their use by legal and quasi-legal bodies. This is important because professional behaviour that does not meet these standards is unethical and may therefore be subject to review by the APS Ethics Committee as well as Registration Boards that use the Code as a guide. The Group further recognized that these standards may be used by Civil Courts as an indicator of the standards of conduct expected of psychologists in Australia. These standards are not exhaustive and where specific conduct is not identified by the ethical standards, the general principles apply. Where it was possible, the Group retained standards that appeared on previous versions of the Code because of their face validity; however, in response to some members' comments during the consultation phase, various textual changes were made to some of these standards. The Group did not incorporate as ethical standards those provisions from the 1997 Code that it considered to be practical guidelines or etiquette rules. These omissions were referred to the APS Ethical Guidelines Committee to consider whether they should be published in the series of Ethical Guidelines that complement the 2007 Code. The Preamble to the 2007 Code indicates that the purpose of these Guidelines is to explain and augment the application of the general principles and specific standards contained in the 2007 Code, and to facilitate their interpretation in particular areas of professional practice. The Guidelines are supplementary to the relevant standards of the 2007 Code, and must be read and interpreted in combination with the 2007 Code. Psychologists who act contrary to the Guidelines may be required to demonstrate that their behaviour was not unethical.

To enhance the enforceability of standards, they were formulated as very general, austere statements at the highest level of abstraction possible with reference to specific behaviour. Where the Group, however, deemed it necessary for educative purposes, it formulated more comprehensive ethical standards.

Examples of standards that were formulated more specifically include those on informed consent (standard A.3) and the use of interpreters (standard.7). In formulating standard C.4.3(c) regarding sexual activity with a client more than two years after termination of the professional relationship, the Group did not proscribe specific behaviour, but provided a process in which psychologists should follow if they wish to engage in sexual activity with former clients after a period of two years from the termination of the service.

Conclusion

The codes of ethics of professional bodies are always pragmatic documents that attempt to reflect the consensus opinion within the profession and will inevitability have limitations (Allan, 2008). The Group, nevertheless, formed the belief that the 2007 Code reflects the image of psychology in Australia as it is: well-regulated, progressive and accountable. As such, the new 2007 Code provides a powerful and clear impression of the ethical principles and standards of behaviour Australian psychologists and members of the APS pursue. The Group also maintained that the explicit, principle-based conceptual framework of the 2007 Code will guide psychologists when they make professional decisions, support them when they feel coerced by clients and other entities and help psychologists and the profession meet their responsibilities to society. The tightly formulated standards should make the 2007 Code relatively easy to enforce by both the APS Ethics Committee and regulatory bodies.

References

Allan, A. (2008). *An international perspective of law and ethics in psychology*. Somerset West, South Africa: Inter-ed.

American Psychological Association. (2002). *Ethical principles of psychologists and code of conduct*. Washington DC: American Psychological Association.

Australian Psychological Society. (1986). *Code of Professional Conduct*. Melbourne, Australia.

Cooke, J. S. (2000). *A meeting of minds: The Australian Psychological Society and Australian psychologists 1944–1994*. Melbourne: Australian Psychological Society.

Cottone, R. R., & Claus, R. E. (2000). Ethical decision-making models: A review of the literature. *Journal of Counseling and Development, 78*, 275–83.

D'Arcy, C., Gridley, H., Sampson, E., & Beckwith, J. (2005). Psychology and social action. *InPsych, 27*, 38–9.

Davidson, G. R., & Sanson, A. (1995). Should the APS have an ethical code of social action? *Bulletin of the Australian Psychological Society*, 2–4.

Dobson, K. S., & Breault, L. (1998). The Canadian Code of ethics and the regulation of psychology. *Canadian Psychology, 39*, 212–8.

Dunbar, J. (1992). *A critical history of codes of ethics: Canadian Psychological Association, 1939–1986.* Unpublished PhD thesis, York University, North York, Canada.

Freckelton, I. (1996). Enforcement of ethics. In M. Coady & S. Bloch (Eds.), *Codes of ethics in professions* (pp. 130–165). Carlton South, Australia: Melbourne University Press.

Garton, A. F. (2004). Psychology in Australia. In M. J. Stevens & D. Wedding (Eds.), *Handbook of International Psychology.* New York: Brunner-Routledge.

Gordley, J. (1984). Legal reasoning: An introduction. *California Law Review, 72*, 138–77.

Keith-Spiegel, P. (1994). The 1992 ethics code: Boon or bane? *Professional Psychology: Research and Practice, 25*, 315–6.

Kendler, H. H. (1993). Psychology and the ethics of social policy. *American Psychologist, 48*, 1046–53.

Kendler, H. H. (1994). Can psychology reveal the ultimate values of humankind. *American Psychologist, 49*, 970–1.

Kendler, H. H. (1999). The role of value in the world of psychology. *American Psychologist, 54*, 828–35.

Louw, J. (1990). *Professionalizing psychology.* Pretoria, South Africa: Human Sciences Research Council.

Louw, J. (1997a). Regulating professional conduct: Part 1: Codes of ethics of national psychology associations in South Africa. *South African Journal of Psychology, 27*, 183–8.

Louw, J. (1997b). Regulating professional conduct; Part II: The Professional Board for Psychology in South Africa. *South African Journal of Psychology, 27*, 189–95.

Parsons, T. (1968). Professions. In D. L. Sills (Ed.), *International Encyclopedia of Social Sciences* (Vol. 12, pp. 536–46). New York: MacMillan.

Pellegrin, K. L., & Frueh, B. C. (1994). Why psychologists don't think like philosophers. *American Psychologist, 49*, 970.

Plaud, J. J., & Vogeltanz, N. (1994). Psychology and the natural ethics of social policy. *American Psychologist, 49*, 967–8.

Prilleltensky, I. (1991). The social ethics of school psychology: A priority for the 1990s. *School Psychology Quarterly, 6*, 200–22.

Prilleltensky, I. (1994). Psychology and social ethics. *American Psychologist, 49*, 966–7.

Professional Board for Psychology. (2002). Ethical code of professional conduct. Retrieved 17 September 2003, from www.psyssa.com/aboutus/codeofconduct.asp.

Psychologist Registration Board v Robinson. (2004). QCA 405.

Psychologists Registration Act of 1976. (Western Australia).

Seymour, F., Nairn, R., & Austin, J. (2004). Comments on Tim Williams' paper, "Setting impossible standards: The model of ethical decision-making associated with the New Zealand Psychologists' Code of Ethics". *New Zealand Journal of Psychology, 33*, 33–4.

Sinclair, C. (1998). Nine unique features of the Canadian Code of Ethics for Psychologists. *Canadian Psychology, 39*, 167–76.

Sinclair, C., Poizner, S., Gilmour-Barrett, K., & Randall, D. (1987). The development of a code of ethics for Canadian psychologists. *Canadian Psychology, 28*, 1–11.

Stroud, W. L. (1994). Why psychologists don't think like philosophers. *American Psychologist, 49,* 968–70.

Tomaszewski, T. (1979). Ethical issues from an international perspective. *International Journal of Psychology, 14,* 131–5.

Viney, L. L. (1973). Toward a more relevant code of professional conduct. *Australian Psychologist, 8,* 106.

Weinberger, L. E., & Sreenivasan, S. (1994). Ethical and professional conflicts in correctional psychology. *Professional Psychology: Research and Practice, 25,* 161–7.

Williams, T. (2004). Setting impossible standards: The model of ethical decision-making associated with the New Zealand Psychologists' Code of Ethics. *New Zealand Journal of Psychology, 33,* 26–33.

Chapter 4
Is a Psychologist Always a Psychologist, Ethically? Some Observations Through a Wide Lens

William Warren

This contribution takes a *road less travelled* in regard to our thinking about the ethical standards expected of psychologists and about the domain that is ethics *writ large*. Perhaps it would be more accurate to say roads less travelled in view of comments from colleagues that the material straddles many different issues. So be it and, that acknowledged, it is an intentionally provocative discussion, that provocation having two levels. One is the simple irritation of our reflection on the ethical dimension of psychological practice by way of moving that discussion beyond the mundane level. The other concerns a deeper aspect that goes to the impossible task that the work of the psychologist might be, and a practical corollary of this being a challenge to the view that a psychologist can simply, or too easily, or ever, opt in and out of being a psychologist.

The occasion of writing an original version of this material was the discussion in 2006 that led to the decision to undertake the project of rewriting the Australian Psychological Society's (APS) Code of Ethics. The catalyst for such a project was the articulated need for the recognition of some fundamental principles that were emerging in the international scene; principles like justice and respect for people and for Peoples, and social responsibility in relation to psychological knowledge and its applications. However, the ideas presented here have a genesis in two earlier papers that raised matters pertinent to the particularly difficult position of someone who would *be a psychologist*. One highlighted the problem of possible conflict between Codes when a psychologist works in contexts where several Codes apply by reason of the different roles or functions being fulfilled (Warren, 1999). The second concerned the problems that arise when money enters into the caring context to corrupt the caring relationship (Howard, 1996; Warren, 2004). The ideas are also an echo of some points made in the context of a discussion of the problems and pros-pects of an applied ethics; that is, whether ethics as discussed by the philoso-phers are somehow always above or beyond the level of application or the practical (Warren, 1992). A proposal to rewrite the APS Code prompted reflec-tion on matters of very long standing in philosophy, yet even within the dis-cipline of philosophy itself some of the perspectives on these matters raised in such reflection are not widely known. This contribution, then, is less an argu-ment and more a chart of a territory that one might travel through, and some points of interest along the journey.

In essence, and to crystallize the discussion, an assertion can be made as follows: that when a psychologist, or perhaps for more limited purposes, an APS member, has interactions with others, the ethical principles developed for psychologists can be argued to apply despite other relationships that might pertain between the parties. For example, a workplace supervisor who is a psychologist, supervising other psychologists or related professionals, will be judged as a psychologist in relation to conduct displayed toward those people. A research team leader psychologist overseeing the work of other psychologists will be similarly judged. The Head of a Department of Psychology in a hospi-tal or a university is in a similar position. Further, in cases such as a psycholo-gist becoming romantically involved with a colleague he or she has supported through some crisis, or working in a wider role such as that of a case worker and perhaps getting more involved with clients than a psychologist might be expected to get, the same assertion will apply.

Codes and Contexts

The issue is focused differently but the same point applies when a psychologist works in a context in which several codes of conduct might apply, each poten-tially expecting different things of him or her. As suggested elsewhere (Warren, 1999) an academic who is an APS member and State-registered psychologist working in, say, an education faculty in a university and is a member of the Australian Association for Research in Education (AARE) would have four Codes impacting on his or her work if the university has its own Code. If that person were a member of the industrial Union (for example, the National Tertiary Education Industrial Union, the NTEU), there would be a fifth, and the list may go on; for example, the recently formulated code pertaining to workers in the problem gambling sector in New South Wales (NSW). Will the individual be expected to uphold the general principles and observe the specific provisions of the APS or a Registration Board Code in force at the time of an alleged breach, irrespective of what other Codes might apply or roles or functions being fulfilled? For present purposes, the answer is suggested to be *yes*.

There were in the 1997 Code specific provisions going to the matter of the relationships between psychologists and other psychologists, as well as between psychologists and members of other professions. *Section H* of the 1997 Code stated in Section *H.1* what is certainly a concomitant, if not an over-riding, responsibility to act with due regard to the needs, special competencies and obligations of colleagues in psychology and other professions. This was strengthened by the then General Principle III, which placed the welfare of clients, the public, and the integrity of the profession above the interests of a psychologist's employer or the [self-]interests of their colleagues. The then *Procedures for Persons Considering Invoking Any Section of the Code* also pointed to the matter of particular things being expected of a psychologist in regard to other psychologists. For example, that there would be an initial approach to a psychologist who another psychologist felt was in breach of the Code. That this last consideration may be difficult in practice does not detract from the apparent thinking underlying it, that is, that psychologists might reasonably be expected to be, for example, assertive, and to be skilled in interpersonal relationships and conflict resolution. These procedures imply a particular or higher standard of conduct in relation to other psychologists. The 1997 Code provisions find expression in the new 2007 Code. For example, Standard A2.2 repeats the old H1 provision, Standard A2.3 the old H5, and Standard C.7.2 provides similar responsibilities in regard to what a psychologist ought to do when he or she becomes aware of breaches of the Code by other psychologists, and Standards B.8.8.1 and B.9 provide specifically for interactions with other professionals. These provisions can be argued to go to the implications of being a member of a profession, and to support the present assertion of something more being expected of one, though just what constitutes a profession is not an easy thing to characterize more generally.

Illustrative of the point being approached here is a relevant determination in NSW in the context of disciplinary proceedings against medical practitioners. This was *Childs v Walton* (Court of Appeal, 13 November 1990, unreported) where the expression *in the practice of medicine* was considered. The argument was followed in other cases, as well as in nursing and it is likely that the argument would apply to the expression *in the practice of psychology* in the various Registration Acts and more generally. It has been followed more recently in relation to medicine (Medical Tribunal of NSW v Jarvis, 2002). The Court of Appeal case (*Childs v Walton*) involved a psychiatrist engaging in a sexual relationship with a patient *after* termination of therapy, whilst the Tribunal matter involved a medical practitioner borrowing money from a patient. In the Appeal case, Samuels JA, with whom the other members of the Court agreed, held that the phrase "in the practice of … does not have a temporal meaning, but rather a qualitative or descriptive character". The phrase "does not circumscribe the period during which the conduct impugned must occur … ; it describes its nature" (p. 12).

The point for us here is that the standards of conduct required of a psychologist go to wider matters than whether he or she is acting in a nominated capacity as a psychologist. If a party in an interaction is a psychologist, then whatever other dimensions there may be and notwithstanding any relationship of sub- and super-ordinancy involved, conduct complained of will be judged in terms of the standards expected of a psychologist. Situations where a psychologist fills a position of line-manager or workplace super-ordinate will have their own dimensions as to the appropriate way of conducting oneself. Enterprise Agreements, Grievance and Meditation policy and procedure, and relevant legislation will impact such a context. However, the fact of being a psychologist brings also its own responsibilities – beyond the level of the common courtesies and manners we all owe to each other – when the super-ordinate is a psychologist, and arguably even more so when another party is also a psychologist or a member of another profession. The practical outcome of the foregoing observations is that while a particular matter might be dealt with *in house* in the context in which it arose and according to industrial agreements and the like, there may well be additional or residual matters of concern to the profession and its ethical *watchdogs*.

Beyond this situation which goes to one's formal role or position, however, is the other scenario noted in the introductory observations; where, for example, a psychologist is assisting a distressed colleague, and the psychologist's conduct comes into question. The 2007 Code deals with this in its interrelated definitions of *professional relationship, psychological service* and *conduct*. The first is premised on the delivery of the second, and the third, *conduct*, raises the matter of judgment on reasonable grounds by others that a psychological service is being provided. The general point arising from our present discussion would be that a wide rather than narrower view be taken. However, and notwithstanding that is as the widest view that is being asserted here, a compromise position might be guided by the following: That where a relationship between a psychologist and another person derives from the psychologist's real or perceived knowledge, skill and understanding, then this will bring into play the ethical standards required of psychologists. It will be no defence to suggest that one was acting in some other capacity than that of being a psychologist, and such things as whether one charges a fee or sees a person outside the normal consulting room or times, will not automatically excuse a psychologist from the standards required.

Further, still, even when a psychologist is acting outside a formal context of psychology and is not even informally approached for advice or assistance, the same high standards will be expected. This is because of a psychologist's understanding of psychological functioning, a deeper or wider understanding than a non-psychologist might be expected to have. Thus, a psychologist's ability to detect when another is, for example, *not well* or otherwise vulnerable, would preclude that psychologist from exploiting or taking an advantage of another. This point is given wider significance and support in observations made by Koocher (2007). Koocher provided examples of what he called *novel naughtiness* in the conduct of psychologists, situations in which psychological knowledge was used in ways that were highly questionable, ethically. For example, psychologists developing advertising material to sway targeted groups to take up smoking a particular brand of cigarette (in one case young working-class females, in another case African-Americans), psychologists contributing in one way or another to the interrogation of people detained under anti-terrorism laws, and personality profiling to assist recruitment of an agent for purposes of espionage. The interrogation matter generated the American Psychological Association's Task Force on Psychological Ethics and National Security (PENS) Report which brought forward principles in relation to psychological ethics in the national security of the United States of America (USA). Clearly, psychologists are seen to have particular knowledge and skill which, in turn, imposes particular ethical responsibilities on them.

The assertion in focus here, then, has two challenging consequences. First, that psychologists will be judged as psychologists in their dealings with other psychologists, other professionals and *clients* (broadly understood), as well as in relation to their conduct where it is their special knowledge and understanding that leads to the relationship. This is notwithstanding other relationships they may have with those people. Second, whatever grounds the relationship, psychologists are in a unique position, in principle, one that perhaps makes the task of being a psychologist a most difficult one, particularly in certain contexts. Indeed, one APS member response to the invitation to comment on a draft of the 2007 Code asked whether, in addition to adopting the principles, endorsing the values and keeping to the standards being then envisaged, a psychologist also had to "walk on water"! However, once inducted or initiated into the field of knowledge, a psychologist's conduct cannot be quarantined from scrutiny on an argument that he or she was acting in some other capacity than as a psychologist.

A Broader Perspective Still

There are, of course, many approaches and perspectives in relation to ethics and morals. Indeed, we already invite a debate in too casually using these terms as if they were interchangeable, as is not uncommon in everyday talk. That issue aside, Broad (1930/1944) has discussed five different types of ethical theory, and within philosophy can be found deontological theories differentiated from teleological theories, and these differentiated from consequentialist theories, as well as existentialist and libertarian theories argued as offering a better account of the human condition and, thereby, our moral and ethical horizons and limits. Yet, philosophical ethics is not conspicuous in clinical psychology courses, as Wheeler's (1998) survey of courses in the UK showed; few courses included such material and there was but lukewarm interest in it. As he notes, though, "without a grounding in the philosophical basis of ethics the practical ethical judgements and actions of psychologists are reduced to the status of blind 'conventionalism' or lucky guesses" (p. 28).

While we are on this high-sounding level let us risk the reader's patience and raise some matters from lesser visited areas of philosophy. These matters arise first in the work of G.W.F. Hegel (1770–1831). Hegel represents a very significant figure in relation to ethics and his work is of a magnitude and impact well beyond what is possible to discuss here. Suffice to note that Hegel wanted to get beyond the position of Kant (1704–1804) so as to develop an understanding of ethics as not merely that which is *commanded*, or which it is one's *duty* to do, but to something that is inherent in life, is natural, is the thing people would automatically do without a need for telling or commanding – other things being equal. His distinction between *Moralitat* and *Sittlichkeit* expresses this. Moralitat, usually translated as morality, referred to rules of conduct laid down by this or that authority, or duties imposed on one by others. Kant's categorical imperative, generally taken as saying that an action is good if it can satisfy the maxim that it can be rationally *universalized*, was too arbitrary for Hegel. Hegel had been interested in *Love* as a human experience, arguing that Jesus had preached an ethic of Love that had been perverted into an ethic of authority by the early Church. Love describes a situation in which one acts in particular ways without coercion or threats of punishment and the like. Thus he envisaged *Sittlichkeit*, or the ethical life, as a feature of mind, that is, love operating, for example, as a natural sociality and an egalitarian outlook. In this, in one's interaction with other people one *just did* what was good.

These are difficult ideas, but two tangents hopefully illustrate them further. One is a reference to the work of the Scottish-Australian philosopher John Anderson (1943/1963a, 1944/1963b) who distinguished rules of conduct (morality) from the science of the good (ethics), and, moreover, argued that it was the philosopher's role to locate what was good, but not to then proselytize or advocate people to do it. Examples of the activities he argued were inherently good were *enquiry, co-operation* and *love;* their opposites, *censorship, competition* and *hate* were evil. A second tangent is to note some ideas in relation to ethics of the nineteenth-century anarchist thinker, Peter Kropotkin

(1842–1921). Kropotkin challenged the pessimistic assessments of human nature put forward by the likes of Thomas Malthus (1766–1834) and Thomas Huxley (1825–1895). Malthus had argued for control and regulation, ostensibly to protect the interests of humankind at large, but in reality for Kropotkin, to protect the interests of the privileged classes. In two significant works, *Mutual Aid* (1902/1939) and, more importantly here, *Ethics* (1925/1992), he argued the essential basis of ethics was in three fundamental aspects of human existence: mutual aid, justice and self-sacrifice. Citing favourably a work by J-M Guyau (1854–1888) the title of which is itself illustrative of the present point being made – *A Sketch of Morality Independent of Obligation or Sanction* (1989) – Kropotkin agrees that ethics was concerned essentially with that growth and development of life which was the aim or goal of Nature itself. Thus, "the moral element in man needs, therefore, no coercion, no compulsory obligation, no sanction from above; it develops in us by virtue of the very need of man to live a full, intensive, productive life" (Kropotkin, 1924/1992, p. 323).

Hegel, Kropotkin and Anderson all conjure with similar ideas of ethics going to features of mind and life, features that are understood in terms of the emotion and associated behaviours captured in the idea of *love*; love as *natural* sociality, or as *egalitarianism*. It is not absurd, therefore, to contemplate the good and the right, equally the evil and the wrong, in terms of what Anderson calls *a way of going on* of mind. To be sure, this idea needs elaboration and he does indeed do this. Here, though, suffice to use these very brief observations to draw attention to a dimension of ethical reflection that finds a place for a notion of an ethical life. That is, conduct that is governed not by sanctions but by an ideal of being the best that a human could be. These ideas appear to be, though, a long way from our familiar Codes of Conduct and the reflection, discussion and determinations that surround them and flow from them.

A Metaphor

It is helpful, or at least interesting, at this point to consider the idea of what metaphor of psychology or, better here of *the psychologist* might lie behind the observations thus far. For example, perhaps one of the most enduring metaphors of teaching is a horticultural one, the metaphor of the teacher as a gardener in, for example, kindergarten, is a strong one in educational thinking. What, though, of psychology? Three metaphors spring to mind for giving a meaning to the work of the applied psychologist.

One metaphor is that of the applied psychologist as *technologist*, one invited to mind by the current interest in manualized treatments, treatment modules and the like. Bunge and Ardila (1987) use the term psychotechnology to refer to the applied dimension of psychology, finding it in the work of Edward Titchener (1861–1918). Titchener (1928) actually used the term *psychotechnics*, referring to applied psychology more generally and, within this domain medical psychology meant psychotherapeutics (p. 33). The implications of the technologist-metaphor for ethical conduct would seem to invite consideration of matters of psychologists' adherence to protocols, skill in applying techniques, and knowledge of variations in applications of modules or protocols to particular groups (the traumatized, those trying to deal with pain and injury, those adjusting to disability, for example). The technologist metaphor invites us to consider differentiations between a technician, a technologist and a professional. However, despite even our wide approach here, discussion of these differentiations would take us too far afield. Suffice to say that it is the notion of a professional that attracts the present discussion.

A second metaphor might be that of the scientist-practitioner, allowing that this might be a metaphor. Here, a particular view of what constitutes science is wedded to application of skills, generating a focus on evidence-based interventions. This is similar to the technology metaphor and might be differentiated from another, the *scholar-practitioner* metaphor, which generates a focus more on humanist or existential interventions. Interestingly, Bunge and Ardila (1987) note that the future might see psychology of health coming to replace psychiatry and clinical psychology, this "broad social and community orientation" taking attention away from science and technology, with different ethical imperatives. These last imperatives might arise as a focus on therapy gives way to a focus on primary prevention; large-scale public interest mental health interventions raise different types of moral and ethical issues than are raised by individual therapy.

What, then, is the metaphor that comes to mind or is *sleeping* in our primary discussion above? A strong contender is the metaphor of the *priest* – though not exactly North's (1972) *secular priest* – or the *elder*, or the person of *high degree* (to draw on Elkin's, 1945/1980 discussion). Can a priest or elder or person of high degree move in and out of being a priest, elder or person of high degree? Even when their conduct is not directly related to their status, or is in connection with even the mundane aspects of life, they will, ideally, bring their higher order outlook to bear. A priest is always a priest, an elder always an elder, a person of high degree always such. There is an interesting link here to Islamic thinking about professional ethics where, as Amine and Elkadi (1989) note, the connection between private life and professional life is very close: "A person who lacks moral values in private life cannot be trusted in professional activities, even with the highest professional and technical standards" (p. 121).

Back to Reality: Sobering and Instructive

Now, all of the foregoing said and a metaphor of the applied psychologist as, for example a priest, elder or person of high degree now exposed, it might be asked whether the position being put here is too difficult for psychological practice, too much to expect of any psychologist? One response to this question is that what is being suggested constitutes an expression of what has been called aspirational ethics. That is, that a psychologist should in all contexts conduct him or herself with the highest level of principles – justice, fairness, respect for people and Peoples, and so on – as an ideal or ideally, but that a lesser standard would be accepted given the impossibility of the level of ethical conduct expected. Yet, the distinction between aspirational ethics and something else takes us back to the distinction between ethics and morals. This seems to be the thrust of Corey, Corey and Callanan's (2002) discussion of this point, where they note that "*Ethics* represents aspirational goals, or the maximum or ideal standards set by the profession", while "*morality* is concerned with perspectives of right and proper conduct ... and involves an evaluation of actions on the basis of some broader cultural context or religious standard" (p. 11). Morality, then, is *relative* while ethics states the ideal to which we should aspire, if we ignore the views of a Hegel, a Kropotkin, or an Anderson which offer a quite different *take* on this distinction. Yet, even accepting this last blind spot, just as conduct cannot be quarantined by one's role, so consideration of that conduct cannot be isolated from considerations of the ebb and flow of philosophical debate going back to the ancient Greeks and which grounds these aspirations. The new Code is framed in a way that directs attention to aspirations by recognizing some higher order principles all of which have a rich history in philosophy.

A second response to the assertion being argued here might be that it is taking psychology too seriously at best, or to charge arrogance, self-aggrandizement; even that one is delusional, at worst! A cursory read of both the history of psychology and reviews of its literature might dispel any special knowledge, deeper insight, or a generally privileged status inhering in the discipline or its practitioners. The response to the theoretical and practical efforts of psychology that was expressed as Radical Psychology (Brown, 1973) is one example of the point. Radical Psychology, with the so-called Anti-Psychiatry movement fuelled by such writers as Laing (1967) and Cooper (1974), argued that psychology as a discipline and as a practice slavishly served dominant social interests (class or gender or race), normalized particular behaviour on arbitrary grounds, breached common ethical principles grounded in respect for persons and generally contributed to that repression and alienation that it might otherwise have been expected to redress. These views underlie the type of priest that North (1972) had in mind, but not that in mind in the present discussion.

Psychological research, no less those practical interventions engaged in by well-meaning psychologists, went relatively unquestioned, ethically, until the advent of scrutiny of the ethical conduct of researchers only after some scandals in research.

In relation to research, though also relevant to our wide discussion here, Chalmers and Pettit (1998) highlight the concerns that arose in 1916 over Udo J. Wile's experiments involving tissue samples taken from the brains of patients suffering from neurosyphilis as an important early marker in the development of more formal scrutiny of professionals. Wile took brain tissue from these patients and injected it into rabbits, the ensuing outcry illustrating one lesser-known force in the evolution of this ethical scrutiny. Pettit (1992) cited Wile's research along with other studies involving experimentation on condemned prisoners, the *bugging* of a jury room, treatment without consent or disclosure and the performance of autopsies, in what became known as the Tuskegee Study which went on over a period of some 30 years.

Chalmers and Pettit (1998) describe the force for change as the "controversy machine", which starts with dubious practice, the appearance of a whistle-blower (usually an insider), the involvement of a community group or newspaper, leading to a public scandal, and then action to prevent that practice reoccurring. The advent of the modern era of ethical scrutiny they suggest, however, was the US Congress decision to make federal funding in the US contingent on research proposals passing ethical review. This was only in 1974, and it heralded the advent of ethical scrutiny. Interestingly, though, the deeper philosophical dimensions of that division of philosophy that is Ethics are not conspicuous. As noted earlier, Wheeler's (1998) survey of the extent of teaching of philosophical ethics in clinical psychology courses in the UK found little interest in such material. Further, there is anecdotal evidence that students in any professional discipline resist all but the practical and/or that which they see as having an immediate survival value. In any event, it can be asked whether the psychology profession was at the controls of the *controversy machine*. The answer is, most likely, no, particularly if the ideas assembled by Brown (1973) or the arguments of the likes of Laing (1967) or Cooper (1974) are reviewed.

Conclusion

The present discussion has ranged widely. Yet, that is a product of the complexity of the field that one is forced to acknowledge in the type of reflection that a discussion of a new Code of Ethics/Conduct invites.

Perhaps those who would work with the mind or the self (presuming these exist), like those who work with the soul (with the same presumption), no less than those who work with the structure and the functioning of the temple in which these are housed, have to take on greater burdens than those who study or work with the material and the natural world. Psychology, as a field of enquiry, has seen controversy and debate as to its *real nature* as well as to its possibilities and potentials. Psychology as a so-called *applied* discipline inherits that controversy, but adds the additional dimension that attracts most of the attention that is framed in Codes, chiefly by reason of the often special vulnerability of those with whom the applied dimension works. However, while it is primarily the efforts to move from what is allegedly psychological knowledge to the use of that knowledge to alleviate human distress that see complaints in terms of unethical conduct, research, organizational and community work equally involve expectations as to ethical practice. Overall, psychology might be too difficult a discipline and the application of its knowledge impossible of ethical practice, in principle, in some contexts. Assuming it is neither too difficult as a field of enquiry, nor impossible of ethical practice, requires that psychologists not only aspire to but also meet the highest standards of conduct in relation to their work. A psychologist is a psychologist is a psychologist, ethically, and in terms of the conclusion drawn by Broad (1930/1944) he or she is required to act more like the *angel* than the *animal*, despite the seeming inherent impossibility of so doing, and this will involve more than a passing acquaintance with ethical thinking:

> One lesson at least has been taught us so forcibly by our historical and critical studies in the theory of Ethics that we ought never to forget it in future. This is the extreme complexity of the whole subject of human desire, emotion, and action; and the paradoxical position of man, half animal and half angel, completely at home in none of the mansions of his Father's house, too refined to be comfortable in the stables and too coarse to be at ease in the drawing room (p. 284).

References

Amine, A. R. C., & Elkadi, A. (1989). Islamic code of medical professional ethics. In R. M. Veatch (Ed.). *Cross cultural perspectives in medical ethics*. Boston: Jones and Bartless Publishers.

Anderson, J. (1963a). The nature of ethics. In his *Studies in Empirical Philosophy*. Sydney: Angus and Robertson Ltd. Original work published 1943.

Anderson, J. (1963b). Ethics and advocacy. In his *Studies in Empirical Philosophy*. Sydney: Angus and Robertson Ltd.

Broad, C. D., (1944). *Five types of ethical theory*. London: Kegan, Paul, Trench, Trubner and Co. Ltd. Original work published 1930.

Brown, P. (Ed.). (1973). *Radical psychology*. London: Tavistok Publications.

Bunge, M., & Ardila, R. (1987). *Philosophical psychology*. New York: Springer-Verlag.

Chalmers, D., & Pettit, P. (1998). Towards a consensual culture in ethical review of research. *Medical Journal of Australia, 168*, 79–82.

Childs v Walton. (1990). Unreported New South Wales Court of Appeal case dated 13 November 1990.

Cooper, D. (1974). *The grammar of living*. London: Allen Lane (Penguin Books).

Corey, G., Corey, M. S., & Callanan, P. (2002). *Issues and ethics in the helping professions*. 6th Edition. Pacific Grove, CA.: Brooks/Cole.

Elkin, A. P. (1980). *Aboriginal men of high degree*. St. Lucia, Queensland: University of Queensland Press. Original work published 1945.

Howard, A. (1996). *Challenges to counselling and psychotherapy*. London: MacMillan.

Koocher, G. P. (2007). *Novel naughtiness: Negotiating negative nuances in behavioural science and mental health practice*. Keynote address, Forty Second Annual Conference, Australian Psychological Society, Brisbane, 25–29 September.

Kropotkin, P. (1939) *Mutual aid: A factor of evolution*. Harmondsworth: Penguin. Original work published 1902.

Kropotkin, P. (1992). *Ethics: Origins and development*. Quebec: Black Rose Books. Volume 8 in *The Collected works of Peter Kropotkin* Translated by L. S. Friedland and J. R. Piroshnikoff. Original work published 1924.

Laing, R. D. (1967). *The politics of experience*. New York: Random House (Pantheon Books).

Medical Tribunal of NSW v Jarvis. (2002). Unreported NSW case, 40025/99 of 29 November 2002.

North, M. (1972). *The secular priests*. London: George Allen and Unwin Ltd.

Pettit, P. (1992). Instituting a research ethic: Chilling and cautionary tales. *Bioethics, 6*(2), 89–112.

Titchener, E. B. (1928). *A beginner's psychology*. New York: The Macmillan Co.

Warren, W. G. (Bill). (1992). Back to basics: Problems and prospects in applied philosophy. *Journal of Applied Philosophy, 9*, 13–20.

Warren, W. G. (Bill). (1999). Psychologists in universities and other institutional settings: Different codes of ethics, different expectations? *APS Division of Research and Teaching (DRAT) Newsletter, 1*(1), 6–19.

Warren, W. G. (Bill). (2004). Ethical considerations in private practice forensic psychology work: An Australian perspective. *International Journal of Forensic Psychology*, Issue 2, 14–20.

Wheeler, J. (1998). The teaching of ethics to United Kingdom clinical psychology trainees: A brief survey. *Clinical Psychology Forum, 113*, 27–9.

Chapter 5
The Australian Psychological Society's 2007 Code of Ethics: An Observer's Perspective

David Collier

I was invited to participate in this project as an observer, which was an experience both intellectually stimulating and morally satisfying. At the conclusion I faced still a number of questions about ethics and ethical codes. This is a good thing if it be known, since the fundamental premise of any discussion of ethics is that the discussion will not answer everything. My outstanding questions related to those challenges inevitable for any professional association trying to provide guidance to a diversity of stakeholders. Those challenges include:

- An association's ethical mission should agree with, and be a guide for, that of their profession generally. This I believe the 2007 Code does. It is responsive to clients' welfare, public needs and the highest standards of professionalism.
- Professional associations derive their income from members' dues and associated fees. The 2007 Code should argue against financial support through deals with the interested industry groups which inevitably risk and create unacceptable conflicts of interest.
- Associations must ensure the editorial independence of their publications and journals.
- Associations should be governed by bylaws adopted by members, association leaderships should be fully accountable to members and all association activities and policies should be publicly disclosed.

In responding to these challenges, most associations recognize the key principles which underlie their development of codes and guidelines. That such principles are not uniformly adopted by all associations is due, in part, to the reality that some organizations are partially dependent on industry or government funding. A policy of "just say no" to such "tagged" funding would be a relatively clear and simple approach to adopt and would be the most acceptable ethically. I accept that it is also simplistic. Difficulties which arise from adopting such a simplistic approach do so because of the need to satisfy the diverse requirements of a membership-based organization which inevitably has a variety of views within its membership.

One way forward is to tackle those challenges through looking at the matter and methodology of ethics and critical thinking. I want to ask you questions about the relationship between ethics and practice. Such questions concern the nature of our moral thinking and how ethics informs our decision-making, the very basis of the 2007 Code.

Is the practice of your profession a moral endeavour? How do ethics inform your decision-making? What are your ethical responsibilities as a member of this profession?

As I understand it, there appear to be seven commonly held elements which will define ethical practice in the profession:

- assessing the appropriateness of treatment
- participating in the informed consent process
- protecting client interests
- providing excellent treatment delivery
- communicating effectively with all involved in treatment
- seeking continued learning
- continuously improving quality

Within all of these elements, your competence, your concern for the client's well-being and your respect for his or her person provides the basis for trust in the treating relationship. If, as has been argued elsewhere, the central paradox in health care delivery is the tension between self-interest and altruism, then your responsibility to the patient in this trust has the greatest force and overrides other obligations.

Our challenge as members of a profession is to critically and ethically examine our own and each other's professional role; the extent to which we achieve excellence in our contribution to client care; to break out of comfortable habits and reflect on new, alternative ways of delivering service as health care professionals; to think about what we are doing in treatment and the consequences for the human mind and spirit of our clients, our colleagues, and ourselves; and to provide a forum for this important dialogue in our practices, our practice programs, and continuing education.

An essential element of understanding this is clarity of goal. We must be certain about what it is that we are trying to achieve, and I am of the view that this certainty cannot be ensured unless you have an acute awareness of ethical conduct. Recognizing what is ethical validates the importance of conduct, provides appropriate reinforcement and helps to foster the development of positive internal goals and standards. These in turn build assuredness and confidence in two critical elements of research and practice: accepting critique constructively and mastering the loneliness of self belief. If you are embarking on a novel line of research, one which is contrary to accepted practice, it will be subject to intense scrutiny. Accept that scrutiny willingly, but believe in yourself. And that is much easier to do if you have the confidence that what you are doing is ethically robust.

The profession has an ethical responsibility to its members to provide the opportunity and the forae to present ideas, to discuss supportively research conducted and the evidence presented and to help their members move onwards with their research and professional growth. It is an ethical imperative to my thinking that the profession must encourage and challenge all members to reach their greatest professional satisfaction open to each person. Equally, we must provide clarity around what the profession's expectations are. The reasoning for this is fundamental to the primacy of the role of ethics in professional practice.

Throughout the months of discussion and development, the Australian Psychological Society's ethics team covered all of these issues and teased out the essential boundaries necessary. There was however, one discussion which the group touched on but then left largely alone and this I believe is worthy of further discussion, and is the topic of this contribution.

What courage can a professional society's Code of Ethics offer a member when the organization for which they work instructs them to behave in a contrary fashion? What if that organization is the government of the day?

The earlier tensions described in the list above pale into insignificance when one looks at the ethical responsibility an association has to support their members in what may be a lonely stand for human dignity in the face of institutional or governmental disregard for human rights. Those professionals working in large institutions or with state or federal entities can find themselves trapped in the dilemma of having to apply their professional code of ethics to work instructions that inherently may be in conflict. To my mind the regulators of the professions must stand ready to draw the attention of such institutions to those occasions when their operating instructions may place a professional employee in a position where that professional's activities are open to a complaint of unsatisfactory professional conduct or professional misconduct. It is the regulators, empowered as they are by statute to protect the public and to maintain the standards of professional practice through recognizing the accreditation of courses and investigating complaints against practitioners, who can most readily take the stand to protect against abuse of professional standards.

We live in an environment where the important freedoms our society has developed over many years are being restricted or are eroding in the face of "operational necessities". In most cases the argument for limitation is based not so much on necessity (though that is frequently the sub-text), but on political judgements centred on what politicians perceive to be good for the wider society or workplace. To counter such an argument refer to the words of John Stuart Mill (1849/1974): "If all mankind minus one were of one opinion, and only one person were of the contrary opinion, mankind would be no more justified in silencing that one person, than he, if he had the power, would be justified in silencing mankind" (p.76). His reasons resonate today as well as when he wrote them down.

It is common in opening this line of thinking to bring into the discussion the analogies which can be derived from the twentieth-century experience of totalitarian regimes. Those experiences gave birth to a charge that still impacts the professional communities – what has been called "the Nazi analogy". In ethical or policy disputes about medicine and the associated professions, no argument can bring debate to a halt more quickly than to invoke a Nazi comparison. Arthur Caplan (2005) wrote authoritatively on this in an article "Misusing the Nazi Analogy", which I will paraphrase for convenience.

He identified that no matter whether the subject is stem cell research, end-of-life care, the conduct of clinical trials in poor nations, abortion, embryo research, animal experimentation, genetic testing or human experimentation involving vulnerable populations, references to Nazi policies or practices tumble forth from critics. "If this is done, then we are on the road to Nazi Germany" has become a commonplace claim in contemporary bioethical debates.

I agree with his view that too often those who draw an analogy between current behaviour and what the Nazis did, do not know what they are talking about. The Nazi analogy is equivalent to dropping a nuclear bomb in ethical battles about science and medicine. Because its misuse diminishes the horror done by Nazi scientists and doctors to their victims, it is ethically incumbent upon those who invoke the Nazi analogy to understand what they are claiming.

A key component of Nazi thought was to rid Germany and the lands under German control of those deemed economic drains on the state – the mentally ill, the alcoholics, the "feeble-minded", and the demented elderly. They were seen as direct threats to the economic viability of the state, a fear rooted in the bitter economic experience after the First World War. The public health of the nation also had to be protected against threats to its genetic health. These were created when people of "inferior" races intermarried with those of Aryan stock. Threats to genetic health also included, by their very existence, those identified by the Nazi apparatchik as genetic degenerates – Jews, Gypsies and Slavs. These theories of race hygiene had gained some prominence in mainstream German scientific and medical circles as early as the 1920s.

What is important to keep in mind about these underlying themes that provided the underpinning for Nazi euthanasia and eugenic practices is that they have little to do with contemporary ethical debates about science, medicine or technology. When critics charge that allowing embryonic stem cell research permits the taking of innocent life to serve the common good, and then attempt to compare it to Nazi research in concentration camps, such claims of resemblance are deeply flawed; moreover, the immorality of Nazi practices is lessened.

Concentration camp prisoners were used in lethal experiments because they were seen as doomed to die anyway and, given the conditions of total war that prevailed, they were considered completely expendable in the service of the national security of the Third Reich.

There are many reasons why a practice or policy in contemporary science or medicine might be judged unethical. But the use of the Nazi analogy in an attempt to bolster an argument is morally repugnant. Over 60 years after the fall of the Third Reich, we owe it to those who suffered and died at the hands of the Nazis to insist that those who invoke the Nazi analogy do so with care.

Against that backdrop to our discussion, and with grateful thanks for Arthur Caplan's clarity of expression and thinking, we must consider the place that a code of ethics ought to play in guiding the individual, the professional associations, the regulatory bodies, the employing organizations and the state in ordering their behaviours and conduct in an ethical manner.

For the individual, the issue in simple terms is one of the wish to balance that individual's continued employment against the need to maintain personal integrity. Ethically, the decision to be made would seem obvious. Should your employer ask of you something which was abhorrent to your personal beliefs and integrity, then it is incumbent on you to resign.

There are many factors which militate against the logic of this decision. In spite of record employment in Australia, there is always a reluctance to give up a position which enables that individual to meet his or her financial commitments. Instead, explanations and excuses for staying compete with the integrity which you wish to display. It is entirely conceivable that the compromise to be made will produce at best a silence in the face of objectionable behaviour, and at worst acquiescence in the very behaviour based on some form of the premise "that there may be reasons for me being asked to do this which I find offensive, to which I am not privy and nor do I need to know, so therefore it is part of my job to act against my conscience".

So, is this response due to fear or to apathy? Arguably, it is essentially a matter of fear, and in our current world, it is primarily a fear of financial loss or inconvenience rather than a personal challenge. Some individuals are blessedly free of fear from an early age, but for most of us we have our fears and weaknesses which we handle on a daily basis. Fear of financial loss increases in proportion to the financial responsibilities we face. I think we can have sympathy for those who acquiesce in the face of this fear, but professional peer support and regulatory recognition of their professional obligations will reinforce the individual courage required to act positively.

But if the reason for one's failure to act is apathy, then this cannot be allowed to absolve individuals of responsibility for their organization's actions. Those individuals who do nothing to prevent an unjust system from taking power indirectly sanction its authority. If there is a lesson to be taken in the practice of ethics from history, it is this. There are always those who stand up and oppose the destruction of principles and standards of practice when governments take control of the institutions of the state. They often stand forth as lone voices of opposition, easily derided, marginalized and then "disappeared". It is a common mechanism for control by a tyranny. As the tyranny strengthens, even quite large groups can be removed, their views cleansed from the communal consciousness. All too often it reaches a climax in the brutalization and murder of entire ethnic groups or social sectors of the tyrannized society.

Why does the society accept these "adjustments"? Perhaps the best words to describe this can be found in the speech of the fictional character Janning, played by Burt Lancaster in the film "Judgment at Nuremburg".

> 'What about those of us who knew better, we who knew the words were lies and worse than lies? Why did we sit silent? Why did we take part? Because we loved our country. What difference does it make if a few political extremists lose their rights? What difference does it make if a few racial minorities lose their rights? It is only a passing phase. It is only a stage we are going through. It will be discarded sooner or later. Hitler himself will be discarded – sooner or later. The country is in danger.'

By the time it is realized that this passing phase has, in fact, become a way of life, it is too late. Dare we suggest that this is already happening in our world? How do those individuals who speak out against institutionalized misconduct fare? In our sound-bite world, the right of access to media given to those with the "focus of interest" such as politicians creates an inherent inequality which all too often sees the individual isolated.

How does the professional association support their members when this happens? The answer that we would like to hear is that their support is to unify their membership against the inequality, that they will raise up public opinion and support their members who may be working in such a situation. Regrettably, this does not always happen. What support there is may be muted or behind the scenes. Associations believe they must deal with the very organizations which may be creating the injustices, the abhorrent behaviours. Perhaps that is true; the lines of communication are terribly important. But for me, the Association must never lose sight of the primacy of ethical integrity. It is my view that once an entity makes even small compromises, for whatever reason, then all of that entity's actions are suspect and the decisions of their office holders open to question.

It is for this reason that when a Code such as this is revised and presented back to the membership as a revitalized document, it is incumbent upon the body which has created it to ensure that the document not only represents those standards clearly to its membership, but also ensures that its own office holders and professional staff adopt and live the Code to the highest standards. That example best supports the membership, best guides the membership as to expected standards and best shows the world the professional expectations and obligations. It was this expectation which was exemplified in the discussions of the ethics committee. Line by line, and word by word, they teased out the complex ethical expectations required by the 2007 Code. Invariably the basic principles that the 2007 Code covers were subject to analysis and reflection and to comprehensive review. When they were finished, the process was renewed and reviewed and discussed yet again. It is the challenge that they, as the Ethics Committee of the Australian Psychological Society (APS), have placed before their own Board, staff and membership.

From the regulators view, where we hear an extraordinarily inventive range of explanations for behaviours which practitioners of repute would not find acceptable, some elements of the "orders are orders" syndrome are beginning to appear. I am proud to report that this does not wash with the Board for whom I am the Registrar; nevertheless, it is concerning. It frequently coincides with the idea that while an individual is a registered psychologist, they were not, at the time of the complaint, "acting" as a psychologist. It is my personal view that the right to be a registered psychologist carries with it the obligation to behave, at all times with the honour, the integrity and the conscience to which all members of the professions ought to aspire.

From the professional association's viewpoint there is the need to provide the opportunity for membership to come together and present on the many activities which make up the work of that profession. These events are the powerhouse not only of the association but also the regulatory bodies in defining what is accepted as best practice. How else can the members hear, explore and explain what it is to be a member of their profession? There have been developments in the role of the Registration Boards, such as that shown in Victoria, where with the passage into law of the Health Professions Registration

Act of 2005, where the Regulatory Boards are empowered under Section 118. "Powers and functions of responsible boards" to take on the following function:

"(b) to approve courses of study that provide qualifications for registration as health practitioners in the health profession regulated by the board". This function derives its moral authority from the activities of the professional association where members use their evidence-based experience and presentations to bring before the membership discussion of matters of practice. How often have I heard members of the Board with which I am associated refer to those experiences when trying to reach a position on a matter, and how much more value and protection is offered by the fact that such experiences are derived from measurement against a wide membership base of thousands rather than the experiences of the practitioner members of the Board who number less than ten?

One of the benefits of a study of the past is that it allows us to look where we have been, to reflect upon that journey and to recognize where the tracks are taking us in our own time. If in accepting this Code as presented the members of the APS can recognize the journey the reviewers have taken and can accept the responsibility that the Code puts upon them when it is fully internalized into their professional behaviour, then we might see standards of practice which provide the greatest benefit and example to all who experience them. To bring together the single practitioner, their professional society, our communities of health practitioners and the society in which we all live, would be a wonderful achievement and one which I believe this code offers.

References

Caplan, A. L. (2005). Misusing the Nazi analogy. *Science*, 309, 535.
Health Professions Registration Act. (Victoria, Australia) 2005.
Mill, J. S. (1859/1974). *On liberty*. Harmondsworth, UK: Penguin.

Chapter 6
The Principles that Underlie the 2007 Code

Alfred Allan

The 2007 Code does not adopt any specific ethical theory. Instead, the Review Working Group (Group) carried on the tradition started by the authors of the 1960 Code by constructing the 2007 Code around principles. Although there are some authors who advocate the use of particular ethical frameworks, such as a virtue approach (see, e.g., Jordan & Meara, 1990; Meara, Schmidt, & Day, 1996), the weight of authority appears to be in favour of a principle-based or principlist approach in ethics in psychology and other health-related professions (Bersoff, 1996; Davidson, 2006). The authors of most of the codes that I will refer to later in this chapter also used a principle-based approach and it appears to have a number of advantages. It is, to start with, practically impossible to draft a totally inclusive code that will provide a solution for every conceivable ethical problem that may confront users of the code. There will therefore always be gaps in codes and stating the principles that underlie these codes explicitly allows users to refer back to them because they provide a higher, more abstract, level of norms if there is no standard to cover a specific situation (Beauchamp & Childress, 1994; Drane, 1982). Furthermore, both the Kohlberg (1976) and Gilligan (1993) models of moral thinking consider reasoning based on principles as more advanced than mere rule following (White, 1991). The articulation of the underlying principles of a code therefore encourages users to function at this higher level of moral decision-making (Bersoff & Koeppl, 1993; Fine & Ulrich, 1988; Knapp & Vandecreek, 2004). This, in turn, enhances objective, systematic and rational decision-making by psychologists. Psychologists are also likely to find it easier to understand, use and remember the content of codes where the standards are structured around, and grounded in, a small number of explicitly stated principles. Principles, furthermore, provide psychologists with a common vocabulary and therefore bring some order and coherence in the discussion of ethical problems (Kitchener, 1984). Finally, even though codes do not explicitly list the virtues the authors of codes believe psychologists should embody, the principles they incorporate usually reflect the virtues they consider important. In this way codes give guidance to trainee psychologists regarding the virtues they should strive to engender in their role as psychologists (Beauchamp & Childress, 1994; Bersoff, 1996; Jordan and Meara, 1990; Meara et al., 1996).

There are theoretically an infinite number of ethical principles that can guide the behaviour of psychologists, and therefore Beauchamp and Childress' (1994) common morality theory was used to identify the principles on which the 2007 Code should be based. These authors argue that the principles of a profession are those beliefs about right and wrong behaviour that are so widely shared by members of a profession that they can be said to "form a stable (although usually incomplete) communal consensus" (p. 5). To find these principles for Australian psychologists, a three-step review was undertaken.

The first step involved a review of the international literature regarding ethics in psychology (see Allan, 2008). An examination of the works of Beauchamp and Childress (1994), Gilligan (1993), Jordan and Meara (1990), Kitchener (1984), Koocher and Keith-Spiegel (2008) and Meara and colleagues (1996) identified 10 possible principles (see Table 6.1)[1]. Most of these principles are derived from Kant's theory (Kant, 1785/1964) but take into account utilitarianism and Gilligan's (1993) notions of care and responsibility.

As a second step, the 1997 Code was examined to determine where it reflects these 10 principles. With the exception of the Pursuit of Excellence and Care and Compassion principles, all the other principles appear in the 1997 Code. Not much attention was given to the Justice principle in the 1997 Code, except

Table 6.1　Principles in the authors' model

• Justice	• Beneficence (do good)
• According dignity	• Care and compassion
• Autonomy	• Veracity
• Nonmaleficence (do no harm)	• Fidelity
• Pursuit of excellence	• Accepting accountability

[1] Broadly defined autonomy, as used here, has two components. The first component reflects the right that competent people have to make their own decisions and to develop their own values, provided that they do not interfere with the welfare of others (self-determination). The second component is that people must respect other people's right to make their own decisions about matters of importance, such as privacy and dignity. Autonomy in the narrow sense includes only the first component.

that the authors state in General Principle III(b) that psychologists must be sensitive to diversity and must not act in a discriminatory manner. Indications of the According Dignity principle could be found in section E.4 ("preserve and protect the respect and dignity of all participants"). The Autonomy principle was reflected in sections A.2 (information that psychologists should provide to clients), B.5 (consent of young people) and D.3 and E.4 which dealt with informed consent by trainees and research participants, respectively. The Autonomy principle in a broader sense of the word also manifested in General Principle III(a) and in a cluster of provisions that dealt with rights such as privacy (B.1) and confidentiality (B.3), disclosure of information about criminal acts (B.6), communication of confidential information to other professionals (B.21) and confidentiality in research (E.11 and E.17).

Signs of the Nonmaleficence principle manifested in General Principles I and II; section B.5 (protection of the interest of young people); section B.18 (termination of the professional relationship); sections B.19 and B.20, which required that psychologists should be competent, maintain their competence and not work beyond; and section E, which dealt with research and the welfare of research participants. Beneficence was not mentioned explicitly in the 1997 Code but elements of this principle could be found in section B.14, where the drafters of the Code required psychologists to help clients locate alternative sources of assistance. Signs of Beneficence could be found in General Principle III (Propriety) where the authors emphasized that the welfare of clients takes precedence over the interest of psychologists and their employers.

Elements of the Veracity principle could be found in section B.14 which stipulated that psychologists had to make advance financial arrangements with clients, whilst aspects of the Fidelity principle could be found in sections B.7 and 8 (non-exploitation of clients).

If the Accepting Accountability principle is accepted as another name for the Responsibility principle it can be traced back to the 1949 Code. In the 1997 Code psychologists' responsibility was limited to their clients and the profession. General Principle I, for instance, provided that psychologists "remain personally responsible for the professional decisions they make". Psychologists' responsibility to their profession was reflected in provisions such as they had to "have the ultimate regard for the highest standards of their profession" (General Principle I). In a similar vein, principle III(c) provided that psychologists had to "refrain from any act which would tend to bring the profession into public disrepute". Inter-collegial loyalty was stressed in provisions that psychologists too should "refrain from making intemperate criticism in a manner which casts doubt on…[a]…colleagues" professional competence' (H.5) but if psychologists knew or suspected a Code violation by another member, they had to follow the procedures for persons invoking the Code (H.6.)

The third step involved a review of the codes of one international, one regional and six national psychology professional bodies set out in Table 6.2 to determine how they correspond with the ten principles set out in Table 6.1.

As in the 1997 Code, the Pursuit of Excellence and Care and Compassion did not manifest as explicit principles in any code. This makes sense, as they are aspirational statements or virtues rather than principles (also see McDowell, 1992). Therefore, although the drafters of the various codes differ in how they define, categorize and name the principles (Allan, 2008), there appears to be eight ethical principles that psychologists across the world share in the early part of the twenty-first century. (See Table 6.3.)

Five of these principles are directly derived from Kant's (1785/1964) theory, namely: Respect for the dignity and rights of people, Justice, Autonomy in the

Table 6.2 Codes reviewed

America
- American Psychological Association's Ethical Principles and Code of Conduct (2002)

Britain
- Code of Conduct, Ethical Principles and Guidelines of the British Psychological Society (1993)
- Code of Ethics and Conduct (2006)

Canada
- Canadian Code of Ethics for Psychologists (2000)

Europe
- European Federation of Psychological Associations (EFPA) Meta-Code of Ethics (2005)

New Zealand
- Code of Ethics: For Psychologists working in Aotearoa/New Zealand (2002)

South Africa
- Ethical Code of Professional Conduct of the South African Psychologist Board (2002)

Universal
- Draft Universal Declaration of Ethical Principles for Psychologists (Ad Hoc Joint Committee, 2005).

Table 6.3 Shared principles

• Respect for the dignity and rights of people	• Beneficence
• Justice	• Veracity
• Autonomy (narrow)	• Fidelity
• Nonmaleficence	• Responsibility

narrow sense, Veracity and Nonmaleficence (including competency and self-care). The Justice, Autonomy, Veracity and Nonmaleficence principles are, strictly speaking, applications of the Respect for the Dignity and Rights of People principle, but because they are so important they seem to have assumed the status of principles themselves. The Respect for the dignity and rights of people principle as used in most codes includes the According Dignity principle in the authors' model and second component of Autonomy as described in footnote 1.

The Beneficence principle as used in the codes is also derived from Kant's theory, but can also be justified by utilitarianism. The Beneficence principle is not always very explicit in the standards of the codes, perhaps because of its more aspirational nature. The exhortation to do good is rather more open-ended than the requirement not to do harm and therefore difficult to make explicit in many cases. The drafters of codes make a distinction between the Veracity and Fidelity principles because the latter principle is based on trust which takes it beyond what Kant had in mind. The Responsibility principle (Accepting accountability in the authors' model) reflects psychologists' accountability to clients, society and the profession and is based on legal or perceived social contracts.

A feature of these eight ethical principles is that they do not have an exclusive self focus, have a strong focus on the needs of others (primarily clients) but also the profession and society.

Respect for the Dignity, Moral and Legal Rights of People

This principle reflects Kant's (1785/1964) belief that humans (persons in contrast to things) are rational and therefore intrinsically valuable, and consequently their dignity and their moral and legal rights must be respected. People, either as individuals or collectives, should therefore never be used as a means to an end, in the Kantian perspective.

Psychologists must respect the dignity of people in all its forms, such as their public reputation, psychological and physical integrity, and their uniqueness. They must therefore communicate respect for other people through their language and actions. They must, furthermore, not harass people or make inappropriate physical contact with them or behave in a manner that may denigrate the character of people or demean or defame them. Respect is also conveyed in subtle ways, such as being punctual, responding to clients' requests expediently, and giving clients space when they need it. Psychologists must be non-judgemental and tolerant, and should avoid imposing their values on clients[2]. They must be particularly sensitive when working with people who are: stigmatized, marginalized, subject to prejudice, or, because of their experience in general, more vulnerable to whatever transpires in the professional relationship.

Psychologists must also respect other people with whom they interact on a professional level. They must, for instance, respect colleagues and be circumspect in what they say about them, because unfair and intemperate criticism of colleagues may defame them and reflect badly on the profession. If psychologists differ, they should debate this in an appropriate forum in a fair manner and refrain from making personal attacks on other people's character or conduct (Davidson, 2000). This does not mean that psychologists should ignore the unprofessional behaviour of their colleagues, but that they must take action in an appropriate and respectful manner if they encounter or become aware of unprofessional conduct. Psychologists are entitled to critique reports or give second opinions when requested, and may disagree with colleagues on professional issues. Their critique or comment on the qualifications, competencies or work of colleagues must, however, be objective and respectful. Any criticism they express must be grounded on facts and they must refrain from using emotive language when offering opinions.

The Respect principle further requires psychologists to respect their clients' moral rights, defined as their universal human rights by the United Nations' Universal Declaration of Human Rights, including those provisions in the Declaration that do not form part of Australian domestic law.

Psychologists must also respect people's legal rights, such as parental and intellectual property rights. For instance, when they review grant or research proposals, or material submitted for publication, they must respect the intellectual proprietary rights of those who made the submissions. Privacy is a right (and a form of dignity) that is highly regarded in Western society. If psychologists expect clients to share information with them, irrespective of how embarrassing or controversial this information may be, they must respect clients' right to privacy. Privacy has two applications. The first application can be called the *right against intrusion or the right to be left alone* (Warren & Brandeis, 1890). This application regulates the extent to which a psychologist can encroach in the client's sphere of intimacy, for example by video or audio taping interviews without permission or asking questions not germane to the client's presenting problem. The second application is the *right to confidentiality*, in accordance with which psychologists must keep secret any confidential

---

[2] This does not mean that psychologists never make judgements, but means that they do not impose their personal values on clients who might hold equally legitimate values.

information obtained from clients, people associated with clients, and colleagues. Psychologists must, for instance, keep material they are asked to review, such as grant applications, confidential.

Rights are not absolute and may be breached if there are overriding ethical obligations to do so. Psychologists may, for example, breach clients' right to confidentiality when it is necessary in order to protect them or other people. In some instances clients themselves may repudiate their right to confidentiality. Nevertheless, given the ethical and practical importance of privacy, the provisions in the codes that allow psychologists to violate their clients' right to confidentiality tend to be very conservative and psychologists must take care to remain within the parameters of these provisions.

Justice

Justice is fundamentally about fairness, rightness and equity (Benn, 1967). Psychologists must treat people without unfair discrimination or favouritism. Discrimination is unfair if a psychologist's actions are based on irrelevant information about the client, such as their age, culture, disabilities, gender, race, religion, sexual orientation or values.

Various forms of justice have been identified, of which two are important for this discussion. *Procedural* justice focuses on the requirement that when psychologists make judgements about the behaviour of other people, they must be objective and fair. Psychologists should therefore be fair when, for instance, they select students for admission to a training program, review grant proposals, decide whom they will admit to a treatment program with a long waiting list, or make other decisions that will affect other people. They should also, where they are obliged to report sexual or other abuse, be fair in their assessment of situations if there is suspicion of such behaviour. An inherent aspect of fairness is that psychologists must be consistent in their decision-making and must be able to explain any apparent inconsistencies.

Distributive justice refers to the notion that benefits, risks and costs should be shared fairly. The premise of this approach is that it is for the common good of a group or society that everyone should be treated fairly at all levels. This form of justice is of particular importance to the profession as one implication of it is that psychologists should endeavour to ensure that all people have fair access to linguistically and culturally appropriate psychological services. In the case of research, psychologists must, for instance, ensure that as far as possible participants who carry the burden and risks are given a reciprocal share of the benefits of the research.

Autonomy

This ethical principle reflects the psychological need that people have to feel in control of their lives (see for example, Deci, 1980; Fiske, 2004; Fiske & Taylor, 2000; Thompson, Sobolew-Shubin, Galbraith, Schwankovsky, & Cruzen, 1993). It also acknowledges competent people's right to make, freely and voluntarily, informed decisions pertaining to their lives. Autonomy is the opposite of paternalism, where others make decisions affecting individuals on their behalf, and by treating clients as autonomous people psychologists demonstrate that they respect their right to make mistakes. In return, their clients must take responsibility for their decisions and behaviour. It is therefore important that clients should have the capabilities required to make the relevant decisions and take responsibility for them. The decisions they make, furthermore, must be free and voluntary choices based on adequate and accurate information about all aspects of the service, including any financial aspects. Psychologists can show respect for their clients' autonomy by engaging them in a shared decision-making process where clients play an active role and the psychologists adopt the role of facilitators. The 2007 Code makes it clear that psychologists should enhance clients' ability to make decisions; if clients are not competent to give legal binding consent, psychologists must, as far as possible, still engage them in an informed consent process and obtain their assent (Standard A.3.7).

Nonmaleficence

Nonmaleficence is the duty that psychologists have to not harm people or engage in behaviour where it is reasonably foreseeable that it could harm others. Psychologists also have a duty to minimize harm when it is unavoidable. It is impossible for psychologists to avoid all harm, but they should engage in conduct that may be potentially harmful only if there are overriding ethical reasons that justify their behaviour; the potential benefits of their conduct outweigh the potential harm and they take steps to restrict the harm. They must also endeavour to correct the detrimental effects of any harm that they caused.

Psychologists must therefore refrain from intentionally or recklessly (that is when they foresee harm but ignore the risk) causing harm to those with whom they work. They must, furthermore, provide services only within the boundaries of their psychological competence, and practice with the care expected of an average, competent and reasonably cautious psychologist in any professional situation they encounter. Psychologists must also maintain their level of competence and keep abreast of new developments relevant to their areas through continuing professional training.

Competent and cautious psychologists are expected to use reliable and valid methods, techniques and procedures that are based on scientifically and professionally derived knowledge. The profession and the law increasingly expect psychologists to restrict themselves to evidence-based practice in psychology (American Psychological Association, 2005; Bohart, 2005).

Nevertheless, psychological competency is not the only competency psychologists require. They are also required to be legally and ethically proficient (*legal-ethical competency*) and have the *cultural competence* to work with people from different cultures and subcultures (Australian Psychological Society, 2003; Davidson, 1999). Furthermore, they must be *physically and mentally* competent to practice. There is a range of physical and psychological factors that can impair the ability of psychologists to practice competently. These include transient problems, such as physical illness, mourning, recovering from a trauma or feeling burnt out or stressed (Mair, 1996; Wood, 1996). Problems that may be more enduring include the problematic use of substances, dementia and acquired brain injuries.

An implication of this principle is that psychologists should continue their professional development and ideally work under ongoing supervision of some nature for the duration of their careers. Psychologists' self-care duty extends to them taking care of their physical and mental health, for instance by adopting a balanced and healthy lifestyle and taking steps to prevent them from being exploited or injured by clients. This will ensure that the standard of their practice remains at the required level and will help them identify and avoid potential problems before they become major issues.

Beneficence

This principle is on the opposite side of the coin from nonmaleficence and refers to the moral obligation of psychologists to act for the benefit of others. In psychology this principle is interpreted as a *prima facie* moral obligation on psychologists to act when their behaviour is likely to avert considerable harm to people, such as their clients, with whom they have a special relationship. The beneficence principle does not require psychologists to do "something beyond the call of duty or from the goodness of one's heart" (Kerridge, Lowe, & McPhee, 2005, p. 52); but it requires psychologists to weigh up the costs and the benefits of actions directed at clients and to choose the option from which clients are likely to benefit most (Beauchamp & Childress, 1994). Given the huge range of situations in which people may find themselves there are few ethical standards in codes that are related to this principle.

Veracity

Psychologists can function optimally only if they and their profession are perceived as truthful (Meara et al., 1996). They must therefore guard against deceiving themselves or others and must be truthful in all their dealings with clients (Jordan & Meara, 1990). This requires psychologists to be accurate and objective when they communicate with clients and ensure that they do not unintentionally mislead them. Psychologists must also take reasonable steps to correct any misrepresentation made by them, even though they may have been made unintentionally. They must also correct any misconceptions held by a client about them, even those they did not contribute to in any manner. They should furthermore actively prevent people from forming misconceptions about them. Clients, for instance, seldom understand the differences between psychologists and psychiatrists, and the differences between specialities within psychology. Psychologists should correct misunderstandings that clients may have about the nature and extent of psychological services that they provide to clients.

Fidelity

In accordance with the Fidelity principle psychologists are in fiduciary (from the Latin word for trust) relationships with clients, because they are entrusted with the interests of clients; therefore, clients' interests take precedence over psychologists' interests and over the interests of others, such as psychologists' employers and colleagues. Whilst some psychologists contest the assertion that they have any power over their clients, clients and ethicists believe that psychologists are indeed in a position of power. (See the Victorian Psychologists Registration Board case: Re Timewell, 2002.) There are various reasons for this perception of a power imbalance between psychologists and clients. Psychologists undeniably have *knowledge and skills*, which most other people do not have, that can give them insights into their clients' situation, personal dynamics and vulnerabilities. The relationship between clients and their psychologists (particularly, but not exclusively when psychologists are therapists) is often very *intense and intimate*. Psychologist-client relationships are also characterized by a degree of *dependency* by clients on psychologists; and people who are dependent are likely to accept the suggestions psychologists make because they fear that they may reject or abandon them (Appelbaum & Jorgenson, 1991). In order to receive assistance, clients must further *share intimate and sensitive information* about themselves with psychologists. Clients furthermore normally consult psychologists when they are hurting and often feeling desperate and are therefore at their most *vulnerable* (Epstein, 1989).

The cumulative effect of these factors promotes the perception of a power imbalance and the belief that clients and society have no choice other than to trust psychologists. The general public expects professional people to be more trustworthy than other people (McKillop, Hills, & Helmes, 1999), and to reassure society and clients that they are worthy of that trust, psychologists must adhere to the Fidelity principle. They must therefore maintain clear boundaries with clients, manage any conflicts of interests with them and avoid exploiting them at any level. All exploitation of clients can be very damaging because even if it does not harm clients psychologically, physically or economically it still erodes the trust, of both individuals and public, in psychologists.

The fiduciary relationship between psychologists and clients does not end the moment the formal professional relationship ends. Psychologists still have the knowledge they had during the relationship and, although the immediacy and form of the relationship may change and fade over time, the essential foundation of that relationship does not disappear. Psychologists therefore remain in a powerful position with regard to their clients for considerable periods following formal termination. While the length of this implicit relationship is open to debate, its primary importance is widely accepted by psychologists.

Responsibility

This principle reflects the responsibilities psychologists have towards a range of parties and entities, but primarily to their clients, society and the profession.

Clients

Psychologists' primary responsibility is towards their clients and emanates from the psychologist-client relationship. When they enter into professional relationships with clients, psychologists undertake to provide professional services in accordance with the ethical principles of the profession and the law of the jurisdiction in which they practice; and they are accountable to clients for this undertaking. The ethical responsibility of psychologists, however, exceeds their legal responsibility. For instance, whereas law requires fault as a prerequisite for compensation, psychologists are ethically responsible to repair harm they caused irrespective of whether they were at fault or not (e.g., Davidson, 2006). In practice psychologists must therefore anticipate the possible harm that could flow from their conduct and take steps to avoid such harm. For example, they must ensure that their clients and other parties (whether they are clients or associated parties) understand the nature and limitations of the relationships between psychologists and each of the parties. Psychologists must also collaborate with other professionals where it is in the best interests of their clients or where they are not competent to provide an adequate service on their own. Psychologists must take steps to ensure that competent colleagues will take care of their clients' welfare if they (the psychologists) are not available, whether temporarily or permanently. They must further take the welfare of their clients into account when they terminate professional relationships.

Profession

The crux of psychologists' responsibility to the profession is to act towards clients, associated parties, colleagues and other professionals in such a way that ensures that clients, other parties, associated parties, other professionals and the general public do not lose confidence in the services and related benefits that psychology as a profession has to offer. They must therefore behave professionally and in a way that will promote the profession and not bring it into disrepute. Psychologists' responsibility to promote the profession requires them to protect the effectiveness of psychological assessment methods and techniques by not rendering those methods open to misuse by publishing them or otherwise disclosing their contents to people who are unauthorized or unqualified to receive such information. They should contribute to the profession and science of psychology by, for example, supervising trainees, serving as office bearers of professional bodies, or doing research that will enhance psychology's contributions to society. Psychologists behave responsibly by obeying the professional rules that govern them and collaborating with authorities if complaints are lodged against them. Psychologists also have a responsibility to respond when they have reason to believe colleagues are involved in criminal activities, or are incompetent, or practicing unethically, or impaired due to physical, mental or addiction problems.

Society

Psychologists, individually and collectively as a profession, have responsibilities to society. Individual psychologists are members of society and are therefore bound by the law and public morality of the jurisdiction in which they live and practice. They must therefore obey the morally defendable law of the jurisdiction. When psychologists' legal obligations conflict with their responsibilities to their clients, they must follow the law. This means, for example, that psychologists, as a general rule, may not refuse to disclose private client information in court when ordered to do so (Anderten, Staulcup, & Grisso, 1980). Psychologists' responsibility to clients is similarly overridden by their responsibility to society when their clients pose an imminent threat of harm to society as such, or to identifiable members of society. Psychologists could also be held responsible for the foreseeable consequences of their deliberate or negligent failure to protect members of the public from harm.

Both individual psychologists and the profession have a social responsibility. The profession's responsibility derives from the notion that society recognizes professions because they serve a social function (Parsons, 1968). According to this notion professions therefore have a right of existence only if, and for as long as, they and their members serve a societal function. Providing a profession meets its responsibility, society will invest in it (e.g., through subsidizing training), give members of the profession privileges (e.g., allowing them exclusive use of the title psychologist) and allow them to regulate themselves to a point. Most psychologists agree, in return, that they must provide services that are useful to society and must ensure that they are competent, do not harm members of society, develop a moral community, and use their professional competencies to the benefit of society and its members (Canadian Psychological Association, 2000). As Davidson discusses in Chapter 9, however, psychologists disagree regarding the degree to which they are responsible to work actively to change those aspects of society that lead to psychological problems.

Conclusion

The 2007 Code is grounded on eight ethical principles that were, for pragmatic reasons, collapsed into three General Principles[3]. The Justice, Autonomy and Rights and Dignity of People principles where collapsed into the Respect for

---

[3] Authors differ in the nomenclature they use to describe the principles and whether they classify them as general principles, principles or applications. For instance, it is common to collapse the principles into three or four general or super-ordinate principles, or to call something a principle that others would see as an application of a principle. For example, whilst some would describe competency as a principle or even a general principle (see the BPS 2006 Code), others would consider it an application of the non-maleficence principle. This does not, however, distract from the fact that these are important moral obligations shared by the international community of psychologists.

the Rights and Dignity of People and Peoples general principle which has a strong deontological character. The Propriety general principle consists of the Nonmaleficence and Beneficence principles and aspects of the Responsibility principle and has a consequentialist nature. Other aspects of the Responsibility principle and the Veracity and Fidelity principles have been collapsed into the Integrity general principle. These General Principles are explicitly stated in the code as the ethical principles of the APS. As the relative weight given to general principles will differ from situation to situation, the Group refrained from appropriating weight to the different general principles. The sequence of the general principles was determined by the logical flow of the document and does not reflect the relative weight of the different general principles. This means that, in contrast to the authors of some codes (see, e.g., the Canadian Code) and scholars (see, e.g., Ross, 1930; Kitchener, 1984), the Group considers all the principles have equal weight, but *prima facie* (Davidson, 2006). Where psychologists find themselves in situations where more than one of these principles place a duty on them, they must study the situation and make a considered opinion regarding which one of the principles are more pressing on them under the circumstances. The 2007 Code follows the trend of most modern codes of ethics in psychology by explicitly linking ethical standards to principles on which they are grounded. It was the belief of the Group that if psychologists cannot find a specific ethical standard in the 2007 Code that provides an answer to the problem facing them, they should be able to work towards a solution by applying the principles that underlie the Code.

References

Ad Hoc Joint Committee. (2005). *Draft: Universal declaration of ethical principles of psychologists*. Unpublished manuscript.

Allan, A. (2008). *An international perspective of law and ethics in psychology*. Somerset West, South Africa: Inter-ed.

American Psychological Association. (2005). *Report of the 2005 Presidential Task Force on evidence-based practice*. Washington, DC: Author.

Anderten, P., Staulcup, V., & Grisso, T. (1980). On being ethical in legal places. *Professional Psychology, 11*, 764–73.

Appelbaum, P. S., & Jorgenson, L. (1991). Psychotherapist-patient sexual contact after termination of treatment: An analysis and a proposal. *American Journal of Psychiatry, 148*, 1466–73.

Australian Psychological Society. (2003). *Guidelines for the provision of psychological services for, and the conduct of psychological research with, Aboriginal and Torres Strait Islander people of Australia*. Melbourne, Victoria: Author.

Beauchamp, T. L., & Childress, J. F. (1994). *Principles of biomedical ethics* (4th ed.). New York: Oxford University Press.

Benn, S. I. (1967). Justice. In P. Edwards (Ed.), *The encyclopaedia of philosophy* (Vol. 4, pp. 298–302). New York, NY: MacMillan.

Bersoff, D. N. (1996). The virtue of principle ethics. *The Counseling Psychologist*, *24*, 86–91.

Bersoff, D. N., & Koeppl, P. M. (1993). The relation between ethical codes and moral principles. *Ethics and Behavior*, *3*, 345–57.

Bohart, A. C. (2005). Evidence-based psychotherapy means evidence-informed, not evidence-driven. *Journal of Contemporary Psychotherapy*, *35*, 39–53.

British Psychological Society. (1993). *Code of conduct, ethical principles & guidelines*. London: Author.

British Psychological Society. (2006). *Code of conduct and practice*. Leicester, UK: Author.

Canadian Psychological Association. (2000). *Code of ethics for psychologists*. 3rd ed. Retrieved 25 September 2000 from www.cpa.ca/ethics.html.

Davidson, G. R. (1999). Cultural competence as an ethical precept in psychology. In P. Martin & W. Noble (Eds.), *Psychology and society* (pp. 162–74). Brisbane: Australian Academic Press.

Davidson, G. R. (2000). Advice for psychologists offering second opinions. *In Psych*, *22*, 12–13.

Davidson, G. R. (2006). Towards an ethical framework for psychological practice. In S. Morrissey & P. Reddy (Eds.), *Ethical and professional practice for psychologists* (pp. 1–13). Melbourne, Australia: Thomson.

Deci, E. L. (1980). *The psychology of self-determination*. Lexington, MA: Lexington Books.

Drane, J. (1982). Ethics and psychotherapy: A philosophical perspective. In M. Rosenbaum (Ed.), *Ethics and values in psychotherapy: A guidebook* (pp. 15–50). New York: Free Press.

Epstein, J. M. (1989). The exploitative psychotherapist as a defendant. *Trial*, *25*, 52–9.

European Federation of Psychological Associations (EFPA). (2005). Meta-code of ethics. Retrieved 12 February 2006 from www.efpa.be/ethics.php.

Fine, M. A., & Ulrich, L. P. (1988). Integrating psychology and philosophy in teaching a graduate course in ethics. *Professional Psychology: Research and Practice*, *19*, 542–6.

Fiske, S. T. (2004). *Social beings*. New York: Wiley.

Fiske, S. T., & Taylor, S. E. (2000). *Social cognition* (3rd ed.). New York: McGraw-Hill.

Gilligan, C. (1993). *In a different voice: Psychological theory and women's development* (2nd ed.). Cambridge MA: Harvard University Press.

Health Professions Council of South Africa. (2002). *Ethical code of professional conduct*. Retrieved 17 September 2003 from www.psyssa.com/aboutus/codeofconduct.asp.

Jordan, A. E., & Meara, N. M. (1990). Ethics and professional practice of psychologists: The role of virtues and principles. *Professional Psychology: Research and Practice*, *21*, 107–14.

Kant, I. (1785/1964). *Groundwork of the metaphysics of ideals*. (H. J. Paton, Trans.). New York: Harper & Row.

Kerridge, I., Lowe, M., & McPhee, J. (2005). *Ethics and law for the health professions* (2nd ed.). Annandale: Federation Press.

Kitchener, K. S. (1984). Intuition, critical evaluation and ethical principles: The foundations for ethical decisions in counseling psychology. *The Counseling Psychologist, 12*, 43–55.

Knapp, S., & Vandecreek, L. (2004). A principle-based analysis of the 2002 American Psychological Association Ethics Code. *Psychotherapy Theory Research Practice Training, 41*, 247.

Kohlberg, L. A. (1976). Moral stages and moralization: The cognitive developmental approach. In T. Lickona (Ed.), *Moral development and behavior: Theory, research and social issues* (pp. 31–53). New York: Holt.

Koocher, G. P., & Keith-Spiegel, P. (2008). *Ethics in Psychology and the Mental Health Professions: Standards and Cases* (3rd ed.). New York: Oxford.

Mair, P. (1996). Psychology in the Australian outback: Rural health services. In P. R. Martin & J. S. Birnbrauer (Eds.), *Clinical Psychology. Profession and practice in Australia* (pp. 480–507). Melbourne: Melbourne Education.

McDowell, B. (1992). The ethical obligations of professional teachers. *Professional Ethics, 1*, 53–76.

McKillop, D., Hills, A. M., & Helmes, E. (1999, October). *Who do we trust? Contemporary views of the status and trustworthiness of lawyers, police officers and others.* Paper presented at the 14th Annual Conference of the Australian and New Zealand Society of Criminology, Perth, Western Australia.

Meara, N. M., Schmidt, L. D., & Day, J. D. (1996). Principles and virtues: A foundation for ethical decisions, policies and character. *The Counseling Psychologist, 4*, 4–77.

New Zealand Psychological Society. (2002). *Code of ethics.* Retrieved 17 September 2003 from www.psychology.org.nz.

Parsons, T. (1968). Professions. In D. L. Sills (Ed.), *International Encyclopedia of Social Sciences* (vol. *12*, pp. 536–46). New York: MacMillan.

Re Timewell. (2002). PRBD (Vic) 1.

Ross, W. D. (1930). *The right and the good.* Oxford: Clarendon Press.

Thompson, S. C., Sobolew-Shubin, A., Galbraith, M. E., Schwankovsky, L., & Cruzen, D. (1993). Maintaining perceptions of control: Finding perceived control in low-control circumstances. *Journal of Personality and Social Psychology, 64*, 293–304.

Warren, S., & Brandeis, L. (1890). The right to privacy. *Harvard Law Review, 4*, 193–220.

White, T. I. (1991). *Discovering philosophy.* Englewood Cliffs, NJ: Prentice Hall.

Wood, W. M. (1996). Professional issues, registration and ethical issues. In P. R. Martin & J. S. Birnbrauer (Eds.), *Clinical Psychology. Profession and practice in Australia* (pp. 77–102). Melbourne, Australia: Melbourne Education.

Chapter 7
Consent, Privacy and Confidentiality

Graham R. Davidson, Alfred Allan
and Anthony W. Love

The educative function of the Code was of specific importance to the Working Group when it drafted the standards concerning informed consent, privacy and confidentiality. The Working Group (Group) needed to rethink, and find a balance between, the applications of guiding principles of autonomy, justice, beneficence, integrity and self-care. Furthermore, there have been important legislative changes (e.g., the changes to the Privacy Act, 1988, that were introduced by the Privacy Amendment [Private Sector] Act, 2000) and court judgements (e.g., Kadian v Richards, 2004; Stapeley v Fisher, 2003) that now impact on the application of these principles. The Privacy Act, for instance, is prescriptive about information that psychologists should provide before collecting client-related information from clients and other parties, and how they should manage such information once they have received it. These provisions and case law have further complicated an area of ethics where there are many exceptions to the general rules of privacy and confidentiality, especially if psychologists work with minor clients (Gustafson & McNamara, 1987; also see Chapter 10). There have also been developments in practice, such as the use of techno-psychology (Grohol, 1999; Koocher, 2007), expansion of rebates by health insurers and Medicare, and the use of centralized electronic filing systems, that challenge the traditional application of the principles of autonomy and integrity. The standards grounded on these principles, such as those found in A.3 to A.7, B.2, and B.4 to B.5, differ somewhat from the standards based on some other principles. They are sufficiently detailed to synthesize evolving ethical and legal expectations in respect of client autonomy and privacy.

Autonomy, which is defined in Kantian theory as free will, can be operationalized as self-freedom or self-determination. Autonomy is a key precept underpinning the Code as well as many other existing codes. It has significance specifically for psychologists who acknowledge the importance of people being able to make free, informed decisions about matters that concern them. However, because people must take responsibility for the consequences of their decisions, it is equally important that they should be competent (i.e., legally and intellectually capable of making, communicating and abiding by a decision), adequately informed about all relevant matters that might influence the decisions they are required to make, and able to make them freely and voluntarily. It has become customary to refer to the requirement that clients should be informed when they make decisions as *informed consent*. However, authors such as Brock (1991) believe that this term suggests a level of passivity on the part of the decision maker and does not reflect the fact that what is involved is a decision-making process involving the active participation of the client. Brock therefore suggests the use of the term *shared decision making*. The Group discussed the use of this term instead of "informed consent" but, whilst acknowledging its merit, decided to retain the term "informed consent" because it is a well-established concept that most psychologists are familiar with and implement in their practice, even if they do not necessarily appreciate all of its contemporary ramifications. However, the group noted that the use of this term may have to be reconsidered during future revisions of the Code.

Privacy and confidentiality, along with informed consent, strictly speaking, are also applications of client autonomy. Having the right to privacy is fundamental to the respect for dignity principle. Right to privacy is predicated on the principle of autonomy – self-determination – because it involves individuals being free to make the decision to be let alone, provides protection from undue, arbitrary interference or intrusion by others into one's personal affairs, and implies having control over one's personal information, including control over how and for what purpose the information is to be gathered, kept, used and discarded. Confidentiality is an expression of the privacy right. Confidentiality constitutes the act of keeping personal information secret. In the context of psychological practice, it involves a conditional duty to protect the privacy of clients' personal information that has been shared with a practitioner by clients or other parties holding the expectation of confidentiality.

However, rights – in this case, to decide about matters that affect one's person and privacy – like duties, are conditional (Ross, 1930). Respect for these rights comes with the caveat that the dignity, personal safety and security, and personal privacy of others must be similarly respected. The challenge confronting psychologists, as recognized by members of the Group, is to determine when a client's rights to decide, and to privacy, should be set aside by the psychologist in preference for the competing duty to protect the welfare of the client or others who might be harmed unreasonably or unnecessarily. In essence, psychologists typically respect client autonomy. However, in exceptional circumstances, re-prioritization of the psychologist's ethical duties might require the psychologist to break confidentiality. For example, if a client is threatening self-harm, and in the psychologist's opinion the threat is real and immediate, then revealing the person's intentions to a crisis assessment and treatment team in order to prevent harm might be justified under the circumstances.

Psychologists, like other parties, also have personal and professional rights that should be respected. They have the right to practice without fearing unreasonably and unnecessarily for their personal safety, reputation or livelihood. They have the right to defend themselves against unreasonable and unjust claims of malpractice or loss of income. In other words, they have the right to protection from undue harm that might result from clients' actions. Thus, questions about when it is appropriate to proceed with a psychological service without the client's express consent, intrude on a client's personal affairs and divulge information about clients and other parties to a service – that is, break confidentiality – are immediately apparent. Answers to these questions often do not rest solely with individual psychologists but may be determined expressly by statute or spelled out the organizational policies and procedures applying to the psychologist's workplace. The Code attempts to impress on members the importance of the dignity and autonomy principles, which are operationalized in the standards relating to informed consent, maintenance of privacy and keeping client information confidential; but it also acknowledges that there are limits to clients' rights to decide about the circumstances under which a service will be provided, personal information will be protected, and confidentiality maintained where the rights of others, including the psychologist, are concerned. Therefore, those sections of the Code, which will be considered in more detail in this chapter, contain both the minimum standards for obtaining clients' informed consent, observing clients' privacy and maintaining confidentiality, *and* the minimum standards for setting aside usual requirements for obtaining consent, protecting clients' privacy and ensuring confidentiality.

Before examining those standards it is important to reflect on psychologists' conditional duty to keep their promises to clients. Keeping and discharging promises (i.e., the duty of honesty) is a component of the integrity principle, along with truthfulness and trustworthiness. While the latter expressions of honesty are central to General Principle C (Integrity) in the 2007 Code, honesty in the form of giving and keeping promises is an ethical cornerstone of informed consent, privacy protection and maintenance of confidentiality. The promises psychologists make to clients are embedded in their charter of client services, practice (or service) brochure, website and other advertising information, and service contract. These documentary materials should contain the information that clients require in order to make an informed judgement about whether or not to avail themselves of the psychologist's services, whether their privacy will be protected or violated, and whether or not personal information they share with the psychologist will remain confidential. The psychologist has an unconditional duty to discharge the promises contained in those documentary materials, if the materials have been properly prepared to reflect the psychologist's duty to respect and protect the client's *conditional* rights, as stated above, to free decision, privacy and confidentiality. The documentary materials, therefore, must accurately reflect the standards contained in the 2007 Code that deal with consent, privacy and confidentiality; and psychologists would be wise to consider exactly what they are promising clients in those documentary materials.

In the remainder of this chapter, we look briefly at the standards that deal with what clients might reasonably expect to be told by the psychologist, in a comprehensible manner, in order to make an informed decision about participating in a service, including promises about limits to consent, privacy and confidentiality.

Consent

The 2007 Code provides that psychologists should fully inform all clients in plain language about the services to be provided, irrespective of the client's competence to make an informed decision to accept the proposed services (A.3). Limitations on the client's competence may be legal ones, for instance, the client is a minor and in the context of the decision to be made is not considered to be a mature minor (Milne, 1995); or they may be psychological; for example, the client is impaired intellectually, emotionally or otherwise psychologically to the point where she or he is unable to make an informed decision. The only exceptions to this general rule are where people have explicitly waived in advance their right to be informed, or where it is not reasonably possible to obtain informed consent, such as in the case of small children (A.3.1). Psychologists, similarly, must obtain consent to provide services from all clients unless the need to obtain consent is not required by law or has been waived by an appropriate research ethics committee (A.3.4). Whilst the Code requires that consent for proposed procedures involving physical contact be documented in an appropriate fashion (A.3.5), it is preferable that all consent documentation should be in writing whenever and wherever possible. This advice aims to ensure the client's consent is obtained when it is required and that the psychologist inadvertently does not neglect to obtain it. Psychologists attempt to obtain clients' consent even where the client's ability to give it is impaired or limited legally. If this is not practical they obtain the consent of people with legal authority to act on the client's behalf (A.3.6). Strictly speaking, parents or guardians have the authority to give consent in the case of people younger than 18 years in all Australian jurisdictions. However, the courts have waived this requirement in the case of so-called mature minors (Department of Health and Community Services v JWB [Marion's case], 1992). Whether minors are judged mature enough to give informed consent will depend on factors such as their ability to understand the nature of the proposed services, their level of cognitive development, including their perceived capacity to comprehend the reasonably foreseeable consequences of accepting or refusing the service being offered and the benefits and risks associated with the service, and whether they have a Medicare card in their own name. In the case of persons who have reached the legal age of consent but who are psychologically impaired, consent should be sought from another who has legal power of attorney or who is appointed as a legal guardian by the court. Where clients are not legally competent to give consent psychologists still respect their dignity by obtaining their assent to provide the service (A.3.7).

Standard A.3.3 specifies the information that psychologists should provide for clients prior to obtaining their consent to the delivery of a psychological service. The information listed represents a minimum standard of disclosure that is acceptable to the profession and reflects published, professional opinion on informed consent. Pomerantz and Handelsman (2004) maintained that clients have a right to know about: the consulting psychologist's professional (e.g., therapeutic, assessment or research) orientation, background and experience as a psychologist, alternative professional orientations that may be available from other psychological services, arrangements regarding appointments, limits of confidentiality, fees and charges, and insurance arrangements and rebates. Pryor (1997) has recommended that clients be informed about: the nature and extent of the professional services to be provided, including the preparation and provision of reports; exactly who will be providing the services; the professional qualifications and affiliations of service providers; the purpose and rationale for the service and criteria for evaluating service outcomes; the provider's expectations of clients, including homework and other preparation required for consultation sessions; the likely costs of the service; the client's right to withhold information and to question the relevance of procedures used in service delivery; what will happen to any personal, assessment or evaluative information gathered in the course of service delivery; the limits of confidentiality, including conditions under which information may be made available to other appropriately qualified professionals; and appropriate means of complaint or redress if the client is dissatisfied with service delivery or outcomes. The type of information provided to clients will depend on the type of psychological service they offer. These services can range from assessment, therapeutic intervention, organizational consulting, research practice or professional supervision and so forth, but core elements of what clients should be told are equally applicable to any psychological service, be it therapy, consulting, research or supervision. Similar expectations about information provision apply in circumstances where a client's consent is sought for gathering information from associated parties (A.7.4) and where other parties are approached for client information (A.7.5). Psychologists have a responsibility to ensure that all parties to a service have an appropriate understanding of the conditions of service delivery prior to the commencement of services (B.4).

Put simply, the information specified in A.3.3, A.7.4 and A.7.5, as well as other information suggested by Pomerantz and Handelsman (2004) and Pryor (1997), when presented to clients in the form of a client charter, service brochure, website materials, research information sheet, supervision plan, service agreement or consent form constitutes the basis for consent and contains the promises the psychologist is offering to the client as well as any other parties to a service. Thoroughness in formulating these professional disclosures is a show of respect for the clients' dignity and autonomy; delivery of the services strictly in accordance with the information given to clients and other parties is a measure of psychologist's fidelity.

Privacy

Privacy has two components. The first is the right that people have against the unjustified intrusion into their private lives, that is, "the right to be left alone" (Warren & Brandeis, 1890, p. 195). The second is the right to exercise control over the agglomeration, storage, dissemination and use of their personal information (Allan, 2008).

Psychologists demonstrate their respect for clients' right to be left alone by only collecting, with their consent, personal information from them that is strictly required to provide the agreed upon service (A.4) and by obtaining their consent to collect information from associated parties of clients, such as their employers or spouses (A.7). In adherence to the privacy principle, psychologists should use client data only for the primary purpose for which it was collected (B.5.5). However, as in the case with other rights, clients as autonomous people can waive their right to privacy by giving consent to psychologists to use it for a secondary purpose (A.5.5 [a]). Even when psychologists have their clients' consent to use or disclose information, psychologists still have a duty to protect their clients' privacy by only using if for the purpose for which the information was disclosed and only to people required to have that information (A.5.4). Psychologists, in certain circumstances, may also release de-identified client data to researchers doing approved research without clients' consent (A.5.5 [b]). This is justified because the benefit of psychological research for the common good outweighs the relatively minor invasion of clients' privacy rights brought about by the release of de-identified information. The release of de-identified data for approved research use is also unlikely to lead to any harm. Psychologists are legally and ethically obliged to keep adequate client records (B.2) and, when there are inaccuracies in records, psychologists respond appropriately to reasonable requests by clients for them to make appropriate corrections, deletions and additions (B2.4). Furthermore, psychologists do not refuse reasonable requests from clients and former clients to access their information for which psychologists have professional responsibility (A.6).

Confidentiality

When clients disclose personal and private information to psychologists, they are entrusting that information to the psychologist with the expectation that the latter ordinarily will hold the information in trust in accordance with the terms and conditions under which the psychological service is being provided. One of the psychologist's conditional duties, therefore, is to protect (keep secret or confidential) clients' personal information. This means, in the context of their professional relationships with clients, that psychologists must ensure that they collect, record, disseminate and dispose of client information in a manner that protects the information entrusted to them (A.5.1 [a]). The professional standard of confidentiality refers to the act of keeping professional secrets. The duty of psychologists to maintain the confidentiality of clients' information continues after the termination of the professional relationship and even the death of clients (Jifkins, 2009a). Psychologists must further take reasonable steps to protect the confidentiality of client information after they leave a specific work setting, or cease to provide services, including as a result of misfortune or their death (A.5.1 [b]).

Whilst psychologists have a clear duty to protect the confidentiality of clients' personal information, that duty is conditional and can be superseded by other duties in certain circumstances. There are, therefore, a number of exceptions where psychologists may be entitled or, in some cases, obliged, to disclose client information. The most obvious exception to maintaining confidentiality is that clients, or people who have legal authority, may explicitly instruct psychologists to disclose information to an identified entity for a specific purpose and within a specified time frame (A.5.2 [a]). Whilst psychologists should take and act on such a directive from a client, they must, in accordance with the principle of beneficence, counsel clients if they believe that the directive to disclose the information is not in the client's best interests.

Psychologists may be required in law to disclose confidential client information without clients' consent and even against clients' wishes (A.5.2 [b]). This exception to the confidentiality rule covers, among other situations, court orders served on a psychologist to disclose confidential information. Subpoenas may take the form of orders to produce records and other documents, attend the court, give oral evidence to the court, or make records and other documents available for inspection or discovery. After establishing the validity of the order and the terms, conditions and content of the required disclosure, and irrespective of whether the psychologist has been successful in obtaining the client's consent for the psychologist to break confidentiality, the psychologist should comply with the court's final ruling (Davidson, 2002). Psychologists who are under investigation by a health practitioners' registration board with which they are registered can also be required by law to produce client files and other information relevant to the investigation (e.g., Queensland *Health Practitioners (Professional Standards) Act*, 1999). There is normally a provision in such legislation for registration boards to seek a court order against a health practitioner who fails to comply with a legal request by a board-appointed investigator to enter a practice premises and/or inspect professional files and other documents, which compels the health practitioner to comply.

There is no *general* legal duty on Australian psychologists to disclose confidential information to protect others, not even where clients threaten to kill or seriously injure another person (Kämpf, McSherry, Thomas, & Abrahams, 2008). There is, however, a range of legislative provisions across the country that allow psychologists to disclose confidential information in tightly defined situations. For instance, there is legislation in some Australian states and territories that mandates psychologists to break confidentiality in circumstances where the psychologist holds a reasonable belief or suspicion that children require protection (Australian Psychological Society, 2008a). All such legislation contains provisions for protecting the identity of persons reporting suspected child abuse or neglect in good faith and for indemnifying them against civil, professional, and/or criminal action for reporting the suspected abuse. Some such legislation provides for legal penalties to be imposed on persons who fail for whatever reason to report suspected child abuse or neglect. In some jurisdictions the duty of psychologists to report offences may go further. For instance, New South Wales citizens, including psychologists, have a duty to inform the police or other appropriate authority if they know, or believe, that another person has committed a serious indictable offence (section 316 of the NSW Crimes Act, 1900); and citizens, including psychologists, have a duty to report acts and intended acts of treason under paragraph 2(b) of section 80.1 of the Commonwealth Criminal Code Act (1995). Psychologists in some states and territories who belong to other specific occupational groups or who are employed under certain legislation are also required legally to report suspected child abuse or other criminal activity. Child safety and correctional workers are cases in point. In some instances, psychologists working as such or employed under other occupational categories may be required by existing workplace policies and procedures to report suspected child abuse or criminal activity.

In all circumstances where court orders, legislative provisions or organizational requirements exist, the Preamble to the 2007 Code states: "Psychologists respect and act in accordance with the laws of the jurisdictions in which they practice. The Code should be interpreted with reference to these laws. The Code should also be interpreted with reference to, but not necessarily in deference to, any organisational rules and procedures to which psychologists may be subject" (p.7); and psychologists "comply…with the law of the jurisdiction in which they provide psychological services" (B.1.2 [d]). If in the psychologist's opinion organizational requirements conflict with the ethical standards of the Code, the psychologist should attempt to resolve those conflicts (B.12.1). Psychologists should inform clients about the legal and organizational limits to confidentiality at the commencement of the professional relationship and subsequently remind them of those limits (A.5.3). This particular standard (A.5.3) requiring disclosure by psychologists to clients of the limits of confidentiality not only recognizes clients' autonomy to make decisions about what personal information they will share with their psychologist but also mandates psychologists to make promises about privacy and confidentiality that are deliverable.

In the absence of mandatory legal provisions, psychologists may have a moral and a civil duty to disclose confidential information if it is the only way of averting an immediate and specified risk of harm to identifiable persons. This duty poses an ethical dilemma between respecting clients' rights to privacy and confidentiality and exercising a duty of care based on the principle of nonmaleficence for the client, other parties and psychologists themselves. This dilemma between maintaining confidentiality and breaking confidentiality in order to prevent harm has received in-depth coverage in the professional literature (McMahon, 1992, 1998, 2006; McMahon & Knowles, 1992, 1995). The dilemma applies in a range of circumstances. It arises in situations where clients are at immediate, specific risk of harming themselves (Australian Psychological Society, 2008b), the psychologist or others (Australian Psychological Society, 2008c). It applies in jurisdictions where reporting suspected child abuse and neglect or other injurious criminal activity is not mandated (Australian Psychological Society, 2008a). It applies arguably in situations where unsolved crimes continue to cause serious pain for direct and indirect victims of those crimes or are indicative of a high risk of reoffending which could place other members of the public at risk of harm (McMahon, 1998). Psychologists should be well prepared to manage such dilemmas, should implement the above guidelines in a thorough, systematic way, and should consult a senior colleague about the need to break confidentiality if they become aware of an immediate, specified risk of harm to clients, other people or themselves. When consulting a senior colleague and in the absence of a client's consent to break confidentiality (A.5.2 [d] [ii]), psychologists do not disclose the client's or other parties' identities (A.5.2 [d] [i]). When they break confidentiality in order to avert immediate risk of harm, they disclose only such information which is reasonably necessary to achieve the purpose of the disclosure and only to people required to have it (A.5.4).

Although the Code does not give priority to the Dignity principle over the Propriety or Integrity principles, that is, it does not prioritize client autonomy over nonmaleficence or fidelity, psychologists should not underestimate the importance of client autonomy. Unless there are compelling reasons in the form of immediate, specified threat of harm, and the threat has been properly assessed, and consultation with senior colleagues has occurred, psychologists should respect clients' rights to privacy and not break confidentiality. They should honour the commitment they have given clients to maintain confidentiality within clearly specified limits (A.5.3). This is why it is so important for psychological service agreements to include clear specifications on the limits to confidentiality.

Although these professional dilemmas for some psychologists may not be a regular occurrence, in both theory and practice they are unavoidable because each ethical duty is co-extensive (they exist simultaneously with other ethical duties) and imperfect (conditional *in situ* on those other ethical duties; Ross, 1930). Each ethical duty is not a duty of perfect obligation, namely, a duty that must be performed without exception. The correct (right) course of action in any set of circumstances requires careful consideration of all of the facts and of one's conditional duties to all parties who have a vested interest in the matter. In determining the correct course of action in circumstances where the client's autonomy, the welfare of the client and other persons, and the psychologist's agreement with the client are in competition, Ross (1930, p. 18) suggested that "It might be said that besides the duty of fulfilling the promises I have and recognise a duty of relieving distress, and when it is right to do the latter at the cost of not doing the former, it is not because I think I shall produce more good thereby but because I think it [relieving distress] is the duty which is in the circumstances more of a duty." What then of the promise (e.g., to respect the client's autonomy and maintain confidentiality)? Ross argued that breaking a promise does not set aside the promise. Reparative action (making amends in some other way) is required to discharge that promise. In Ross's theory of *prima facie* (conditional) duty, all other things being equal, fidelity (keeping a promise) takes precedence over other duties. In order to ensure that psychologists deliver on their promises to respect clients' autonomy by safeguarding their privacy and maintaining confidentiality, it is very important to make realistic promises about the limits to confidentiality and to review these contractual responsibilities on a regular basis during service delivery. Davidson (2006) has mapped out a set of ethical reasoning steps based on Ross's theory of *prima facie* duty to assist psychologists to determine the right course of action toward clients and other parties and to monitor the impact of those actions.

The focus of the discussion so far has been on situations where the psychologist's contractual agreement with a client regarding privacy and confidentiality comes into conflict with the psychologist's other ethical responsibilities to the client and/or other parties. The difficulty of determining the right course of action may be increased when psychologists provide services to multiple clients (B.5). It is very important in those circumstances to ensure that privacy rights and limits to confidentiality are negotiated in advance with the clients so that their several and joint best interests are respected. This may involve careful consideration of the type of information and parts of records to which the clients may have shared access and the type of information and parts of records that are specific to the individual clients, which can be accessed only by the individual in question (Jifkins, 2009b). The psychologist should ensure that each party to a service involving multiple clients should have a clear understanding of the procedure for indication that the information they provide should not be shared without their consent with other parties to the service. The need to negotiate arrangements for privacy protection and limits to confidentiality severally and jointly applies irrespective of whether the multiple clients are a couple, family members, work colleagues or employees and their employer.

There are other circumstances under which psychologists might reasonably disclose client information on a need to know basis. These include consensual disclosures to third party payers (B.4) and when third parties (e.g., Medicare or health insurers) can require access to certain information on the psychological service being provided. Finally, psychologists have conditional rights to defend themselves against allegations of unethical and unprofessional conduct and against civil actions relating to such allegations. They also have a legal right to pursue lost earnings if clients withhold payment of fees for services (Koocher, 1995). Standards on disclosure of these limits to confidentiality and release of information on a need to know basis also apply in all these circumstances.

To allow clients to make informed decisions regarding the information they will share with them, psychologists must inform clients at the onset of the professional relationship, and as regularly thereafter as is reasonably necessary, of the limits of confidentiality and the foreseeable use of information that they will generate in the course of the relationship. Psychologists should not consider that providing clients with appropriately worded statement setting out these various limits to confidentiality as an impediment to the establishment of a trusting relationship between clients and themselves. Nowell and Spruill (1993) found that student participants in their study said they would be more willing to self-disclose if they were promised absolute confidentiality than if they were promised limited confidentiality. There was, nevertheless, no difference between those participants who were told in a general fashion there were limits to confidentiality in circumstances where clients posed a risk of harm to themselves or others, and participants receiving detailed explanations of the limits relating to risk of harm, child abuse and neglect, court orders, third party arrangements, and so on. However, Kremer and Gesten (1998) found that student and client participants indicated that they would be less likely to disclose information to a psychologist when told about managed care requirements (health insurers may require inspection of case files prior to settlement of treatment claims and that the psychologist has no control over files relinquished to health insurers) than when they received a standard explanation or a standard explanation with a rationale of the limits of confidentiality. Nevertheless, the promise of absolute confidentiality *prima facie* is unethical because it is a promise on which psychologists may be unable to deliver. Therefore, psychologists, in an appropriately worded fashion, should explicitly set out the limits to confidentiality in the knowledge that the level of detail they provide may have little influence on clients' willingness to self-disclose, unless it is directly related to health insurance cover or health rebates. Notwithstanding, the conditions pertaining to Medicare and other health insurance schemes should be disclosed to clients who are likely to make use of those schemes.

Conclusion

The framers of the new 2007 Code were acutely aware of the changing context within which the concepts of consent, privacy, and confidentiality are to be adopted and implemented by psychologists. Evolving applications of the principles of autonomy, justice, beneficence and integrity have altered along with the legal and professional landscape over recent decades, and changes in legislative provisions and technology over that period have rendered long-cherished views on concepts such as privacy and confidentiality decrepit according to more than one critic. Psychologists need to be aware of these changes and modify their practices accordingly. The Group recognized that the 2007 Code, as well as laying out minimum ethical standards of practice, needs to contain standards that are sufficiently open-ended and flexible to cope with unforeseeable legislative and other changes that have implications for psychological practice. Otherwise, it was thought, the 2007 Code would potentially be obsolete within a very short time.

The Group acknowledged, and signalled to members, the conditional nature of rights and duties, which must be considered in terms of the facts of each individual case. In western cultures, autonomy is usually given primacy as an ethical precept. It follows that individual clients are free to decide for themselves about professional service options, such as agreeing to receive a particular treatment, or revealing private information to psychologists for the purposes of service provision. In order to make autonomous decisions, people need to be informed fully about the pertinent features of any service offered by psychologists. In addition, psychologists have a duty to keep their promises, both explicit and implied, to clients. This duty is based on the principle of fidelity. Under usual circumstances, clients are fully informed, and provide explicit consent; confidentiality ensues because psychologists honour their promises. Psychologists recognize under usual circumstances that the decisions and related information belong to clients; and clients have a right to decide who is privy to that information. The psychologist is merely the custodian who acts in the clients' best interests by protecting the shared secrets.

These rights and duties are not absolute. Many factors can interfere with the usual circumstances and change the decisional balance. For example, with regard to the exercise of autonomy, the starting assumption is normally that a client is competent and free to choose between competing options. Any challenge to these assumptions leads to realignment of ethical principles; autonomy might be given lesser importance and nonmaleficence – the avoidance of harm – given precedence. A young child who does not possess the cognitive maturity to appreciate the value of psychotherapy would, for example, surrender autonomy in relation to the decision and a supervising parent might make the decision in the child's best interests on the child's behalf.

Consent as an application of the autonomy principle must be updated regularly to take account of changes in the client's circumstances and the particulars of service delivery. The conditions that applied when a client was initially free to make an autonomous decision in relation to psychological services might not prevail throughout the service. For example, a person's fluctuating mental status may be reflected in changed intentions to inflict self-harm. If, in the psychologist's professional judgement, a client is no longer able to make a competent, informed decision, then constraints on professional behaviour, ensuring confidentiality, may no longer apply and the psychologist may be required, ethically, to break the confidence and reveal the risk of self-harm to other parties.

No Code can ever hope to encompass concrete standards that apply in each and every practice setting or provide comprehensively for future legislative changes; at best, it can articulate the core ethical principles and minimum ethical standards for practice in ways that allow for their flexible application; and the APS can be alert to legislative and other changes affecting practice, and inform members of those changes. However, the responsibility for ensuring ethical conduct in this vital area of practice remains the responsibility of individual psychologists.

References

Allan, A. (2008). *An international perspective of law and ethics in psychology*. Somerset West, South Africa: Inter-ed.

Australian Psychological Society. (2008a). *Guidelines for reporting child abuse and neglect, and criminal activity*. Melbourne, Australia.

Australian Psychological Society. (2008b). *Guidelines relating to suicidal clients*. Melbourne, Australia.

Australian Psychological Society. (2008c). *Guidelines for working with people who pose a high risk of harm to others*. Melbourne, Australia.

Brock, D. W. (1991). Shared decision making. *Kennedy Institute of Ethics Journal, 1*, 28–47.

Criminal Code Act. (1995). Commonwealth.

Crimes Act. (1900). New South Wales.

Davidson, G. R. (2002). Dealing with subpoenas: Advice for APS members. *In-Psych, 24*(5), 31, 33–4.

Davidson, G. R. (2006). Toward an ethical framework for psychological practice. In S. A. Morrissey & P. Reddy (Eds.), *Ethics and professional practice for psychologists*. (pp. 1–13). Melbourne, Australia: Thomson.

Department of Health and Community Services (NT) v JWB (Marion's case) (1992). 175 CLR 218.

Grohol, J. M. (1999). Best practice in e-therapy: Confidentiality and privacy [Electronic Version]. Retrieved 28 October 2007, from www.ismho.org/issues/9902.htm.

Gustafson, K. E., & McNamara, J. R. (1987). Confidentiality with minor clients: Issues and guidelines for therapists. *Professional Psychology: Research and Practice, 18*, 503–508.

Health Practitioners (Professional Standards) Act. (1999). Queensland.

Jifkins, J. (2009a). Managing confidentiality following a client's death. *InPsych, 31*(1), 26–7.

Jifkins, J. (2009b). Legal aspects of managing client records. *InPsych, 31*(2), 30–1.

Kadian v Richards. (2004). NSWSC 382.

Kämpf, A., McSherry, B., Thomas, S., & Abrahams, H. (2008). Psychologists' perceptions of legal and ethical requirements for breaching confidentiality *Australian Psychologist, 43*, 194–204.

Koocher, G. P. (1995). Confidentiality in professional practice. *Australian Psychologist, 30*, 158–63.

Koocher, G. P. (2007). Twenty–first century ethical challenges for psychology. *American Psychologist, 62*, 375–84.

Kremer, T., & Gesten, E. (1998). Confidentiality limits of managed care and clients' willingness to self–disclose. *Professional Psychology: Research and Practice, 29*, 553–8.

McMahon, M. (1992). Dangerousness, confidentiality, and the duty to protect. *Australian Psychologist, 27*, 12–16.

McMahon, M. (1998). Confidentiality and disclosure of crime related information. *In–Psych, 20*(1), 12–13, 19.

McMahon, M. (2006). Confidentiality, privacy and privilege: Protecting and disclosing information about clients. In S. Morrissey & P. Reddy (Eds.), *Ethics and professional practice for psychologists.* (pp. 74–88). Melbourne, Australia: Thomson.

McMahon, M., & Knowles, A. (1992). Psychologists' and psychiatrists perceptions of the dangerous client. *Psychiatry, Psychology and Law, 1*, 207–15.

McMahon, M., & Knowles, A. (1995). Confidentiality in psychological practice – a decrepit concept? *Australian Psychologist, 30*, 164–8.

Milne, J. (1995). An analysis of the law of confidentiality with special reference to the counselling of minors. *Australian Psychologist, 30*, 169–74.

Nowell, D., & Spruill, J. (1993). If it's not absolutely confidential, will information be disclosed? *Professional Psychology: Research and Practice, 24*, 367–9.

Pomerantz, A. M., & Handelsman, M. M. (2004). Informed consent revisited: An updated written question format. *Professional Psychology: Research and Practice, 35*, 201–5.

Privacy Act. (1988). Commonwealth.

Privacy Amendment (Private Sector) Act. (2000). Commonwealth.

Pryor, R. (1997). Charting client consent. *InPsych, 19*(5), 6.

Ross, W. D. (1930). *The right and the good.* Oxford: Clarendon Press.

Stapley v Fisher. (2003). WADC 278.

Warren, S., & Brandeis, L. (1890). The right to privacy. *Harvard Law Review, 4*, 193–220.

Chapter 8
The 2007 APS Code in Relation to Professional Ethics Education

Anthony W. Love

Professional ethics has gained increasing public interest in recent years, and there is widening exposure to media coverage of related topics, such as surrogate parenting. This interest has been coupled with a growing scepticism regarding the trustworthiness of professionals to self-regulate their own members. There are several reasons for the rise in distrust, including evidence of gross and minor violations by professionals, often first raised by consumers, who now have greater awareness of their power in professional relationships. Such distrust has led to rising social expectations of the external accountability of professional practitioners. Growing public interest and increasing distrust are indicators of the greater care that professions need to invest in the ethics education of its members (Robertson & Walter, 2007).

Professional Ethics Education

To ensure that they assist members to act ethically, professions such as psychology need to address a number of considerations. The first is that it must have a Code of Ethics, which is made readily available to members. A profession also requires a set of procedures for evaluating and disciplining members' conduct. Such procedures include standards of practice against which individual behaviour can be compared, and rules for ensuring members are treated justly. It must also consider the ethics education and training needs of two different groups. There are currently practising psychologists who require ongoing professional development that is relevant to their practice. Their educational needs are very different from the second group: students of psychology who are planning to become practitioners. It must be remembered that the latter group will be practising until around the middle of this century. It is imperative that they are helped in developing a conceptual scaffold for understanding ethical challenges that exist today and for those that might emerge in the future. In developing a new APS Code of Ethics (Code), the contributors therefore tried to ensure that it would be relevant to practitioners today and also meet the emerging needs of the profession over the next two decades (Koocher, 2007).

All psychologists need a suitable framework for applying ethics in their practice. Rest and Narvaez (1994) have proposed that the basis for making moral judgements in a specific situation requires moral sensitivity to the ethical implications of that encounter. In other words, we need to interpret a situation in terms of moral implications and connections before we can begin to judge which actions, if any, might be morally appropriate in that situation. This requirement is not difficult if the situation is relatively straightforward. However, professional issues are rarely simple. It is often the additional layers of complexity that create barriers to appreciating the full moral implications of actions and events. Thus nurturing moral sensitivity, Rest and Narvaez assert, helps establish an important foundation on which to build better ethical practice. This theoretical position has a great deal of merit and it undoubtedly underpins the moral intuitions that practitioners have in relation to specific situations. When asked, many will say that they just felt that something was wrong or inappropriate in a given situation, and hence felt impelled to act in a specific way. They might not be able to spell out why it was so, but they know in their hearts that it was. Thus, most practitioners will generally act intuitively in an ethical manner because of their tacit understanding of the ethical implications of a situation rather than their explicit awareness of the issues involved (Narvaez & Block, 2002).

This analysis underscores the importance of knowledge building in ethical theory (Raes, 1997). To act intuitively is commendable, and it is a character virtue that psychologists would want to nurture. It has two limitations, however, which have been highlighted by the contributions of psychological theories to ethical reasoning and decision-making (e.g., Kohlberg, 1984). Few practitioners have had any formal training in ethical theory or moral philosophy; most had not read much literature on the topic (Davidson, Garton, & Joyce, 2003). If we do not have the appropriate cognitive framework or schema for making that intuitive response more explicit, then we run the risk of not understanding comprehensively the ethical implications in a situation. A cognitive schema for ethical implications provides mental checklists for us to consider. Have I missed something important? Did I fully appreciate the layers of complexity in this context? What are the principles I need to consider? In other words, a cognitive framework can actively assist us make better informed intuitive assessments, especially if we practice applying the framework's principles regularly and deliberately until they become second nature to us (Haidt, 2007). The Code is concerned with how members behave, and with their professional deportment and not with how they arrive at their ethical judgements; but making explicit links between the two increases opportunities for deeper learning.

Secondly, a purely intuitive response to the ethical situation can lead to poorly considered ethical actions (Greene & Haidt, 2002). By acting on spur-of-the-moment ethical intuitions, there is always the danger of compounding the problem rather than helping solve or alleviate it. For example, it is widely understood that "doing good" is a central value and key motivation for action with many of the helping professions, including psychology (Beauchamp, 2003). Implicit motivation to do good in a specific context can overwhelm some of the other important considerations that need to be factored in but which might be missed or neglected in the heat of the moment. The intention of many welfare officers in the 1950s was to help Aboriginal children perceived to be at risk; it was not to create harm. Unfortunately, there was apparent neglect of other important psychological imperatives, such as children's need to develop a sense of identity through attachment to the family. As a result, great harm was done to many victims under the guise of beneficence. This is not an historical anomaly, as the issue of paternalism in health care is still hotly debated (e.g., Whitney & McCullough, 2007).

A new Code, it was decided, should have an internal structure that lent itself to ease of understanding and ready adoption by the intended users. The more it could provide an intellectual scaffold for improving knowledge of ethical implications, the more useful it may prove to members, was the vision of the Review Working Group. In the next section, the internal structure of the Code (Australian Psychological Society, 2007) is described in some detail. However, it was also recognized that knowledge of professional standards and legal considerations are important factors in psychologists' determination of best courses of action open to them. The rapid developments on both these fronts could quickly render a Code obsolete or irrelevant, a challenge now encountered by all professions (e.g., Steinberg, Bloch, Riley & Zelas, 2000). Hence, the Review Working Group decided that to meet this challenge, the 2007 Code would incorporate a framework of general principles and specific standards, as well as a supplemental process that would ensure members were kept abreast of best practice developments. This was achieved by reaffirming the need for Ethical Guidelines that would supplement and reinforce the 2007 Code, showing how its principles were to be interpreted in practice, and which could be updated at regular intervals and with relatively short lead times to ensure they reflected current community and professional standards.

The Place of the APS Code in
Professional Ethics Education

From the beginning, the Review Working Group determined that the new Code would occupy a particular position with regard to the regulation of practice by members. The Review Working Group thought it vital that the 2007 Code not be perceived as a set of normative rules, providing a carefully defined set of prescribed and proscribed behaviours for psychologists. Nor was it a tool for controlling members through a series of punishments for specific breaches. Rather, the Review Working Group wanted the 2007 Code to embody both best practice aspirations and set minimal standards for competent practice for APS members. In this way, the emphasis was to be placed on each member's self-determination of and personal responsibility for his or her own professional conduct. Ultimately, it was agreed that it was preferable for the Society to promote members' ethical behaviour through principled judgement, rather than by coercion to comply.

What are the principles that provide the framework for the 2007 Code? Following much debate and review of other professional codes, including relevant international codes as well as a careful consideration of current approaches to applied ethics (e.g., the so-called principlist perspective, as exemplified by Beauchamp and Childress, 2001), a set of principles was agreed upon as a framework for structuring the specific content. These principles address three considerations: the persons to whom psychological services are provided, the character and integrity of the psychologist providing those services, and the professional relationship that is developed. This tripartite schema is both easily accessible for and already meaningful to most members, as it reflects the central elements of the professional relationship.

The first area relates to the fundamental importance of respect for persons. The 2007 Code in fact refers to "Respect for the rights and dignity of people and peoples" (p. 6). Thus, it distinguishes between the individuals and the groups to which they belong. The intention is to prevent, once again, any apparent insensitivity to difference and to special needs that others might have, discouraging attempts to squeeze them into a "one size fits all" solution to ethical practice. There are no simple solutions to most problems that members encounter. We are all required, as psychologists, to respect the wishes and preferences of others, even if they do not fit our personal views of what is best for the individual. The Code specifically enumerates the right to autonomy and justice. While it is tempting to interpret these concepts within a narrow perspective, based perhaps on our own background and assumptions, it must be borne in mind that the definition of concepts such as autonomy will differ for different cultures and peoples. For example, in many communities it is not always appropriate for a practitioner to discuss a person's condition solely with the individual, even if he or she is a competent adult. Thus, it might be important to establish with the person just where the boundaries of autonomy begin and end, and help that person negotiate the tricky path between family expectations and dominant cultural assumptions about who needs to make decisions.

The status of the individual within society is changing rapidly in this period of history and it was considered vital that practitioners keep abreast of evolving perceptions and their impact on social conventions and legal implications. For example, the insistence on protecting rights to privacy has become more strident in recent times, reflecting a growing anxiety in public discourse around fears of ever-extending encroachment on the private domain (Westin, 2003). In Australia, both State and National legislation has been introduced that bears directly on the conduct of psychologists. Professional psychologists need to understand both General Principle A, enacted in Standard A4, pertaining to Privacy, and the legal requirements for best practice, outlined in the relevant Guideline.

The second general principle is Propriety, and according to the 2007 Code, it "incorporates the principles of beneficence, non-maleficence (including competence) and responsibility to clients, the profession and society" (p. 6). These principles are clearly related to approaches adopted by most current applied ethics textbooks and will be familiar to students working from these texts. For example, in the opening chapter of the recent volume by Morrissey and Reddy (2006), Graham Davidson provides an excellent overview of concepts such as beneficence and nonmaleficence. Davidson (2006) has asserted that an understanding of these principles, which are *prima facie* duties of psychologists, allows them to determine the correct course of our conduct, and thus act ethically, even in novel circumstances. It can be seen that the 2007 Code is designed to incorporate this common approach to understanding ethics into its basic framework. The emphasis here is on considering fundamental aspects of the relationship between the client and the psychologist when determining professional conduct.

The third general principle is Integrity. It refers to the character and virtues of psychologists, which in their professional dealings at least, if not their personal lives, have to meet a standard that is unimpeachable. The very nature of psychological practice requires the establishment of a relationship with clients built on intrinsic trust (Beauchamp & Childress, 2001). Trust is an ephemeral and easily damaged aspect of any relationship. With strangers, individuals usually build trust over time. They might approach a new relationship with a preparedness to trust the other, but it would be imprudent to trust everyone without any reservation. Exploitation might soon follow. A professional relationship is very different. The consumer usually approaches a new professional relationship with expectations about how professionals can be trusted. While this sentiment has diminished somewhat in recent decades, it is still strongly held by most. It has been argued that this is part of the social contract that allows professions to function with a high degree of autonomy. It is basic to the integrity of the profession that its members be trustworthy, so most clients approach psychologists with this mental set. They are prepared to trust professionals they consult without the professionals having to establish their bona fides anew each time. This means that psychologists have a dual responsibility with respect to their personal integrity. If they do not display the virtues expected of them, then they not only harm the particular client whose trust has been abused, but they also damage the reputation of the profession as a whole. That is why high standards of professional integrity, consensually agreed to by those who choose to belong to the profession, are expected of all practitioners, whatever their personal views might be on specific issues.

The approach of creating general principles from which to derive the standards ensures each standard can be understood and analysed by students and members of the profession. It also means that new dilemmas might create the need for new standards, but these can rationally be derived from the same general principles that are embodied in the 2007 Code. Professional conduct that does not meet the spirit of these general principles becomes the subject of consideration by others and where it can be shown that individuals have not met the standards provided by the 2007 Code, that behaviour will be determined to be unethical.

In the 2007 Code, each of the General Principles is accompanied by an explanatory statement outlining how it has been embodied in the standards it covers. Examples of professional practice considered to represent aspects of the general principle are provided. Under General Principle A, for example, the explanatory statement indicates that respect for the rights and dignity of people and peoples is reflected in the importance of "people's privacy and confidentiality" (p. 11). Thus, an important distinction for learners is made in an area that often creates confusion and misunderstanding. Confidentiality, for example, is often thought of as a principle that psychologists must follow rather than seen as a process that flows from the ethical principle of respect for rights and dignity. This approach clarifies the distinction between principles and processes. When combined with other General Principles, such as Propriety, the appropriate conduct for psychologists with regard to confidentiality becomes a much clearer, if no less difficult, course to navigate in consultation with a client.

Nevertheless, the 2007 Code does provide certain prescriptive and proscriptive statements regarding practice in key areas where there is consensus that there is no room for the exercise of personal judgement by practitioners

(Skene, 1996). The most obvious of these is the complete banning of sexual relationships with clients. Standard C.4.3 (a) states that psychologists "do not engage in sexual activity with a client or anybody who is closely related to one of their clients;" (p. 29). It comes under General Principle C: Integrity, and reflects the current community view that in circumstances where a relatively less powerful individual is vulnerable to exploitation, the person with the greater power has to exercise personal restraint for the greater benefit of all. While this view has not necessarily prevailed in the past, it is clearly the expectation that the community currently has of professionals who work with clients who are often vulnerable to exploitation. This point demonstrates the important role played by community standards in the shaping of professional ethics. For those learning about the ethical standards of psychology and how ethical judgements are to be exercised, based on the general principles outlined in the 2007 Code, understanding the proscription should be straightforward. While other areas might be open to interpretation, it is clear that there is no room for compromise on these tenets of standard best practice.

Despite the advantages offered by its clear structure and explicit statement of general principles, the limitations of the 2007 Code as a guide to learning about professional conduct have to be borne in mind. While creating and publicizing it is a central component of the APS's approach to ensuring members conduct themselves ethically, there are other provisions that the APS has developed to ensure this goal is achieved. The Guidelines, for example, serve as a bridge between the relatively minimal details provided by the 2007 Code and more specific, theoretically informed understandings of ethics. They take into account those other aspects mentioned in this chapter, including community standards, legal considerations, and widely accepted views on best psychological practice in given circumstances. While the Guidelines are extremely helpful in unpacking the practical implications of the 2007 Code, individual psychologists are expected to develop a deeper understanding of the 2007 Code through an appreciation of its conceptual underpinnings. This step requires sound education in professional ethics at the undergraduate or pre-professional level, as well as ongoing professional development in the area.

Conclusions

The developers of the 2007 Code deliberately adopted a framework that will enable APS members to establish a coherent cognitive schema for scaffolding their knowledge and understanding of the 2007 Code. It asserts that three essential elements – the client, the psychologist, and the professional relationship – form the core of professional practice. General principles, familiar to anyone who has studied applied ethics, can be directly related to these elements. Thus, considering the client immediately brings to bear issues of autonomy. Reflecting on the role of the psychologist raises issues such as fidelity for consideration. While this approach is no guarantee of sensitivity to the ethical implications of professional activities, a cognitive framework such as this, according to most theorists, is likely to promote the possibility of considered reflection. With continued application, these more conscious, deliberate thought processes can become internalized and automated, so that the intuitive responses of practitioners become better informed, and possibly more closely aligned to current perceptions of best practice.

The implications for education in professional ethics for psychologists are that educators can take advantage of this opportunity to step back and reconsider their ethics curricula in relation to the ethical development of the next generation of practitioners (Mattick & Bligh, 2006). It is essential to provide students with a basic understanding of the principles of and tools for sound, ethical decision-making in their professional lives, as well as the skills to understand and analyse social trends. It is also important to direct members' capacity for empathic understanding and their personal resonances to these vital questions (Cadore, 1996). In pre-professional courses, it means that instructors might move from reliance on learning specific standards spelled out in the 2007 Code. Learning about specific content is important but not sufficient. Instead, the 2007 Code can be examined from a principle-based perspective, with an emphasis on considering how general principles are translated into specific standards. Such approaches can help to begin fostering a deeper understanding and appreciation of ethical reasoning and how it can relate to practice, thereby consolidating decision-making frameworks and promoting better ethical behaviour. A developmental perspective would suggest that orienting students to the ethical implications of psychology could begin from their initial contact with the discipline, in the first year of their undergraduate courses.

In terms of ongoing professional development, it is clear that more emphasis is needed on the further education of professional psychologists to ensure their knowledge is expanded and consolidated, and their understanding of best practice guidelines stays current. At this level, a deeper understanding of the essential tensions between different principles, such as autonomy and beneficence, can be refined. The need to manage, as much as solve, these conflicts is the important point here (Wertheim, Love, Peck, & Littlefield, 2006). The APS could provide improved opportunities for practice in ethical reasoning and feedback on performance with real-world ethical dilemmas to help improve ethical sensitivity and foster better decision-making among its members. To this end, a requirement that further courses in professional ethics be a mandatory component of professional development activities would be a very helpful initiative.

References

Australian Psychological Society. (2007). *Code of ethics*. Melbourne, Australia.

Beauchamp, T. (2003). Methods and principles in biomedical ethics. *Journal of Medical Ethics, 29*, 269–74.

Beauchamp, T., & Childress, J. (2001). *Principles of Biomedical Ethics* (5th ed.). New York: Oxford University Press, 2001.

Cadore, B. (1996). Reflections on education in biomedical ethics. *Ethical Perspectives, 3*, 194–9.

Davidson, G. R. (2006). Toward and ethical framework for psychological practice. In S. Morrissey and P. Reddy (Eds.), *Ethics and Professional Practice for Psychologists* (pp. 1–13). Melbourne, Australia: Thomson Social Science Press.

Davidson, G. R., Garton, A. F., & Joyce, M. (2003). Survey of ethics education in Australian university schools and departments of psychology. *Australian Psychologist, 38*, 216–22.

Greene, J., & Haidt, J. (2002). How (and where) does moral judgement work? *Trends in Cognitive Sciences, 6*, 517–23.

Haidt, J. (2007). The new synthesis in moral psychology. *Science, 316*, 998–1002.

Kohlberg, L. (1984). *Essays on moral development, Vol. 2: The psychology of moral development*. San Francisco: Harper & Row.

Koocher, G. P. (2007). Twenty-first century ethical challenges for psychology. *American Psychologist, 62*, 375–84.

Mattick, K., & Bligh, J. (2006). Undergraduate ethics teaching: Revisiting the Consensus statement. *Medical Education, 40*, 329–32.

Morrissey, S. & Reddy, P. (Eds.). (2006). *Ethics and Professional Practice for Psychologists*. Melbourne, Australia: Thomson Social Science Press.

Narvaez, D., & Block, T. (2002). Moral schemas and tacit judgement or how the defining issues test is supported by cognitive science. *Journal of Moral Education, 31*, 297–314.

Raes, K. (1997). Teaching professional ethics: A remark on method. *Ethical Perspectives, 4*(2), 243–45.

Rest, J. R., & Narvaez, D. (1994). *Moral development in the professions*. Hillsdale, New Jersey: Lawrence Erlbaum.

Robertson, M., & Walter, G. (2007). Overview of psychiatric ethics I: Professional ethics and psychiatry. *Australasian Psychiatry, 15*, 201–6.

Skene, L. (1996). A legal perspective on codes of ethics. In M. Coady and S. Bloch (Eds.). *Codes of Ethics and the professions* (pp. 111–129). Melbourne, Australia: University of Melbourne Press.

Steinberg, B., Bloch, S., Riley, G., & Zelas, K. (2000). Revising the code of ethics of the Royal Australian and New Zealand College of Psychiatrists: Process and outcome. *Australasian Psychiatry, 8*, 105–9.

Wertheim, E., Love, A. W., Peck, C., & Littlefield, L. (2006). *Skills for resolving conflict* (2nd ed.). Melbourne, Australia: Eruditions Publishing.

Westin, A. F. (2003). Social and political dimensions of privacy. *Journal of Social Issues*, 59(2), 431–53.

Whitney, S. N., & McCullough, L. B. (2007). Physicians' silent decisions: Because patient autonomy does not always come first. *The American Journal of Bioethics*, 7, 33–8.

Chapter 9
Exploration of Psychologists' Social Responsibilities: How Does the 2007 APS Code of Ethics Measure Up?

Graham R. Davidson

"*The concept of personal individual ethics needs to be extended to the social and cultural environment, because the environment influences the ethical behaviour of psychologists and the quality of life of all citizens. A morally responsible perspective includes a political role for psychologists, which encompasses strategies to shape that environment.*" (Pettifor, 1996, p. 1)

This chapter examines the precept of social responsibility and explores its relevance for the Australian Psychological Society (2007) Code of Ethics, hereafter called the 2007 Code. Such an enterprise is not new for Australian psychology (e.g. Butler, 1998; Davidson, 1998; Davidson & Sanson, 1995) but is as complex now as it was previously, especially in the after-light of the Code of Ethics Working Group's (Group) work over some 18 months of reviewing and revising the 2007 Code. The key questions continue to be about what psychologists mean by "social responsibility" and how to codify the precept, that is, stating within a code of ethics for psychologists the standards that are thought to represent socially responsible professional practice. These questions are not solved by focusing narrowly on philosophical debates about whether the science of psychology and psychologists as scientist-practitioners have legitimate roles to play in alleviating human suffering and contributing to the social good, but by expanding that debate to include an examination of the social role and function of contemporary psychology and its codes of ethics.

This chapter examines the meaning of social responsibility and related terms. It then attempts to clarify the issues which must be considered within any discussion or debate about what socially responsible psychological practice entails. It expands the precept of social responsibility to incorporate the precept of cultural competence. It examines the General Principles and Standards contained in the 2007 Code in order to determine (a) whether and to what extent the 2007 Code has sufficiently embraced the precept and (b) professional conduct that may constitute socially responsible or irresponsible conduct. The chapter finishes with some reflections on whether the 2007 Code succeeds in promoting socially responsible psychological practice.

Social Responsibility and Related Terminology

The term "social responsibility" does not appear in the 2007 Code. This is a matter worthy of comment later in the chapter. There is a diversity of meanings ascribed to social responsibility, when the term is used in related professional codes of ethics.

The American Psychological Association's (2002) Ethical Principles of Psychologists and Code of Conduct (hereafter the APA Code [2002]) General Principle B: Fidelity and Responsibility refers to psychologists' "professional and scientific responsibilities to society". The statement of this General Principle places emphasis on exercising and accepting professional responsibility to promote beneficence and non-maleficence. Its intention appears to be very similar to the values and standards articulated in the 2007 Code's General Principle B: Propriety Explanatory Statement and Standard B.3 (a)–(h) Professional Responsibility. However, the APA (2002) General Principle B: Fidelity and Responsibility alludes to pro bono responsibilities, "Psychologists strive to contribute a portion of their professional time for little or no compensation or personal advantage" (p. 3).

The Canadian Code of Ethics for Psychologists (Canadian Psychological Association, 2000; hereafter the CPA Code) General Principle IV: Responsibility to Society embraces expectations about propriety, including responsibility and caring but, as a point of divergence from the APA Code (2002), places considerable emphasis on using psychological knowledge for, and directing psychological practice toward, developing and modifying social systems and structures for the good of persons whom they affect. When social structures and policies are not in those persons' best interests, the CPA Code requires psychologists to advocate for the structures and policies to be changed: "psychologists involved have a responsibility to speak out in a manner consistent with the principles of this Code, and advocate for appropriate change to occur as quickly as possible" (p. 28). The specific standards forming CPA Code General Principle IV: Responsibility to Society are grouped to demonstrate an ethical commitment to knowledge acquisition, beneficial application of that knowledge, respect for society and social engagement (called Development of Society). Psychologists' responsibilities to speak out and/or take action against harmful, unfair or discriminatory social structures, policies and practices are repeated in Clauses IV.22 and IV.29. The CPA Code therefore embraces the APA Code's (2002) emphasis on propriety but extends the precept of responsibility to encompass qualified advocacy.

To use a very different comparison, the Ethics in Social Work, Statement of Principles (International Federation of Social Workers, 2004; hereafter the IFSW Statement) Principle 4.2: Social Justice states that "Social workers have a responsibility to promote social justice, in relation to society generally, and in relation to the people with whom they work." They do so by challenging all forms of discrimination, recognizing and respecting diversity, using resources available to them equitably and challenging oppressive, unfair or harmful policies and practices. The IFSW Statement's conceptualization of social advocacy is not dissimilar from that which is found in the CPA Code. However, the IFSW Statement goes a step further by imposing an expectation that social work practitioners will promote social justice, as expressed, with *people with whom they work*. While the CPA Code carries a similar expectation with regard to respect for diversity, its enjoinment of psychologists to advocacy appears to be directed to social structures, policies and practices generally rather than toward advocacy on behalf specifically of *people with whom they work*.

One is able to see in these three professional codes some progression from conceptualizing social responsibility in terms of accountability for knowledge generation and application for individual and social benefit, to active sharing of knowledge for that purpose and finally to professional intercession on behalf of people and peoples with whom one works professionally. These differences are clearly evident in the issues that will be canvassed next in this chapter. To finish the task of definition, social responsibility and social ethics will be used interchangeably. When used in the broader sense, they cover ethical engagement in social issues, social and public policy issues, public interest issues, social advocacy and other forms of social action. In the narrower sense, social responsibilities are those relevant standards that are prescribed by the relevant code of ethics.

The Scope of Social Responsibilities

Although the APA and CPA Codes provide psychologists with generic standards of social responsibility, psychologists themselves are left with decisions about how, when and on what they should act in order to fulfil their responsibilities to society. Campos (1995) explored the scope of social responsibility by formulating an Ethical Code of Social Action based on the 1992 APA Code (APA, 1992). Campos maintained that psychologists, in order to show respect for human rights and dignity (Principle D), and concern for human welfare (Principle E) and social responsibility (Principle F), which the 1992 APA Code required, were committed to social action at a number of levels. Starting from the 1992 APA Code as the base, Campos identified four aspects of social responsibility that underscore ethically and professionally responsible social action. There is the responsibility to be involved: Psychologists are committed to the amelioration of social problems through social action that is based on sound psychological knowledge. There is the responsibility to act: Psychologists find and implement effective interventions that ameliorate social problems. There is a responsibility not to evade or equivocate about social problems and human rights violations: Psychologists respond to problems and violations using the best available psychological knowledge at the time. Finally, psychologists need to confront their personal social, cultural and political prejudices by recognizing the equal importance of all persons whose dignity, rights and welfare needs are under threat.

Davidson and Sanson (1995) examined the implications of Campos' social action framework in more detail in an attempt to determine when and how psychologists might practice in a socially responsible fashion. In order to embrace the social action framework, psychology as a profession and psychologists as professionals need to contemplate the following questions:

- Is it possible to distinguish psychologists' social responsibilities from their own personal morality or is their commitment to such responsibilities dependent on them having a personal commitment to goodness?
- How then might ethical standards and guidelines sufficiently encompass personal morality and constructions of goodness? How much should codes of ethics rely on psychologists' personal opinions on what constitutes a social problem or human rights issue?
- With which social problems and/or human rights issues should psychologists become involved professionally? Is engagement with a particular social problem or human rights issue arbitrary or happenstance?
- Are psychologists who do not engage intentionally or unwittingly with social problems or human rights issues acting unethically if, in all other respects, their professional conduct is in keeping with their professional code of ethics?
- What does it mean to take social action? Does social action involve some form of public action which extends beyond making appropriate use of psychological knowledge to influence social policy or to implement tried and tested psychological interventions? What types of other social action are ethically justifiable?

Davidson (1998) explored the concept of social action further in relation to whether social responsibility mandates various forms of social advocacy. Davidson and Sanson (1995) made the case strongly that the social responsibility precept mandates psychologists, when circumstances arise, to plead the case for psychologically informed social policy development and to promote the use of tried and tested psychological interventions that alleviate social problems. However, commentators have tended to be silent on the professional ethics of advocacy that takes the form of abetting a client to obtain justice or rectify a human rights infringement.

Davidson (1998) also briefly explored the relationship between social responsibility and social protest. Does social responsibility mandate social protest against what one perceives to be unfair or otherwise immoral legislation or political policies? Is only lawful social protest ethical? Might unlawful protest against an immoral law or political act be ethically justifiable? These questions have relevance for how individual psychologists resolve ethical conflicts between their professional responsibilities and personal moral values. They are also relevant for how professional societies such as the APS engage in debate about social policy issues on which party-political differences exist, when the path of least resistance and professional self-interest may result in tacit acceptance of the prevailing party-political line. Just to debate, and not to denounce unfair and unjust social policies may constitute a repudiation of social responsibility.

The Science vs. Values Debate

Mandating psychologists to engage in social policy debate and development assumes that psychology as an empirical science has a legitimate role to play in influencing social and political values that underscore social policy. It also assumes that psychology is sufficiently knowledgeable to make a contribution to social policy debate. The latter assumption depends on whether psychology is able to defend its contributions based on the evidence it has accumulated, which may demonstrate the social benefits of some social interventions over others.

Let us start with the latter of these assumptions. Ellsworth (1991) took the position, in relation to the APA's presentation of "amicus briefs" in court, that "In science, the search for knowledge is never complete; to keep silent until our understanding is perfect is to keep silent forever" (p. 77). Following this line of thinking, Davidson and Sanson (1995) argued that the enterprise of commenting on social policy formation and implementation based on scientific knowledge available at the time is as legitimate as formulating and implementing preventive, therapeutic and other psychological interventions based on scientific knowledge available at the time, provided that psychologists are confident that the available evidence is scientifically sound. Furthermore, the scientist-practitioner paradigm is predicated on the notion that scientific knowledge needs to be applied and tested in practice in order to advance the science and underscore the practice. Psychologists' reluctance to engage with social policy debate and formulation based on the argument that scientific knowledge about the social issue in question is still being refined may be more indicative of their limited commitment to social ethics than of their idealization of perfect science. However, the question about psychology's role in the values debate remains.

Naysayers for psychology having an active role in debate about social policy, and for psychologists engaging actively with social issues, have included commentators such as Robinson (1984), Hillerbrand (1987), Waterman (1988) and Kendler (1993, 1994). A central tenet of their position is what is known as the naturalistic fallacy, which is attributed to the British philosopher, G. E. Moore (1903). Moore argued that the fallacy is committed whenever an indefinable (or ill-defined) moral value which might be used to describe something is subsequently used for definitional purposes as a natural property of that something. For example, ascription of value judgements such as better, more, preferred, desired and so on to observable outcomes of events such as political elections or the impacts of a child safety intervention made on the basis of other indefinable values such as good or bad is a naturalistic fallacy. Kendler (1993) and others have also argued that one commits the fallacy if one attempts logically to justify a value judgement using only factual information (the *is – ought* distinction). According to this line of argument, therefore, the evidence generated by psychological inquiry cannot be used as the sole basis for determining or defending what one regards as the moral thing to do. The naysayers have argued that this logical fallacy places limits on psychology's ability to contribute to social *qua* moral debates. They have also questioned whether the science of psychology may judge the legitimacy of social issues, decide who has the authority to determine what a social issue is, and reach consensus on what a socially responsible course of action for addressing the issue is.

Hillerbrand (1987) questioned whether social responsibility is a value position that can be mandated by professional codes or whether such a value position at best can only be aspirational. If professional codes have only aspirational status, their purpose becomes directing practitioners' attention toward certain value positions and not regulating professional conduct. Engagement with social agenda and all subsequent social action then become a matter of choosing personally to be engaged. Such engagement, critics maintain, cannot be mandated.

Proponents of socially responsible social action such as Brewster Smith (1985, 1990, 2000), Butler (1998), Davidson and Sanson (1995), O'Neill

(2005), Prilleltensky (1989, 1990, 1994, 1997) and Pettifor (1996, 2004) have argued that neither psychological science nor professional practice are value-free or apolitical. For psychology to be socially accountable it must examine and acknowledge the social, cultural and political values from which its research questions and professional techniques are derived. Psychologists should understand the values that underscore their research and professional practice and should work to ensure that their research findings and professional skills are used for the public good and not for social detriment. Brewster Smith (1985, 1990) maintained that vigorous political debate, and not rational, disinterested discussion, is necessary for members of professional associations such as the APS or the APA to have shared opinions about what is in the public good, and that such debate will need to take into consideration: members' personal and professional values, the importance of the social issues in question to psychology and society as a whole, the likely contributions that psychological research and practice may make, the likelihood of psychology receiving public and political support for its contributions, and the level of consensus amongst psychologists about the issues and possible solutions.

Other proponents of socially responsible scientific inquiry have taken the debate about scientific objectivity one step further. Writing about the confrontational nature of conducting research with people and communities from refugee backgrounds (also see Davidson, Murray, & Schweitzer, 2008), Mackenzie, McDowell, and Pittaway (2007) maintained, in cases where researchers are witnesses to human rights violations and criminal acts of sexual and other violence, that "when a human being is in need and the researcher is in a position to respond to that need, non-intervention in the name of 'objective' research is unethical" (p. 316). Responding ethically in such circumstances, according to Mackenzie and colleagues, may require direct intervention in the lives of research participants or associated parties, active moral protest against those human rights violations or direct assistance for victims or associated parties who wish to advocate on behalf of themselves or other victims. They argue that research with refugee populations that does not offer some form of benefit to vulnerable research participants directly through skills development, personal and community capacity building, improved social and health conditions, or changes to unjust public policies and practices, is unethical. It is simply insufficient morally to rely on the expectation that one's research will not cause harm to research participants; it must deliver benefits or actively prevent further harm. Mackenzie and associates acknowledged that showing respect for vulnerable research participants' rights to decide what they should do, providing advocacy support to bring about good, and preventing immediate harm, present researchers with the difficult ethical dilemma of balancing vulnerable individuals' (already) limited autonomy with the duties of beneficence and nonmaleficence. Vulnerable participants' rights to decide may be preserved without diminishing the principles of beneficence and non-maleficence, if psychologists researching or practising under such circumstances obtain participants' consent to intervene, protest or provide advocacy support, as well as their consent for the initial research activity or service delivery. In other words, social action designed to benefit or prevent further harm to vulnerable participants, to be ethical, must be negotiated with those who stand to benefit or be harmed by the psychologist's actions. Kakkad (2005) made a similar case for pursuing psychological research with social justice agendas that make psychology relevant for communities and peoples who have been oppressed, traumatized or otherwise victimized; but also expanded the argument to cover psychological therapies that are designed for ameliorating the suffering of traumatized clients whilst influencing public policy and instigating systemic change.

Commentators such as O'Neill (2005) and Prilleltensky (1989, 1997) have also maintained that psychologists collectively in their research and practice, under the guise of autonomy, and at the expense of justice, have privileged the psychology of individual differences over the psychology of systems. Psychologists, in doing so, are agents for the inequitable social status quo and not for equitable social change. Prilleltensky (1997) argued for the development of what he labelled *emancipatory communitarian approaches* in psychological research and practice, which seek to find a balance between individual autonomy and distributive justice concerns, provide a social context for ethical decision-making, and effect changes in individuals as well as in the social systems of which they are a part.

It appears that the rhetoric for an amoral, apolitical psychological science and its professional practice has disappeared in the last decade from psychology's debates about its responsibilities to society. However, the question about how to codify social responsibility as a professional standard has not been finally settled.

One possible solution to the problem of how to apply the social responsibility precept is to examine the professional knowledge and skills that psychologists require in order to deliver psychological services in a socially responsible fashion. The term that is generally used to describe this particular aspect of socially responsible practice is *cultural competence* (Acevedo-Polakovich et al., 2007; Dana, 2002; Davidson, 1999; Paniagua, 2005).

Cultural Competence

The precept of cultural competence draws on a number of ethical principles from which professional standards for psychologists have been derived. These have included General Principles A: Competence, B: Integrity, D: Respect for

People's Rights and Dignity, and F: Social Responsibility from the 1992 APA Code; and General Principles II: Competence and III: Propriety from the 1997 APS Code (Dana, 1994; Davidson, 1999). (Note that the 2002 APA Code contains a revised set of General Principles. Psychologists bound by that Code may defer to General Principles A: Beneficence and Nonmaleficence, D: Justice, and E: Respect for People's Rights and Dignity, when exploring the ethical parameters of cultural competence.)

The 1997 APS Code offered little guidance on the ethical standards that a culturally competent practitioner should observe, other than General Principle II: "Members shall bring and maintain appropriate skills and learning in their areas of professional practice"; and General Principle III (b): "Members must be sensitive to cultural, contextual, gender and role differences and the impact of those on their professional practice on clients. Members must not act in a discriminatory manner nor condone discriminatory practices against clients on the basis of those differences." However, the meaning of the relevant general principles in the 1997 APS and 2002 APA Codes for culturally competent research and psychological service delivery have been clarified considerably by the publication respectively of the 2003 APS Guidelines for the Provision of Psychological Services for, and the Conduct of Psychological Research with, Aboriginal and Torres Strait Islander People of Australia (ATSI), and the 2003 APA Guidelines on Multicultural Education, Training, Research, Practice, and Organisational Change for Psychologists. The 2003 APS ATSI Guidelines require Australian psychologists to demonstrate: awareness of relevant research with Aboriginal and Torres Strait Islander peoples, knowledge about and respect for indigenous value systems and authority structures, an acknowledgement of language differences, awareness of socio-political issues and one's own attitudes and beliefs about those issues and appropriate reaction against situations of prejudice and discrimination. Davidson (1999) explored the concept of culturally competent psychological practice further under the rubric of (a) *knowledge* about clients' cultures, including an appreciation of clients' social and cultural circumstances, (b) *awareness* about one's own attitudes and beliefs about the clients' cultures, and feelings and about the impact of one's professional style on the clients' progress, and (c) *skills* of self-monitoring, communication and counselling – a framework that reflected ethical debate about and empirical research into the precept. Each of these dimensions of cultural competence can be codified further into specific research and professional practices. Fowers and Davidov (2006) have argued that multiculturalism, expressed in terms of cultural competence, is a virtuous pursuit in the Aristotelian sense for psychologists. The aim of being culturally competent is to bring about good for clients, whilst eschewing the negative influences of racism and prejudice. Such competence fosters the virtue of openness to difference and otherness, it underscores the acquisition of practical wisdom, and it extols courage in the form of actions that are designed to bring about fair, just and beneficial outcomes for recipients of psychological services. The endgame of analysing culturally competent practice is to acknowledge value differences between the psychologist and client where values may be incommensurate but equally fundamental and correct, understand social and cultural variations in behaviour, and exploit value conflicts and situational variations that strengthen rather than weaken the alliance between the psychologist and client. This approach opens the door for prescribing professional conduct that is universally acceptable and proscribing professional conduct that is always culturally unacceptable, resulting in standards of professional practice to which both psychologists and their clients subscribe.

While there is acknowledgement that cultural competence may be defined in different ways and that each definitional approach has its limitations, there is continuing support for the view that cultural competence embodies all three awareness, knowledge, and problem-solving skills dimensions (Sue, Zane, Hall, & Berger, 2009). Placing emphasis on the problem-solving skills dimension of cultural competence suggests that psychologists can learn to be culturally competent. Placing emphasis on the cultural knowledge dimension suggests that psychologists, having such knowledge and experience, can be culturally literate in the client's and in their own culture. Culturally literate psychologists with culturally appropriate problem-solving skills are capable of having culturally appropriate and relevant communications with clients, understanding clients' needs and selecting suitable interventions to address those needs, selecting and administering culturally sensitive forms of assessment (Davidson, 1997; Ridley, Hill, & Wiese, 2001), and ensuring that appropriate emphasis is placed on individual clients in the family and community contexts from which they come. Nevertheless, Sue and colleagues acknowledge that the models of cultural competence adopted by psychology have focused primarily on the psychologist–client dynamic mainly to the exclusion of institutional and systemic factors that influence health service delivery.

Vera and Speight (2003), in contrast, maintained that culturally competent counselling and psychotherapeutic services alone are insufficient demonstrations of psychologists' social responsibilities. They argued that social responsibility is only fully exercised within a transformational framework that is committed to systemic changes through social policy reform, designed to give greater emphasis to distributive justice than to autonomy, and to emancipate people and communities from social, economic and political oppression. They also argued for the adoption of a broad definition of the term "cultural" to encompass a range of social and lifestyle differences. Vera and Speight's construal of social justice is similar to Prilleltensky's (1997) notion of *emancipatory communitarianism* above, and regards social action in the form of advocacy as an essential component of social responsibility. Prilleltensky (2008) has continued to champion the need for a *transformational* psychology committed to types of research and practice that have the express purpose of changing socio-political structures which perpetuate the iniquitous exercise of political power. It seems for Prilleltensky that such a psychology of liberation can be achieved only by directing resources in the first instance toward social critique and professional activism, rather than toward the amelioration of individual clients' suffering and enhancement of their well being, which should follow systemic change, although he acknowledges that political awareness raising and social action should advocate for amelioration of suffering and justice in the immediate term as well as socio-political change in the long term. All psychological research and practice, according to Prilleltensky, should therefore be *psycho-political*, or power-focused, when it comes to the question of enhancing individual and collective well being.

The 2007 APS Code

This section turns its attention to the question about whether the 2007 APS Code, through the revised General Principles, embraces the precept of social responsibility and, through the Standards, provides Australian psychologists with direction about socially responsible psychological practice. Attention is focused specifically on whether the Code:

- Permits psychologists to engage professionally with social issues by making a contribution evidentially to social policy development and implementation;
- Mandates psychologists to be engaged professionally with social issues and provides guidance on the types of issues with which they engage;
- Permits psychologists to engage in other forms of social action, including social advocacy and social protest;
- Articulates standards for practising psychology in a culturally competent fashion; and
- Flags the need for a communitarian as well as an individualistic perspective on social ethics.

The Preamble to the 2007 Code explains that the Code contains an expression of psychologists' responsibilities to their clients and *the community and society at large*, as well as to colleagues and other professionals. Those responsibilities are expressed in the form of three general principles: A: Respect for the Rights and Dignity of People and Peoples; B: Propriety; and C: Integrity. *Peoples* is a term that is new to the 2007 Code. The Definitions section states that peoples are "distinct human groups with their own social structures who are linked by a common identity, common customs, and collective interests"

(p. 9). General Principle A: Respect for the Rights and Dignity of People and Peoples incorporates rights to justice and autonomy. Those rights and human dignity are achieved by placing emphasis on people's "diversity and uniqueness … and right to linguistically appropriate services", as well as on fair treatment and "fair access to psychological services" and their benefits. The ethical standards relating to A.1: Justice proscribe unfair discrimination (A.1.1), require demonstrable understanding of the sequelae of unfair discrimination (A.1.2), and mandate "assist[ance to] clients to address unfair discrimination or prejudice that is directed against [them]" (A.1.3).

Taken collectively, these sections of the Preamble, General Principles and Standards arguably commit psychologists to using psychological knowledge in ways that benefit people and enhance human rights and dignity. Psychologists are not prevented from using their knowledge to affect the course of social policy development in ways that help psychology achieve the General Principle of respecting human rights and dignity. On the contrary, while making a contribution to social policy development and change is not mandated, the tone of these sections is that using psychological knowledge to achieve these stated principles is encouraged.

These sections of the 2007 Code are explicit about psychologists having responsibilities to peoples as well as to individual people. They set forth the requirements for psychologists to eschew discrimination, act respectfully, and take professional responsibility (B.3) for peoples as a whole as well as for individual clients.

Social advocacy for fair, just and beneficent treatment of people and peoples is expected, but A.1.3 might be read as a prohibition against engaging in any form of advocacy on behalf of direct clients; the psychologist is mandated to assist clients themselves to address unfair discrimination and prejudice. The reasons that emerged in the Group discussions for prohibiting direct forms of advocacy were that such advocacy may inadvertently usurp clients' autonomy (cf. Mackenzie, McDowell, & Pittaway, 2007), be difficult to mandate and enforce, and engage the psychologist in an additional professional relationship (that of advocate as opposed to assessor, therapist etc.) which may impair the psychologist's judgement when fulfilling the primary professional relationship. (See C.3.1 on multiple relationships.)

The 2007 Code neither prescribes, nor prohibits psychologists from, participating in social protests. However, the Preamble and B.1.2 (d) specifically state that psychologists must act lawfully and interpret the 2007 Code with reference to the law. These sections suggest that psychologists engaging in lawful social protest are acting ethically but psychologists engaging in unlawful behaviour, whether it is for the purpose of protesting against something they consider immoral or for some other purpose, are acting unethically. The 2007 Code therefore requires psychologists to restrict any social action to that which is lawful.

With which specific topics of public interest and social policy development and implementation might and/or should psychologists engage? The 2007 Code is expressly silent on this question but psychologists should not interpret this silence as a license for unfettered personal choice on the issues and topics with which they might engage. Heed should be paid to General Principle A: Respect for the Rights and Dignity of People and Peoples, which directs psychologists' attention to conduct that promotes equity and the protection of people's human, legal and moral rights and enhances human dignity. Attention is also directed toward redressing unfair discrimination (A.1: Justice), which may involve efforts to ensure that social policy and resource distribution do not discriminate unfairly against community groups and peoples. General Principle B: Propriety maintains an emphasis on the welfare of clients and other members of the public. Standard B.1: Competence requires psychologists to practice within the limits of their established psychological knowledge (B.1.2 [b]) and education and training (B.1.2 [a]). General Principle C: Integrity mandates psychologists to identify and avoid conflicts of interest (esp. C.3.4 on declaring vested interests). Although financial interests receive attention, acting with integrity pertains to all personal interests, which might include religious, political, environmental and other social affiliations. The requirement is for these vested interests to be declared rather than avoided, unless there is the likelihood that they will impair the psychologist's professional judgement.

Finally, the 2007 Code pays due attention to standards of culturally competent professional practice without making specific reference to cultural competence. When judging the standards, it is important to recognize that clients by definition may be individuals, families, groups, or communities and also that professional responsibilities are directed at people and peoples. Unfair discrimination is proscribed (A.1). Respectful conduct covers linguistic and non-linguistic conduct (A.2.1 [a]). In order to practice competently, psychologists must have appropriate knowledge and skills (B.1.1). This includes psychological knowledge of human cultural diversity. There are additional responsibilities placed on psychologists to ensure that ethical standards are maintained when interpreters are used (B.7). Selection, administration and interpretation of psychological assessment data must be appropriate and accurate (B.13.3) and based on research knowledge (B.13.4).

Strengths and Limitations Regarding Social Ethics

In summary, the 2007 Code provides direction on the ethics of socially responsible psychological practice (social ethics). It stops short of mandating social action in the form of either social policy engagement or social advocacy. It proscribes direct advocacy on behalf of current clients. It forbids unlawful protest. It provides indirect guidance on how psychologists determine the social issues with which they may engage professionally. It provides minimum standards for practising psychology in a culturally competent fashion. It strongly endorses professional conduct that is respectful of people and their cultures, preserves human rights and promotes equity.

Although there is recognition of peoples and acknowledgement that communities may be clients, the 2007 Code is limited in respect to specific standards that must be observed when working directly with communities and cultural groupings, the assumption being here that practising with communities or these groupings is no different from practising with individuals, couples, families or organizational groups, to all of whom standard B.5: Provision of Psychological Services to Multiple Clients, and all of the other standards, apply equally. What is missing here is some guidance on the apportionment of professional responsibilities to communities or cultural groupings as a whole and to the individual persons, families and groups who constitute them. This should be a matter for consideration in the next round of revisions.

Although there is acknowledgement that clients may be organizations or communities, the 2007 Code remains client-focused and *not* systems-focused (cf. Prilleltensky, 2008; Vera & Speight, 2003). Thus, psychological practice is about services that psychologists provide to clients and not about how they engage with the development and implementation of social and political systems. This limitation compares unfavourably with the considerable emphasis in the CPA Code on using psychological knowledge for, and directing psychological practice toward, developing and modifying social systems and structures for the good of those persons whom they affect. Notwithstanding the increased emphasis in the 2007 Code on distributive justice, it leans clearly toward a model of ethics that is based on *benevolent individualism* rather than on *emancipatory communitarianism* (Prilleltensky, 1997). Whether it is possible to mandate professional conduct from a communitarian perspective or whether such a perspective is one to which psychology should aspire is a matter for further debate. The "proof of the pudding" for communitarianism would be the development of specific ethical standards that reflect communitarian ideals *and* which are enforceable.

Reflection on the Work of the Group and Conclusion

The limits placed by the 2007 Code on social advocacy and social protest as well as the limitations associated with modelling a code of ethics to reflect the professional relationship between psychologists and their clients – be they individual or multiple clients – offer an appropriate starting point for reflecting on those discussions that occurred within the Code of Ethics Review Working Group as the 2007 Code was being drafted. In my opinion, all members of the Group sought an outcome to the review that strengthened APS members' ethical commitment to social ethics. Notwithstanding, discussion of the General Principles and Standards frequently returned to three key questions. Was it possible to link the General Principles exclusively to specific ethical Standards? Is it possible to enforce specific ethical Standards that are included in the 2007 Code? Is it possible legally to defend decisions to enforce the 2007 Code, if a breach of the Code has been apprehended and a psychologist appeals the decision in court or before a tribunal? Such are the realities of enforcing codes of ethics.

Writing and linking the General Principles and ethical Standards presented the first challenge. The original draft of the 2007 Code actually contained four General Principles, the last of which was called Social Responsibility. However, when the Group carefully examined the definitions of each of the four draft General Principles and the accompanying explanatory statements, as well as the ethical Standards that had been attributed initially to Social Responsibility, two things became clear. First, there was considerable redundancy in definitional terms between Social Responsibility and the other draft General Principles. Further redrafting suggested to the Group that the statement of Social Responsibility could be covered comprehensively by some minor redrafting General Principle A: Respect for the Rights and Dignity of People and Peoples and General Principle B: Propriety. The second clarification that emerged was that every ethical Standard assigned to the draft Social Responsibility principle could be (and subsequently was) placed under the three remaining General Principles. The assumption may be made from this clarification that socially responsible psychological practice seeks fairness and justice, protects people's rights, respects people's dignity, safeguards people's welfare and honours the trust people place in the profession and its members.

Articulating each General Principle in the form of enforceable ethical Standards presented the second challenge. There was extensive debate about three issues as the ethical Standards were being drafted. First, the ethical Standards together constitute the minimum standards of conduct that might reasonably be expected of psychologists (see the Preamble). The ethical standards are not an exhaustive set of expectations and nor can they, or do they, articulate ethical ideals to which psychologists may aspire. They are the minimum Standards for ensuring that psychologists meet their responsibilities to clients, society, colleagues and the profession. Second, the ethical Standards apply to psychologists' conduct *qua* psychologists and/or APS members. Unless otherwise stated (e.g. see the definition (b) of Conduct and ethical Standard C.1: Reputable Behaviour), the 2007 Code does not apply to psychologists' personal conduct. Therefore, a personal commitment to social ethics becomes a matter of personal morality. Third, the ethical Standards must be able to be enforced in order for the 2007 Code to have authority. Conduct is defined as any act (of commission) or omission. Members of the Group struggled frequently with the wording of ethical Standards because of the perceived difficulties that may arise if a psychologist was found *not* to have acted in a particular way. Some examples of this dilemma included whether a psychologist could be compelled to engage in social advocacy, whether a psychologist could be compelled to endorse a particular public interest position that might be contrary to his or her personal beliefs, and whether a psychologist could be compelled by a client to advocate directly on the client's behalf, if the psychologist held the opinion that direct advocacy usurps clients' autonomy or in other ways is not in the best interests of clients. Aspects of social ethics in hindsight lend themselves less to regulation and more to aspiration to ethical best practice than do other ethical standards of professional practice.

Administering codes of ethics assumes an additional level of difficulty if decisions taken against psychologists on the basis of those codes are tested via the legal process. Legal considerations may include whether the code of ethics being applied is widely accepted by the professional community, whether the interpretation of the code that has been applied in a specific circumstance is one with which a reasonable person with knowledge of the profession may agree, and whether the professional conduct in question constitutes a clear breach of the relevant code or a section thereof. Members of the Group were cognizant of the need to draft enforceable ethical Standards that meet these additional criteria.

However, codes of ethics are premised on more than what is considered professionally and legally to be acceptable professional practice. They are also premised on a philosophical appreciation of what is morally good and bad or right and wrong, in which the notion of goodness is not necessarily simple and clear. There has already been some discussion in this chapter about dilemmas that ensue from considering one's professional obligations to respect clients' autonomy, prevent future harm and, at the same time, seek justice on their and others' behalf. Hillerbrand (1987) also commented on competing moral expressions of good, in the form of "divergent themes [that] arise [from] contrasting views of social action as commitments of caring *or* justice" (p. 112, my emphasis), thus highlighting the tensions that exist between rights-based and care-based ethics. The existence of these competing moral theories is not sufficient reason for psychologists to put precepts such as social responsibility and social action in the "too hard basket". On the contrary, they are tensions that frequently emerge in everyday psychological practice. Davidson (2006) and other commentators have recommended that psychologists familiarize themselves with, and adopt, ethical decision-making models that assist them to resolve these ethical tensions and thus determine how they should act professionally in any given set of circumstances. This includes determining the socially responsible course of action for their clients, the community and the profession in consultation with clients and other key stakeholders.

References

Acevedo-Polakovich, I. D., Reynaga-Abiko, G., Garriott, P. O., Derefinko, K. J., Wimsatt, M. K., Gudonis, L. C., et al. (2007). Beyond instrument selection: Cultural considerations in the psychological assessment of U.S. Latinas/os. *Professional Psychology: Research and Practice, 38*, 375–84.

American Psychological Association (APA). (1992). Ethical principles of psychologists and code of conduct. *American Psychologist, 47*, 1597–611.

American Psychological Association (APA). (2002). Ethical principles of psychologists and code of conduct. *American Psychologist, 57*, 1060–73.

American Psychological Association. (2003). Guidelines on multicultural education, training, research, practice and organisational change for psychologists. *American Psychologist, 58*, 377–402.

Australian Psychological Society (APS). (1997). *Code of ethics.* Melbourne, Australia.

Australian Psychological Society (APS). (2003). *Guidelines for the provision of psychological services for, and the conduct of psychological research with, Aboriginal and Torres Strait Islander people of Australia.* Melbourne, Australia.

Australian Psychological Society. (2007). *Code of ethics.* Melbourne, Australia.

Brewster Smith, M. (1985). Ethics and advocacy: Rejoinder. *American Psychologist, 40*, 1142–3.

Brewster Smith, M. (1990). Psychology in the public interest. What have we done? What can we do? *American Psychologist, 45*, 530–6.

Brewster Smith, M. (2000). Values, politics and psychology. *American Psychologist, 55*, 1151–2.

Butler, P. V. (1998). Psychology as history, and the biological renaissance: A brief review of the science and politics of psychological determinism. *Australian Psychologist, 33*, 40–6.

Campos, L. P. (1995). Should the CPA have an ethical code for social action. *California Psychologist*, Feb., 31.

Canadian Psychological Association. (2000). *Canadian code of ethics for psychologists.* Ottawa, Canada.

Dana, R. H. (1994). Testing and assessment ethics for all persons: Beginnings and agenda. *Professional Psychology: Research and Practice, 25*, 349–54.

Dana, R. H. (2002). Multicultural assessment: Teaching methods and competence. *Journal of Personality Assessment, 79*, 195–9.

Davidson, G. R. (1997). The ethical use of psychological tests: Australia. *European Journal of Psychological Assessment: ITC Bulletin, 13*, 132–9.

Davidson, G. R. (1998). In pursuit of social responsibility in psychology: A comment on Butler (1998). *Australian Psychologist, 33*, 47–9.

Davidson, G. R. (1999). Cultural competence as an ethical precept in psychology. In P. Martin & W. Noble (Eds.), *Psychology and society* (pp. 162–74). Brisbane: Australian Academic Press.

Davidson, G. R. (2006). Toward an ethical framework for psychological practice. In S.A. Morrissey & P. Reddy (Eds.), *Ethics and professional practice for psychologists* (pp. 1–13). Melbourne, Australia: Thomson.

Davidson, G. R., Murray, K. E., & Schweitzer, R. (2008). Review of refugee mental health and wellbeing: An Australian perspective. *Australian Psychologist, 43*(3), 160–74.

Davidson, G. R., & Sanson, A. (1995). Should the APS have an ethical code of social action? *Bulletin of the Australian Psychological Society, 17*(5), 2–4.

Ellsworth, P. (1991). To tell what we know or wait for Godot? *Law and Human Behavior, 15*, 77–90.

Fowers, B. J., & Davidov, B. J. (2006). The virtue of multiculturalism: Personal transformation, character, and openness to the other. *American Psychologist, 61*, 581–94.

Hillerbrand, E. (1987). Philosophical tensions influencing psychology and social action. *American Psychologist, 42*, 111–8.

International Federation of Social Workers. (2004). Ethics in social work, statement of principles. Retrieve on 12 March 2007 from www.ifsw.org/en/p38000324.html.

Kakkad, D. (2005). A new ethical praxis: Psychologists' emerging responsibilities in issues of social justice. *Ethics and Behavior, 15*, 293–308.

Kendler, H. H. (1993). Psychology and the ethics of public policy. *American Psychologist, 48*, 1046–53.

Kendler, H. H. (1994). Can psychology reveal the ultimate values of humankind. *American Psychologist, 49*, 970–1.

Mackenzie, C., McDowell, C., & Pittaway, E. (2007). Beyond "do no harm": The challenge of constructing ethical relationships in refugee research. *Journal of Refugee Studies, 20*, 300–19.

Moore, G. E. (1903). *Principia ethica*. Cambridge: Cambridge University Press.

O'Neill, P. (2005). The ethics of problem definition. *Canadian Psychology, 46*, 13–20.

Paniagua, F. A. (2005). *Assessing and treating culturally diverse clients: Practical guide*. Thousand Oaks, CA: Sage.

Pettifor, J. L. (1996). Ethics: Virtue and politics in the science and practice of psychology. *Canadian Psychology, 31*, 1–12.

Pettifor, J. L. (2004). Professional ethics across national boundaries. *European Psychologist, 9*, 264–72.

Prilleltensky, I. (1989). Psychology and the status quo. *American Psychologist, 44*, 795–802.

Prilleltensky, I. (1990). Enhancing the social ethics of psychology: Toward a psychology at the service of social change. *Canadian Psychology, 31*, 310–9.

Prilleltensky, I. (1994). Psychology and social ethics. *American Psychologist, 49*, 966.

Prilleltensky, I. (1997). Values, assumptions and practices: Assessing the moral implications of psychological discourse and action. *American Psychologist, 52*, 517–35.

Prilleltensky, I. (2008). The role of power in wellness, oppression, and liberation: The promise of psychopolitical validity. *Journal of Community Psychology, 36*, 116–136.

Ridley, C. R., Hill, C. L., & Wiese, D. L. (2001). Ethics in multicultural assessment: A model of reasoned application. In L. A. Suzuki, J. G. Ponterotto, & P. J. Meller (Eds.), *Handbook of multicultural assessment: Clinical, psychological and educational applications.* (pp. 29–46). San Francisco, CA: Jossey-Bass.

Robinson, D. N. (1984). Ethics and advocacy. *American Psychologist, 39,* 787–92.

Sue, S., Zane, N., Hall, G. C. N., & Berger, L. K. (2009). The case for cultural competency in psychotherapeutic interventions. *Annual Review of Psychology, 60,* 525–48.

Vera, E. M., & Speight, S. L. (2003). Multicultural competence, social justice and counseling psychology: Expanding our roles. *The Counselling Psychologist, 31,* 253–72.

Waterman, A. S. (1988). On the uses of psychological theory and research in the process of ethical inquiry. *Psychological Bulletin, 103,* 283–98.

Chapter 10
Reviewing the APS Code of Ethics with Young People in Mind

Marie R. Joyce

Participation on the committee reviewing the APS Code of Ethics was an opportunity to reflect in the company of colleagues who brought searching, open minds to a domain already familiar to us all. Each committee member was invited to contribute both general thinking and analysis, and reflections from a particular perspective, in my case the perspective of children and young people. The processes of review took us into realms outside our everyday operations, to consider and consult about legal, philosophical and organizational issues, including human rights considerations.

This chapter will explore some of the key ethical issues for psychologists in working with children and young people, and will begin with addressing the importance of the legal contexts of ethical decision-making concerning minors. Two major areas, informed consent and confidentiality, will be discussed as they represent the most important ethical issues psychologists working with young people have to face. It is worth noting at this point that the new code does not explicitly mention young people as the previous code did. Rather, it emphasizes general principles and the ethical standards that arise from them, as they impinge on, and apply to, each and every area of practice.

The last sections of the chapter explore my reflections and reading during the review process: I was led to new applications of contemporary philosophical ethics, with implications for the meaning of education or training in ethics, and for the role of professional development and supervision in ethical decision-making.

Legal Context

One of the challenges facing professionals is to keep abreast of the changing legal contexts in which they work. In a country such as Australia, with both Commonwealth and State laws, there is much to know. The Commonwealth has recently passed an act affecting families and services to families: the *Family Law Amendment (Shared Responsibility) Act 2006*, amended the *Family Law Act (Cth)* which was passed in 1975. This Act of Amendment aimed to change the culture in the management of marital separation where children are involved and it introduced a new presumption of shared parental responsibility. This means that parents are understood to have an equal role in decision-making about major long-term issues affecting their child, including for example the child's name, education and major health issues. The concept of shared responsibility explicit in this Act is one that has implications for psychologists working with children and their parents and particular significance for those psychologists who are preparing Parenting Plans for the Family Court.

Within each state and territory there are changing legal contexts. For example, in Victoria the *Children, Youth and Families Act 2005* replaced the former *Children and Young Persons Act 1989*. Of particular interest in this new Act, which preceded the amendment of the Commonwealth legislation, is the prominence of the concept "the best interests of the child". Both Commonwealth and State changes to the law emphasize the priority of the child's needs over that of their parents. This concept is at the heart of the Victorian legislation which defines three *Best Interests Principles*, the third of which enunciates eighteen further specific principles. In addition, these are followed by extensive *Decision-making Principles*. Throughout this legislation value is placed on taking primary account of the child's needs and wellbeing, while also respecting the family unit and making every effort to preserve it. In addition, specific and separate sections are devoted to acknowledging the particular needs of indigenous children and families.

The scope of the *Best Interests Principles* can be clarified with some examples: Division 2, Section 10. *Best interests principles* (3), for example, states:

> … consideration must be given to the following, where they are relevant to the decision or action —
>
> (a) the need to give widest possible protection and assistance to the parent and child as the fundamental group unit of society and to ensure that intervention into that relationship is limited to that necessary to secure the safety and wellbeing of the child;
>
> (b) the need to strengthen, preserve and promote positive relationships between the child and the child's parent, family members and persons significant to the child;

(c) the need, in relation to an Aboriginal child, to protect and promote his or her Aboriginal cultural and spiritual identity and development by, wherever possible, maintaining and building their connections to their Aboriginal family and community;

(d) the child's views and wishes, if they can be reasonably ascertained, and they should be given such weight as is appropriate in the circumstances.

Thoughtful analysis and consultation as set out in this legislation may be helpful to psychologists who are assessing the "best interests of the child".

Key Ethical Considerations

In practice, the two particular areas in which psychologists face complex ethical decision-making where young people and their parents are involved are the gaining of informed consent and the protection of confidentiality.

Informed consent

The gaining of consent from children and their parents is addressed in standard A.3.6 of the 2007 Code:

A.3.6. *Psychologists* who work with *clients* whose ability to give consent is, or may be, impaired or limited, obtain the consent of people with legal authority to act on behalf of the *client*, and attempt to obtain the *client*'s consent as far as practically possible.

Great complexity exists in this area due to uncertainty regarding how limited a particular young person's ability to give informed consent is, expressed in notions of perceived "maturity". The process of deciding whether the young person can give informed consent is by no means a straightforward one. Guidance can be found in the legal definition in Victoria which refers to whether the young person has achieved "sufficient understanding and intelligence to enable him or her to understand fully what is proposed" (Secretary, Department of Health and Community Services v JWB and SMB, 1992, p. 79, line 174).

Even when careful attempts are made, as in the APS *Guidelines for Working with Young People* (2009), to tease out factors of importance in this decision, there can remain tensions between the desire to pay respect to the child's wishes and accountability to each parent or carer.

The 2007 Code gives an emphasis to respecting those clients judged not able to give informed consent by urging compliance, nevertheless, with the information-giving procedures as far as possible. That is, even though a young client is deemed not mature enough to give informed consent, it is the ethical responsibility of the psychologist to explain the psychological service to be provided as clearly as possible and to take into account the wishes of the young person as appropriate. This is further exemplified in the 2007 Code, where it refers to the collection of client information from associated parties:

> A.7.3. *Psychologists* who work with *clients* whose consent is not required by law still comply, as far as practically possible, with the processes described in A.3.1., A.3.2., and A.3.3.

Tan, Passerini and Stewart (2007), in addressing issues of informed consent in UK mental health care settings, cite Kennedy and Grubb, who in 2000 wrote that there are three components considered essential for informed consent:

1. The adequate and appropriate provision of treatment information, including the risks and benefits of the proposed treatment and other options,
2. The absence of coercion, and
3. The presence of capacity to make a treatment decision (Kennedy & Grubb, 2000, cited in Tan et al., 2007, p. 193).

Tan and colleagues note that two of these three requirements are external to the client and challenge the psychologist to manage the environment ethically. The focus of ethical discussion is most often on the last requirement, which brings the psychologist's professional judgement to the fore. Tan and associates provide a clinical practice algorithm to assist in this kind of decision-making. Conceptually, they analyse "consent" into verbal and behavioural components which may be particularly evident in decisions regarding treatment in serious mental health contexts: verbal consent, verbal refusal, and the absence of verbally expressed views, each of these in any possible combination with behavioural co-operation, resistance or compliance (Tan et al., 2007). Where a young person is being admitted to hospital, treatment is likely to involve the family as well and they recommend considering consent then as from the family group.

The desirability of freedom of decisions by young people to participate in research is highlighted by Heath, Charles, Crow and Wiles (2007). They draw attention to the complexities of gaining informed consent from young people for research participation, especially when the young people are in institutions where gate-keepers decide on their behalf, for example, not to participate. Heath and colleagues express concern regarding the tension between the system of gate-keeping and the ethical framework of researchers who wish to prioritize the *agency* and capabilities of young people to decide for themselves whether to participate or not.

Kendall and Suveg (2008) have examined the participation of young people in randomized clinical trials (RCTs) from an ethical perspective and have proposed six recommendations to guide psychologists in the three phases of these trials – prior to treatment, during and following treatment. This guidance places emphasis on anticipating eventualities, such as a child wanting to withdraw from the research, and planning clearly for them in advance.

Mudaly and Goddard (2009) explored a rights approach to ethical issues in research with children who have been abused and found that many ethical questions remain unresolved; however, they provided an analysis of ethical issues of a study in which young people in this context were encouraged to give voice to their experiences and in which risks were minimized.

Whenever it is proposed to receive informed consent from a minor, a professional judgement must be made regarding the maturity of the young person. In the context of the delivery of psychological services to young people, decision-making regarding the ability of young clients to give consent may include considering questions such as:

- Is it ethical to provide a psychological service to *this* young person without the direct consent of their parents or guardians?
- How should one respond to the request from the young person that the parent be excluded from knowing all or part of the nature of the problem, reasons for referral, or findings of an assessment?
- How should one respond when parents make the referral and the young person expresses initial reluctance or unwillingness to participate?

Such questions can arise with added complexity in education settings, which exemplify the organizational contexts of psychologists, but with the added issue that many clients are minors. Different education settings from kindergarten, to primary school, secondary school and special settings may operate under different government and legal systems. State education, private school systems and individual private schools may have different types of agreement in place between parents and educational institutions. Standard B.12.1 and standard B.12.2 of the 2007 Code provide reminders of possible conflict between the demands of the organization and the principles of the Code.

Standard B.12.1. Where the demands of an organization require *psychologists* to violate the general principles, values or standards set out in this *Code*, *psychologists*:

(a) clarify the nature of the conflict between the demands and these principles and standards;
(b) inform all parties of their ethical responsibilities as *psychologists*;

(c) seek a constructive resolution of the conflict that upholds the principles of the *Code*; and

(d) consult a senior psychologist.

Standard B.12.2. *Psychologists* who work in a team or other context in which they do not have sole decision-making authority continue to act in a way consistent with this *Code*, and in the event of any conflict of interest deal with the conflict in a manner set out in B.12.1.

Some schools make explicit in their agreement with parents at enrolment what are the expectations regarding possible referral to a psychologist within the school. Others assume a kind of implicit understanding. Psychologists are required to clarify these matters at the beginning of their employment in the school. The need for personal professional judgement, however, remains with the psychologist, including regarding the matter of perceived maturity of the particular young person.

Other common areas of difficulty include expectations regarding record keeping, access to information about the young clients, the purpose of assessments and communications about the reports, along with possible systemic problems such as informal communications which can easily lack confidentiality. In the wider school context I note recent expectations of psychologists to undertake other roles in the school at the same time as their role of psychologist: for example, the psychologist may be asked (or expected) to teach classes in psychology, or to act as a team coach in a particular sport. These situations call for careful ethical decision-making by psychologists who may benefit from consideration of documents relating to multiple relationships and boundaries (Australian Psychological Society, 2008).

Confidentiality

Section A.5 of the 2007 Code addresses confidentiality, and standard A.5.2 and standard A.5.4. of the Code clearly link the communication of confidential information to the provision of consent by the individual concerned. This, however, does not take account of minors who cannot give informed consent. In this domain there are diverse "push and pull" factors: the right to privacy of the child, the best interests of the child, the age and maturity of the child, the rights and responsibilities of the parents and the protection of the integrity of the family unit. In a context where family members are alienated from one another and in conflict, decisions about the child's best interests may be fraught. Further, it is more common than not for the information that is gained from the child to be about events and experiences involving the family members who may be seeking to be informed. Psychologists working with young people have to address the question of how to respond to the request from a young person that a parent be excluded from knowing all or part of the nature of the problem, reasons for referral or findings of an assessment.

Melton, Ehrenreich and Lyons (2001) note that psychologists' duties regarding confidentiality with child clients are not clear under US statutes and frequently go unmentioned. The argument for full disclosure could include the view that mental health treatment of a child, to be effective, generally ought to include family members and that parents need to be aware of their child's needs to be able to carry out their duty of care (Melton et al., 2001). They note further that this argument operates *against* the notion of the mature minor. Issues about a psychologist's duty to warn when there is a risk of self harm also need serious consideration in relation to minors. No working solution in the face of these problems is offered by the authors beyond the suggestion that "the clinician is well advised to establish a policy regarding disclosures to parents, to discuss that policy with clients when beginning treatment, and to document carefully both the policy itself and the reasons for any exceptions to it" (2001, p. 1085).

Koocher and Keith-Spiegel (1993) present further guidelines:

> Although a mental health professional is not legally obligated always to seek permission of a child client before disclosing confidential information, it is ethically mandatory to attempt to get such permission. This implies a recognition of the child's cognitive, social, and emotional developmental levels with appropriate allowances. It also implies an understanding of children's special dependency and vulnerability with respect to adults and of the resulting levels of protection that confidentiality may afford (p. 82).

The exercise of professional judgement in working with children and adolescents clearly requires a sound knowledge of developmental psychology, a component often missing from clinical psychology training in Australia. Whether a psychologist approaches development from cumulative learning or cognitive constructivist paradigms, such knowledge provides a basis for judging age-appropriate behaviour, for understanding the developmental context of presenting problems and for recognizing age-stage asynchronicity. Knowledge of developmental psychopathology is a further distinctive body of knowledge which elucidates the natural history of pathological processes in childhood and adolescence, and is desirable for practitioners working with troubled young people.

At the heart of professional decisions regarding confidentiality is a consideration of the relationships within the child's family. An ethicist whose philosophy is beginning to appear in the writings of psychologists is Emmanuel Levinas (1961/1969, 1982/1985) and it is notable that his ethics is relational at its core (Birrell, 2006; Parry, 2008). As this is consonant with the emergence of greater emphasis on respect for children and young people a brief account will now be presented. Consistent with this emphasis, Barnes (2007) has called for an ethics of care, beyond the rationale of rights, and documented the voices of young people expressing clearly their desire for respect and advocacy.

Emmanuel Levinas

Levinas was a twentieth-century philosopher who was a student of Husserl and Heidegger and shared their phenomenology and existentialism. This shared approach was based not on empiricism but on a person's internal subjective experience. Levinas rejected an approach that put this in opposition to objectivity; rather, through his focus on *intentionality*, he highlighted inter-subjectivity and saw intentionality as always orienting the person to the external world. Vandenburg (1999) writes that Levinas proposes a new approach to knowledge:

> We encounter others, face-to-face, in this moment, with urgency and immediacy. Their presence, their face, their eyes harken to us, make ethical demands for us to be responsible for them … and knowing occurs within this context. … Ethics is not a category of knowing, it is a condition for knowing (p. 33).

The philosophy of Levinas is not the thinking of an unrealistic romantic – a Lithuanian Jew, he spent years in a German prison camp and well knew the evil capabilities of the human heart. He held that the responsiveness of each human to the other was at the very heart of existence and ethics, and preceded systems of knowledge and truth. Vandenberg, in his 1999 essay, has shown how this view of human attunement as the basis for human ethics is consonant with much developmental psychology, especially recent research on infancy showing infants' early responsiveness to the quality of care. Beyond infancy, it is apparent in the relationships of a family, "the apparent extreme claims about the primordial ethical nature of human life, the asymmetry of responsibility, the centrality of love, mystery and death are essential features of parent-child relationships (Vandenberg, p. 36)". Such a philosophy offers deepening possibilities to a psychologist's way of relating to clients, so that no client, child or adult would ever be an object of clinical service or research. It also raises questions about how to conduct education in ethics.

A growing focus in ethics education, for example in the medical profession, is on virtue ethics. Bolsin, Faunce and Oakley (2005) state that the proponents of virtue ethics stress:

the character of the agent as a crucial addition to knowledge about principles, rules, and duties, as well as the consequences of their performance or non-performance. Proponents ... focus on an agent's motive, emotion, and whole "plan of life", as well as isolated moments of choice and discrete actions (p. 614).

The 2007 Code has as its focus core ethical principles and their application to the work of psychologists. While it might be argued that the 2007 Code implies a professional person of overall moral character and integrity, the question remains regarding how such professional character is achieved. This has important consequences for the "training" of psychologists as ethical professional people. Ethics education must be much more than teaching about the 2007 Code and giving practice in decision-making. As Vandenberg (1999) argues:

... ethics does not simply arise from 'moral dilemmas' that force difficult decisions. Rather, our daily, in this moment, journey is a moral one, every action a decision about how to comport ourselves in the face of ethical demands engendered by being with others. Simple gestures, such as feeding and giving, for instance, are common, yet profound ethical acts of care for another (p. 34).

A virtue ethics approach also has implications for professional development and the processes of supervision. The very interactions that take place in these contexts would need to have a formative influence beyond the internalization of standards and learning of "professional rules".

The work of psychologist, George Kunz (1998), which draws on the philosophy of Levinas, proposes an alternative paradigm for psychology recognizing the paradox of power and weakness. His reflections on Levinas remind us that professions and disciplines, while naming ethical principles, can be acting in their own self interest, a point also made by Coady and Bloch (1996). At the heart of Levinas' ideas is the possibility of a radical altruism which, like virtue ethics, focuses on the person and his/her *responseability*. These philosophical views are on a very different track from utilitarianism, moral contractualism and cultural or psychological relativism. Their insights may be important for us in considering our ethical responsibilities and how we communicate and uphold them within our profession, especially with the most vulnerable, including children and young people.

The final section of this chapter turns now to an important source of international understanding and agreement about the rights of children, the UN Convention on the Rights of the Child, a convention paid little attention in Australian university psychology courses, in my experience.

The UN Convention on the Rights of the Child

Melton, Ehrenreich and Lyons (2001), in arguing that the law can be a guide-post and a framework to assist decision-making, have discussed the importance of the 1989 United Nations Convention on the Rights of the Child. They proposed that, even though it may not be legally enforceable, "its comprehensiveness and conceptual coherence make it an excellent tool for policymakers, program administrators, and clinicians puzzled by ethical issues involving child clients" (p. 1089). One of these authors (Melton, 1990, 1991) formulated six principles derived from the Convention as a guide to mental health work with children:

1. The provision of high-quality services for children should be a matter of the highest priority for public mental health services.
2. Children should be viewed as active partners in child mental health services, with heavy weight placed on protection of their liberty and privacy.
3. Mental health services for children should be respectful of parents and supportive of family integrity.
4. States should apply a strong presumption against residential placement of children for the purpose of treatment, with due procedural care in decision-making about treatment and with provision of community-based alternatives. When out-of-home care is necessary for the protection or treatment of the child, it should be in the most family-like setting consistent with those objectives.
5. When the state does undertake the care and custody of emotionally disturbed children, it also assumes an especially weighty obligation to protect them from harm.
6. Prevention should be the cornerstone of child mental health policy (Melton et al., 2001, pp. 1089–1090).

Conclusion

Decisions about psychological interventions with children bring us into complex legal and ethical territory. As emphasized earlier, psychologists need to be aware of their commonwealth and state or territory laws in relation to children and their rights. However, there will still remain many grey areas where what is recommended is to "clarify with all parties" aspects of involvement and responsibility, but little guidance is offered as to how to conduct this clarification. The greatest complexities emerge in managing the tensions between the child's rights and wishes in the context of the "mature minor" and accountability to each parent or carer. A sound understanding of development is needed on which to base decisions regarding the mature status of a young person.

This chapter has considered a range of factors affecting ethical decision-making in this domain. These included Victorian legal principles emphasizing the best interests of the child, issues relating to informed consent and confidentiality, light shed by the philosophy of Emmanuel Levinas and the UN Convention on the Rights of the Child. Some implications for ethics education of psychologists are suggested. The weight given by the law and in psychological literature to the child's privacy, the stress on family integrity and prevention as the cornerstone may all give us pause in reflecting on our 2007 Code and our practice.

References

Australian Psychological Society (APS). (2007). *Code of ethics*. Melbourne, Australia.

Australian Psychological Society (APS). (2008). *Guidelines for managing professional boundaries and multiple relationships*. Melbourne, Australia.

Australian Psychological Society (APS). (2009). *Guidelines for working with young people*. Melbourne, Australia.

Barnes, V. (2007). Young people's views of children's rights and advocacy services: A case for "caring" advocacy? *Child Abuse Review*, 16, 140–52.

Birrell, P. (2006). An ethic of possibility: Relationship, risk and presence. *Ethics and behavior*, 16(2), 95–115.

Bolsin, S., Faunce, T., & Oakley, J. (2005). Practical virtue ethics: Healthcare whistle-blowing and portable digital technology. *Journal of Medical Ethics*, 31, 612–18.

Coady, M. M., & Bloch, S. (Eds.) (1996). *Codes of ethics and the professions*. Carlton South: Melbourne University Press.

Heath, S., Charles, V., Crow, G., & Wiles, R. (2007). Informed consent, gatekeepers and go-betweens: Negotiating consent in child- and youth-orientated institutions. *British Educational Research Journal*, 33(3), 403–17.

Kendall, P. C., & Suveg, C. (2008). Treatment outcome studies with children: Principles of proper practice. *Ethics and behaviour*, 18(2), 215–33.

Koocher, G. P., & Keith-Spiegel, P. C. (1993). *Children, ethics and the law. Professional issues and cases*. Lincoln: University of Nebraska Press.

Kunz, G. (1998). *The paradox of power and weakness. Levinas and an alternative paradigm for psychology*. Albany: State University of New York Press.

Levinas, E. (1961/1969). *Totality and infinity* (Alfonso Lingis, Trans.). Pittsburgh: Duquesne University Press.

Levinas, E. (1982/1985). *Ethics and infinity*. (Richard Cohen, Trans.). Pittsburgh: Duquesne University Press.

Melton, G. B. (1990). Promoting children's dignity through mental health services. In C. P. Cohen & H.A. Davidson (Eds.) *Children's rights in America: The UN Convention on the Rights of the Child compared with United States law* (pp. 239–58). Washington, DC: American Bar Association, Center on Children and the Law, and Defense for Children International-USA.

Melton, G. B. (1991). Socialisation in the global community. Respect for the dignity of children. *American Psychologist, 46*, 66–71.

Melton, G. B., Ehrenreich, N. S., & Lyons, P. M. (2001). Ethical and legal issues in mental health services for children. In C. E. Walker & M. C. Roberts (Eds.) *Handbook of clinical child psychology* (3ʳᵈ Ed.) (pp. 1074–93). New York: John Wiley & Sons, Inc.

Mudaly, N., & Goddard, C. (2009). The ethics of involving children who have been abused in child abuse research. *International Journal of Children's Rights, 17*(2), 261–81.

Parry, D. (2008). Ethics as first philosophy and its implications for psychotherapists and counsellors. *Existential Analysis, 19*(1), 156–75.

Secretary, Department of Health and Community Services v JWB and SMB. (1992). FLC 92–293.

Tan, J. O. A., Passerini, G. E., & Stewart, A. (2007). Consent and confidentiality in clinical work with young people. *Clinical Child Psychology and Psychiatry, 12*, 191–210.

Vandenberg, B. (1999). Levinas and the ethical context of development. *Human Development, 42*, 31–44.

Chapter 11
Boundaries and Multiple Relationships

Sabine Hammond

One of the most challenging ethical issues for professional psychologists involves maintaining and managing professional boundaries. In this context, psychologists need to consider such questions as: "When am I acting as psychologist?" "Is it acceptable or even beneficial to cross boundaries?" "Under what circumstances do boundary crossings become boundary violations?" "Are multiple relationships acceptable or should they be avoided?" "Which multiple relationships are unacceptable and raise the risk of harm to the clients?"

This chapter addresses these questions and provides an overview of boundary and multiple relationship issues, with specific reference to the 2007 Code. The focus will be on non-sexual boundary and multiple relationship issues in psychological services in a broad sense. Violations of sexual boundaries is addressed in Chapter 12 by Allan and Thomson. The question of when a psychologist is a psychologist (Cook & Hammond, 2006) is addressed in Chapter 4 by Warren.

The challenges raised by boundary issues and multiple relationships are reflected in registration board statistics. Complaints about inappropriate mixing of roles, conflict of interest and boundary violations accounted for a high percentage of complaints. In Victoria, approximately 10 per cent of complaints to the Psychologists Registration Board (PRBV) in the past five years involved boundary violations and multiple relationships (Hammond & Freckleton, 2006; Psychologists Registration Board of Victoria, 2005, 2006, 2007), with sexual misconduct or impropriety accounting for on average an additional 3.5 per cent of complaints. The PRBV investigates many non-sexual boundary violations through confidential informal hearings. The outcomes of formal hearings available over the Internet (www.psychreg.vic.gov.au) reflect the range of serious non-sexual boundary violations and multiple relationships that were considered serious unprofessional conduct, including the development of friendships soon after the termination of the professional relationship, social activities with clients, meeting clients for therapy in a café, or purchasing a property adjacent to a former client's home.

Definitions: Boundaries and Multiple Relationships

A large proportion of the literature about boundaries and multiple relationships derives from and refers to client-therapist relationships. It makes sense to assume that clients in this type of relationship may be most vulnerable to boundary crossings and violations. However, the 2007 Code refers to a much broader spectrum of practice, as illustrated in the definitions of the code. A "professional relationship or role is the relationship between a psychologist and a client which involves the delivery of a psychological service" (p. 9). A psychological service "means any service provided by a psychologist to a client including but not limited to professional activities, psychological activities, professional practice, teaching, supervision, research practice, professional services, and psychological procedures" (p. 10). The 2007 Code clearly defines clients not only as persons seeking therapy but refers to clients as "a party to a psychological service" (p. 8) and notes that psychologists have responsibilities not only to their clients, but also to the community, to society, and other professional relationships.

The development of the 2007 Code involved healthy discussion among members of the Review Working Group on the implications of these definitions and the specific standards on boundaries and multiple roles for all APS members and the wide range of professional services they deliver. For example, special challenges were raised about whether the provisions of the new code adequately addressed the roles of organizational psychologists. For example, the question was raised (E. Allworth, personal communication, 23 March 2007) of how well standards pertaining to boundaries and multiple relationships applied to such client groups as organizations, communities, third party payers and so on, and whether it would be unethical (a) for an organizational psychologist to have a close personal relationship with the sister/brother of an Human Relations manager who commissions their services (e.g., for psychological assessments of job candidates, job analysis, 360° surveys, consultation on change management or similar) in his or her organization, (b) to accept referrals for medico-legal assessments from one's brother/sister-in-law who is a lawyer, or to greet the brother/sister-in-law with a kiss and a hug before a meeting? Whilst the responses to these questions may be obvious relative to therapeutic relationships, they may not be as clear-cut in the larger organizational or community contexts.

In recent years, both the APS Ethics Committee and registration boards have addressed concerns about psychologists acting inappropriately in their private lives. Whilst many psychologists might argue that it is desirable for psychologists to have good boundaries in all of their interpersonal relationships, in order to avoid bringing the profession into disrepute (cf. section C.2.3.), the 2007 Code addresses specifically psychologists' professional relationships, that is, when psychologists act in a professional role. This distinction between professional and private conduct is important, as the field struggles with delineation of the professional and private roles of psychologists and where to draw the demarcation line. However, discussion of when a psychologist is or is not a psychologist goes beyond the focus of this chapter (Cook & Hammond, 2006; Pipes, Holstein, & Aguirre, 2005; Warren, Chapter 4 in this book).

What are Boundaries?

Boundaries define the roles of psychologist and client and, once engaged in a professional relationship, their specific roles. Boundaries provide a foundation for professional relationships by fostering a sense of trust, safety and predictability for the client, and the belief that the psychologist will always act in the client's best interests (Australian Psychological Society, 1999/2008; Glass, 2003).

The 2007 Code, specifically, General Principle B, Propriety, in standard B.1.2. addresses the expectations of psychologists with respect to boundaries by first focussing on boundaries of professional competence:

> *Psychologists only provide psychological services within the boundaries of their professional competence. This includes, but is not restricted to: (a) working within the limits of their education, training, supervised experience and appropriate professional experience; (b) basing their service on the established knowledge of the discipline and profession of psychology; (c) adhering to the Code and the Guidelines; (d) complying with the law of the jurisdiction in which they provide psychological services; and (e) ensuring that their emotional, mental, and physical state does not impair their ability to provide a competent service* (p. 18).

Boundaries refer to the limits of the professional relationship with the client and allow one to distinguish between the expectations and interactions that would be considered appropriate, as compared to inappropriate, within that relationship (Somers-Flanagan, Elliot & Sommers-Flanagan, 1998). How clear and firm boundaries should be has been the focus of debate, especially with respect to the therapeutic relationship (Lazarus & Zur, 2002; Zur, 2007). In response to criticisms that boundaries introduce a rigid cookbook nature to the relationship between psychologist and client, Koocher and Keith-Spiegel (2008) have pointed out that the structure provided by clear and firm boundaries may be in itself therapeutic.

Standard B.3, Professional responsibility, refers explicitly to the notions of boundaries discussed above: "Psychologists are aware of, and take steps to establish and maintain proper professional boundaries with clients and colleagues" (p. 20).

What are Boundary Crossings?

Boundary crossings are generally defined as departures from commonly accepted practice (Australian Psychological Society, 1999; Gutheil & Gabbard, 1993; Remley & Herlihy, 2005; Smith & Fitzpatrick, 1995). Boundary crossings may be appropriate and predominately benign, and may represent attempts to adapt treatment for an individual client (Glass, 2003). Glass also distinguished between *aggregated* and *grey* areas of boundary crossings. Aggregated boundary crossings are defined as profuse, prolonged, unquestioned and/or unconnected to any obvious therapeutic intent, and that could be seen to verge on malpractice (Glass, 2003). On the other hand, grey areas refer to deviations from the standard or established therapeutic technique that are greater than those of boundary crossings, but are not inherently steps towards boundary violations, for example, scheduling double sessions for a client who travels from a great distance (Glass, 2003) or meeting with a client at a location convenient to the client but possibly not as confidential as the psychologist's office. At times, it may not be clear whether this may be a true boundary crossing or adapting one's practice flexibly to the needs of the client. Pope and Keith-Spiegel (2008) note that:

> Nonsexual boundary crossings can enrich therapy, serve the treatment plan, and strengthen the therapist-client working relationship. They can also undermine the therapy, sever the therapist-patient alliance, and cause immediate or long-term harm to the client (p. 638).

Psychologists must constantly decide whether or not to cross a boundary that can have a profound influence on the progress of therapy. These choices are often subtle but multifaceted and therefore require serious consideration.

Generally these boundary crossings work best when discussed by the psychologist and client (Gutheil & Gabbard, 1998).

The Slippery Slope Towards Boundary Violations

The literature notes that often, boundary violations may begin seemingly innocently, as boundary blurring or crossings, and may be perceived by the psychologist as beneficial for the client (Corey, Corey & Callanan, 2007). Boundary violations are deviations from appropriate techniques and accepted practice that are typically harmful and exploitative of the client's and/or psychologist's needs. Boundary violations are typically not discussed between the psychologist and client (Gutheil & Gabbard, 1998). Violations involve conflict of interest in or dual intimate, therapeutic, work and social relationships because of the power differential between psychologist and client (Koocher & Keith-Spiegel, 2008).

In the 2007 Code, the potentially harmful effects of boundary violations are addressed in General Principle C Integrity by noting the power differential in the relationship: "Psychologists recognise that their knowledge of the discipline of psychology, their professional standing, and the information they gather place them in a position of power and trust. They exercise their power appropriately and honour this position of trust. Psychologists keep faith with the nature and intentions of their professional relationships" (p. 26). The principle is clarified further in the explanatory notes: "Psychologists are aware of their own biases, limits to their objectivity, and the importance of maintaining proper boundaries with clients. They identify and avoid potential conflicts of interest. They refrain from exploiting clients and associated parties" (p. 26). The 2008 Guidelines for managing boundaries and multiple relationships address the factors that psychologists should consider if a conflict of interest occurs. The Guidelines stress the importance of seeking independent advice from senior psychologists, of informing all parties involved in the potential or actual conflict, of developing a harm-minimization plan should the client wish to proceed with the multiple relationship, and considering to discontinue the professional service to the client.

The General Principle is further specified in Standard C.4., Non-exploitation, which addresses both exploitation and sexual relationships: "C.4.1. Psychologists do not exploit people with whom they have or had a professional relationship" (p. 28). and "C.4.2. Psychologists do not exploit their relationships with their assistants, employees, colleagues or supervisees" (p. 28). Finally, Standard C.4.3 explicitly addresses sexual relationships. (See Allan & Thomson, Chapter 12.)

Dual or Multiple Relationships

Multiple relationships occur when the psychologist is in another, significantly different relationship with a client, such as a social, financial or professional role (Pope & Vasquez, 1998). These roles may be concurrent, as when a psychologist hires a client to be a house cleaner. Or they may be consecutive, as when a psychologist goes into business with a client on termination of the therapy relationship (Koocher & Keith-Spiegel, 2008). The Australian Psychological Society's Guidelines for managing boundaries and multiple relationships (1999; 2008) also note that the goals of these relationships may not necessarily be compatible. For example, the therapeutic goal of the house cleaner client might be to establish a positive sense of self-esteem, which may be undermined when the psychologist has to complain about the poor standards of the house cleaning services, and thereby create the potential for harm for the client. Schank and Skovholt (2006) have identified eight reasons that make multiple relationships problematic. They noted that these relationships 'may be pervasive, difficult to recognize, sometimes unavoidable, the subject of conflicting advice, potentially harmful, and a risk to consumers and professionals, and they may affect a range of others (consumers, other professionals, the profession of psychology, and society)" (p. 36).

A range of variables has been identified in the literature that increases psychologists' risk or vulnerability for boundary crossings, violations or engaging in potentially problematic multiple relationships (Knowles, 2006). The APS Guidelines for managing boundaries and multiple relationships (2008) identify a range of risk factors including factors associated with the work setting, financial issues, and the type of clients. Koocher and Keith-Spiegel (2008) provide extensive examples that illustrate these risk factors and the problems that can result from multiple roles and relationships.

In its definitions, the 2007 Code identifies four conditions when multiple relationships can occur:

> … *when a psychologist, rendering a psychological service to a client also is or has been: (a) in a non-professional relationship with the same client; (b) in a different professional relationship with the same client; (c) in a non-professional relationship with an associated party; or (d) a recipient of a psychological service provided by the same client* (p. 9).

Similar to the APA Ethical Principles, the 2007 Code does not prohibit all dual or multiple relationships. In Standard C.3. Conflict of Interest, the strong language of the prior Code of Ethics (2003) has been attenuated from "avoid" to "refrain" from multiple relationships under conditions of impaired competence by the psychologist or risk of harm or exploitation to the client.

C.3.1. Psychologists refrain from engaging in multiple relationships that may: (a) impair their competence, effectiveness, objectivity, or ability to render a psychological service; (b) harm clients or other parties to a psychological service; or (c) lead to the exploitation of clients or other parties to a psychological service.

C.3.2. Psychologists who are at risk of violating standard C.3.1., consult with a senior psychologist to attempt to find an appropriate resolution that is in the best interests of the parties to the professional service.

C.3.3. When required by over-riding ethical considerations, their organisational requirements, or by law to enter into a multiple relationship, psychologists at the outset of the professional relationship, and thereafter when it is reasonably necessary, adhere to the provisions of standard A.3. (Informed consent).

C.3.4. Psychologists declare to clients any vested interests they have in the services they deliver, including all relevant funding, licensing and royalty interests.

Whilst this wording allows psychologists much more flexibility in their ethical decision-making, according to Koocher and Keith-Spiegel (2008), it is also less specific and may place less-experienced psychologists at greater risk of role violations.

In the 2007 Code, psychologists also are given explicit responsibility for ensuring that there are no multiple relationships when delegating tasks or using interpreters: Standard B. 6.(b): "psychologists who delegate tasks involved in the provision of psychological services to assistants, employees, junior colleagues or supervisees ... take reasonable steps to ensure that the delegate is not in a Multiple Relationship that may impair the delegate's judgement", B.7.(b), with respect to use of interpreters, "take reasonable steps to ensure that the interpreter is not in a multiple relationship with the client that may impair the interpreter's judgement."

Problem-Solving and Decision-Making About Boundary Issues and Multiple Relationships

In investigations by the registration boards, psychologists investigated for boundary violations and multiple relationships often identify total avoidance of multiple relationships as their future strategy to deal with such issues. Avoidance of multiple relationships has been strongly advocated by past ethics codes (e.g., 1997 APS Code). Over the past few years, there has been increasing debate in the literature as to whether psychologists can always avoid multiple relationships (Knowles, 2006; Younggren & Gottlieb, 2004; Zur, 2007).

Whilst there is relative agreement that sexual relationships should always be avoided during the professional relationship, there is less agreement on whether and after what time upon termination of the relationship, an intimate relationship should proceed (see Allan & Thomson, Chapter 12). Much of this discussion, especially involving non-romantic relationships (Pope & Keith-Spiegel, 2008; Sonne, 2005), has addressed specific settings such as rural and remote areas (Schank & Skovholt, 1997, 2006), other small or embedded communities (Johnson, Ralph, & Johnson, 2005; Staal & King, 2000), or specific therapy modes (Hill & Mamalakis, 2001; Pepper, 2004). Clouding this discussion to a considerable extent is that most literature addresses the therapeutic professional relationship, which is undoubtably one of the most vulnerable ones to boundary violations. Moreover, the literature is generally focussed on psychologists' views and responsibilities. Moleski and Kiselika (2005) noted that there is little research that addresses clients' perception and understanding of boundaries across settings and clients. Such understanding would be especially important with respect to clients from different cultural backgrounds who may have different understanding of how acceptable certain boundary crossings may be.

A recent Doctor of Psychology thesis (Van Megchelen, 2008) addressed client perceptions of boundaries. Key findings of this qualitative study with current and former psychology clients from urban (non-embedded) and rural (embedded) settings were: 1. Many clients did not have a clear idea of what a therapeutic boundary was. They also showed low awareness of boundary issues or how to deal with potential boundary crossings. Many clients did not want to be informed at the outset of treatment about how boundaries were to be maintained because they believed it was the psychologist's role to do the right thing and provide professional treatment. 2. Client understandings of boundary crossings were socially constructed, varied significantly according to the context of the situation. 3. There was some similarity in how clients from embedded and non-embedded communities understood and dealt with boundary issues; however, the rural embedded sample deemed it harder to manage boundaries. The findings suggest that clients trust their psychologist to act ethically and maintain proper boundaries, making it even more imperative for psychologists to address boundary issues in a thoughtful, deliberate and ethical manner.

It is noteworthy that the 2007 Code, like the 2002 APA Ethics Code, is now acknowledging the likelihood that dual or multiple relationships cannot always be avoided, and should be managed thoughtfully. The 2007 Code also stresses that exploitative, potentially harmful relationships should be avoided.

However, with the definition of clients in the 2007 Code, certain multiple relationships seem to be difficult to avoid, therefore requiring special attention to minimize possible harm. For example, a senior psychologist may serve both as the clinical supervisor and the administrative supervisor pursuing very different goals in each role. In university settings, it is not uncommon that the psychologist is at the same time the student's lecturer, the research supervisor and/or the clinical supervisor, and if holding an administrative role, the training director, clinic director, or head of school. In organizational psychology settings, where the client is an organization, whether the relationship between the psychologist and any member of the organization involves a dual relationship needs to be carefully clarified.

It is also important to consider that not all dual or multiple relationships can be anticipated (Knowles, 2006; Sonne, 2005). A colleague from a rural area recently shared her very frustrating experience at a dinner party, when her husband was clearly delighted to be seated next to a very nice couple, where the female partner had been his own wife's recent former client. Frustration and reportedly a considerable marital argument resulted from the psychologist wanting to leave the dinner party as early as possible, and not being able to tell her husband why without violating confidentialty. Sonne (2005) refers to such examples as incidental or accidental contacts, that is, not constituting boundary violations or multiple relationships.

There is some disagreement in the literature about whether psychologists could be more relaxed about some multiple relationships (e.g., Lazarus & Zur, 2002; Zur, 2007). I myself recently did not accept a referral, when the potential client mentioned that she was employed at my child's school. However, it is worthwhile contemplating whether I might have acted differently if I were not in a major metropolitan area with excellent referral sources, but in a rural setting or *the expert* for this problem, or selected because the client thought I would be especially sensitive to the nature of her problems (see Zur, 2007).

When psychologists can anticipate that the relationship with the client might involve dual or multiple relationships, psychologists need to evaluate systematically whether the boundary crossing will be a step onto the slippery slope placing both psychologist and client at risk or potentially beneficial. A helpful framework for classifying multiple roles and conflict of interest is provided by Pearson and Piazza (1997). These authors have distinguished between five types of multiple relationships: circumstantial relationships, structured multiple relationships, shifts in professional role, personal and professional role conflicts and predatory relationships.

Circumstantial multiple roles are co-incidental and likely to occur in small, embedded or rural communities, for example when the client is also the school teacher of the psychologist's child or the co-worker of the psychologist's spouse (Campbell & Gordon, 2003; Johnson et al., 2005; Shank & Skovholt, 1997). In *structured multiple relationships*, the psychologist and the client have more than one role. Some authors (Behnke, 2005) have noted that such relationships occur almost by definition, for example in university settings where staff members may have two or three roles, such as lecturer, research and clinical supervisor in any one semester. *Shifts in professional roles* may occur when psychologists move roles, for example, when a psychologist moves from a junior to a senior position and becomes supervisor to a colleague previously at the same professional level. *Personal and professional role conflicts* occur when personal relationships are followed by professional ones or vice versa (see also Johnson et al., 2005). Finally, *predatory professionals* use their professional role to take advantage of the client. Sexual relationships with clients fall into this category and are clearly considered as serious professional misconduct during the psychologist client-relationship (APA, 2002; APS, 2007; see also Allan & Thomson, Chapter 12; Koocher & Keith-Spiegel, 2008). However, authors also caution about intimate, sexual relationships with former clients, even after a time delay of two years or more, because of the potential exploitative nature of such relationships. Business relationships with current and former clients can similarly move from a professional/personal role conflict into the predatory category.

Ethical Decision-Making About Multiple Relationships

There is extensive literature on ethical decision-making in general (e.g., Miner, 2006), and with specific reference to managing risk with respect to boundary crossings and multiple relationships (e.g., Knowles, 2006; Sonne, 2005; Younggren & Gottlieb, 2004).

Barnett, Vasquez, Lazarus and Moorehead-Slaughter (2007) also identified seven considerations to help psychologists evaluate whether or not to cross a boundary. (1) Is the crossing motivated by the client's best interest rather than the psychologist's own need? (2) Is the boundary crossing consistent with the treatment plan? (3) Is the boundary crossing sensitive to the client's problems, history, cultural background and values? (4) Is the rationale for the boundary crossing documented in the client's record? (5) Is the boundary crossing discussed with the client in advance? (6) Has the power differential between psychologist and client been considered? (7) Has the psychologist engaged in consultation or supervision with a colleague prior to the boundary crossing? Moreover, Knowles (2006) suggested that psychologists consider the size of the power differential between psychologist and client, whether the professional relationship is anticipated to be short-term or longer-term in duration, and whether or not the client may want to return for further services by this psychologist after the relationship has been terminated.

Schank and Skovholt (2006) have identified a large number of strategies for minimizing risk of boundary violations and multiple relationships, with special focus on rural communities. Schank and Skovholt stressed the importance of knowing relevant ethics codes, laws and regulations but also that the ethics codes may not be sufficient for making such ethical decisions in rural areas.

These authors suggested involving clients actively in the decision-making process by obtaining informed consent and addressing the likelihood of out-of-therapy contact directly. They further noted the importance of being aware of broader community standards. Similar to other authors, they also note the importance of ongoing consultation and supervision, professional development, and careful documentation.

By anticipating what dual relationships or role conflicts might arise in their work settings, and by engaging in systematic decision-making and risk analysis, psychologists can prevent the blurring of professional boundaries, or crossing of boundaries. Through such risk analysis, psychologists are more likely to engage in a multiple role relationship with good awareness of the potential problems and with backup from professional colleagues through supervision and consultation.

Conclusion

Issues involving professional boundaries and multiple-role relationships within psychological services are very complex. This is particularly true for non-sexual multiple relationships, which may result from initial good intentions by the psychologist but, via the "slippery-slope" phenomenon, may result in serious boundary violations and role blending that is ultimately harmful to the client. The 2007 APS Code of Ethics and the 2008 Guidelines for managing professional boundaries and multiple relationships recognize the importance of careful ethical decision-making by psychologists about engaging in such relationships, rather than forbidding them completely.

Whilst boundary crossings and multiple relationships may not be avoidable at all costs, the onus remains on the psychologist to engage in thoughtful decision-making, consultation and supervision to assure that a decision in favour of a boundary crossing or a dual role is truly in the client's best interest and will not result in harm at some time in the future. This is a very difficult process indeed.

References

American Psychological Association (APA). (2002). Ethical principles of psychologists and code of conduct. *American Psychologist, 57*, 1060–73.

Australian Psychological Society (APS). (1997). *Code of ethics.* Carlton South, Australia.

Australian Psychological Society (APS). (1999). *Guidelines for managing professional boundaries and multiple relationships.* Melbourne, Australia.

Australian Psychological Society (APS). (2007). *Code of ethics*. Melbourne, Australia.

Australian Psychological Society (APS). (2008). *Guidelines for managing professional boundaries and multiple relationships*. Melbourne, Australia.

Barnett, J. E., Vasquez, M. J. T., Lazarus, A. A., & Moorehead-Slaughter, O. (2007). *Boundary issues and multiple relationships: Fantasy and reality. Professional psychology: Research and practice*, 38, 401–10.

Behnke, S. (2005). On being an ethical psychologist. *Monitor on psychology*, 36(7), 114–5.

Campbell, C. D., & Gordon, M. C. (2003). Acknowledging the inevitable: Understanding multiple relationships in rural practice. *Professional psychology: Research and practice*, 34, 430–4.

Cook, P., & Hammond, S. A. (2006, September). *When is a psychologist a psychologist: Policy development towards improved professional standards*. Raising professional standards. Forum presented at the Joint Conference of the Australian Psychological Society and the New Zealand Psychological Society, Auckland, New Zealand.

Corey, G., Corey, M. S., & Callanan, P. (2007). *Issues and ethics in the helping professions*. Belmont, CA: Thomson Brooks/Cole Publishing Company.

Glass, L. L. (2003). The gray areas of boundary crossings and violations. *American Journal of Psychotherapy*, 57(4), 429–44.

Gutheil, T. G., & Gabbard, G. O. (1993). The concept of boundaries in clinical practice: Theoretical and risk-management dimensions. *American Journal of Psychiatry*, 150(2), 188–96.

Gutheil, T. G., & Gabbard, G. O. (1998). Misuses and misunderstandings of boundary theory in clinical and regulatory settings. *American Journal of Psychiatry*, 155(3), 409–14.

Hammond, S. W., & Freckelton, I. (2006). Being the subject of a complaint to a regulatory board: Complaints happen. In S. Morrissey and P. Reddy (Eds.). *Ethics and professional practice for psychologists* (pp. 150–62). South Melbourne, Australia: Thompson Learning.

Hill, M. R., & Mamalakis, P. M. (2001). Family therapists and religious communities: Negotiating dual relationships. *Family Relations*, 50(3), 199–208.

Johnson, W. B., Ralph, J., & Johnson, S. J. (2005). Managing multiple roles in embedded environments: The case of aircraft carrier psychology. *Professional psychology: Research and practice*, 36, 73–81.

Koocher, G. P., & Keith-Spiegel, P. (2008). *Ethics in psychology and the mental health professions: Standards and cases* (3rd ed.). New York: Oxford University Press.

Knowles, A. (2006). Boundaries, dual relationships and professional practice. In S. Morrissey & P. Reddy (Eds.), *Ethics and professional practice for psychologists* (pp. 89–101). South Melbourne, Australia: Thomson/Social Science Press.

Lazarus, A., & Zur, O. (2002). *Dual relationships and psychotherapy*. New York: Springer Publishing Company.

Miner, M. H. (2006). A proposed comprehensive model for ethical decision-making (EDM). In S. Morrissey, & P. Reddy (Eds.), *Ethics and professional practice for psychologists* (pp. 25–37). South Melbourne, Australia: Thomson/Social Science Press.

Moleski, S. M., & Kiselica, M. S. (2005). Dual relationships: A continuum ranging fro the destructive to the therapeutic. *Journal of Counselling and Development, 83*(1), 3–11.

Pearson, B., & Piazza, N. (1997). Classification of dual relationships in the helping professions. *Counsellor Education and Supervision, 37*, 89–99.

Pepper, R. S. (2004). Confidentiality and dual relationships in group psychotherapy. *International Journal of Group Psychotherapy, 51*(1), 103–14.

Pipes, R. B., Holstein, J. E., & Aguirre, M. G. (2005). Examining the personal-professional distinction: Ethics codes and the difficulty of drawing a boundary. *American Psychologist, 60*(4), 325–34.

Pope, K., & Keith-Spiegel, P. (2008). A practical approach to boundaries in psychotherapy: Making decisions, bypassing blunders, and mending fences. *Journal of Clinical Psychology, 64*, 638–52.

Pope, K. S., & Vasquez, M. J. T. (1998). *Ethics in psychotherapy and counseling* (2nd ed.). San Francisco, CA: Jossey-Bass.

Psychologists Registration Board of Victoria. (2005). *Annual Report 2005.* Melbourne, Australia.

Psychologists Registration Board of Victoria. (2006). *Annual Report 2006.* Melbourne, Australia.

Psychologists Registration Board of Victoria. (2007). *Annual Report 2007.* Melbourne, Australia.

Remley, T. P., Jr., & Herlihy, B. (2005). *Ethical, legal, and professional issues in counseling.* Upper Saddle River, NJ: Pearson Education.

Schank, J. & Skovolt, T. (1997). Dual relationship dilemmas of rural and small community psychologists. *Professional Psychology: Research and Practice. 28*, 44–49.

Schank, J. A., & Skovolt, T. M. (2006). *Ethical practice in small communities: Challenges and rewards for psychologists.* Washington, DC: American Psychological Association.

Smith, D., & Fitzpatrick, M. (1995). Patient-therapist boundary issues: An integrative review of theory and research. *Professional Psychology: Research and Practice, 26*, 499–506.

Sommers-Flanagan, R., Elliot, D., & Sommers-Flanagan, J. (1998). Exploring the edges: Boundaries and breaks. *Ethics and Behaviour, 8*(1), 37–48.

Sonne, J. L. (2005). *Nonsexual multiple relationships: A practical decision-making model for clinicians.* Retrieved on 1 June 2008 from http://kspope.com/site/multiple-relationships.php.

Staal, M. A., & King, R. E. (2000). Managing a multiple relationship environment: The ethics of military psychology. *Professional psychology: Research and practice, 31*(6), 698–705.

Van Megchelen, T. (2008). *How do clients of psychology services perceive and maintain therapeutic boundaries? A qualitative research inquiry.* Unpublished Doctor of Psychology thesis, Australian Catholic University, Melbourne, Australia.

Younggren, J. N., & Gottlieb, M. C. (2004). Managing risk when contemplating multiple relationships. *Professional psychology: Research and practice, 35*(3), 255–60.

Zur, O. (2007). *Boundaries in psychotherapy: Ethical and clinical explorations.* Washington, DC: American Psychological Association.

Chapter 12
The Regulation of Sexual Activity Between Psychologists and Their Clients and Former Clients

Alfred Allan and Donald M. Thomson

As discussed by Hammond in Chapter 11, multiple relationships are actively discouraged in the 2007 Code of the Australian Psychological Society (APS) because of the concern that they may impair psychologists' objectivity and effectiveness to render a psychological service; harm clients and lead to the exploitation of clients. However, only one form of multiple relationship is explicitly regulated in most codes of ethics for psychologists (Allan, 2008), namely sexual activity between psychologists and their clients, even though there is no evidence that sexual activity between psychologists and clients occur more frequently than other multiple relationships. In fact, recent research in the Unites States of America (USA) suggests that only 2 per cent of psychologists have engaged in a sexual boundary crossing and that the prevalence of such behaviour may be decreasing (Lamb & Catanzaro, 1998; Lamb, Catanzaro, & Moorman, 2003). The Review Working Group (Group), nevertheless, decided to follow the example of the authors of other codes and to retain the standards of the 1997 Code that prohibits sexual activity between psychologists and associated parties. This decision followed a robust discussion of the issue during which the Group debated arguments that authors make to support the prohibition of sexual activity between psychologists and their clients.

The first argument is that clients cannot be considered to be *autonomous* people when it comes to sexual relationships with their psychologists (Moleski & Kiselica, 2005). There is a risk that clients may be dependent, vulnerable and powerless while they are receiving psychological services and may therefore be easy targets for psychologists to manipulate and exploit. Psychologists who engage in sexual activity with clients are seen to have failed in their obligation to promote autonomy (Moleski & Kiselica, 2005). Some scholars believe that sexual activity between psychologists and their clients is such a flagrant abuse of power that it should lead to a charge of rape if it includes sexual penetration (Masters & Johnson, 1976). It is therefore not surprising that tribunals virtually always consider sexual activity between psychologists and their current clients as unethical (see, e.g., Atkins & Stein, 1993; Re Hall, 2003; Re Psychologist, 1997, 2001; Re Walsh, 2005) and that sexual relationships between psychologists and their clients have been explicitly identified as criminal offences in some states in the USA (Borruso, 1991; Haspel, Jorgenson, Wincze, & Parsons, 1997). Even in jurisdictions where there is no specific legislation proscribing it, courts may find psychologists guilty of a criminal offence if they find that the sexual activity was coerced or that the sexual activity was fraudulently misrepresented as legitimate therapy.

Furthermore, even if clients are considered to be autonomous, some authors argue that the risk of harm to them is so high that the *nonmaleficence* principle outweighs the autonomy principle when it comes to psychologist-client sexual relationships (Moleski & Kiselica, 2005). For instance, Webb (1986), argues that sexual activity with clients does not only disregard "the intent of the therapeutic relationship, but it perverts it into a real intrusion into the patient's world of fears, hopes, and guilt … the patient usually suffers the greatest damage because he or she has trusted and depended on the … [psychologist] … for guidance and protection in the therapeutic relationship" (p. 1149).

There is some evidence that psychologist-client sexual contact is detrimental to clients (Aviv, Levine, Shelef, Speiser, & Elizur, 2006; Ben-Ari & Somer, 2004; Nachmani & Somer, 2007; Pope & Bouhoutsos, 1986; Somer & Saadon, 1999). For instance, data collected by Aviv and his colleagues from 918 Israeli psychiatrists, psychologists and social workers whose clients revealed sexual activity with their most recent former therapist indicate that 3 per cent of the clients had to be hospitalized; 6 per cent attempted suicide; and 0.03 per cent committed suicide. However, these findings must be interpreted with care because it is difficult to assess the claims made by clients that they have suffered psychological damage as a result of sexual activity with their psychologists. It is virtually impossible to establish what symptoms pre-existed the sexual activity and the samples used may not be representative because it is very likely that it is primarily clients who feel aggrieved that will report such activity, such as where there was an acrimonious end to their relationships. Nevertheless, even though the likelihood of sexual activity between psychologists and their clients may be low, it cannot be ignored because of the extent of possible harm to clients should it occur, and because the clients involved are often people who have been victimized in the past or are otherwise vulnerable (Somer & Saadon, 1999). Such exploitive behaviour also harms the well-being of society because such behaviour may discourage people in need of mental health treatment from using the services of psychologists. It further brings the profession in disrepute and can have a negative impact on the livelihood of psychologists.

A final argument in support of prohibiting sexual activity between psychologists and clients is that society forbids people who are entrusted with the interests of others, from taking advantage of them to satisfy their own needs because such exploitation repudiates the *trust* that is essential in relationships of this nature. Sexual behaviour with clients is seen as a betrayal of the client's trust and, at the least, an exploitation of the client's transference feelings (Appelbaum & Gutheil, 1991; Appelbaum & Jorgenson, 1991; Lakin, 1988; Quadrio, 1994; Simon, 1994a, 1994b; Steere, 1984).

However, these three factors on their own do not justify the singular attention to sexual activity found in codes of ethics because they are also relevant in other multiple relationships, such as, for instance, when a psychologist exploits a client financially. It appears to us that the key issue that justifies the prohibition of psychologist-client sexual activity is that the personal intimacy that invariably accompanies it will always impair psychologists' effectiveness, objectivity and judgement. Psychologists who have close, personal relationships with people may, for instance, not have the objectivity to make proper professional judgements in respect of them or the readiness and ability to be as challenging and persistent with them as they should be. Sexual activity is therefore unacceptable even in the absence of exploitation.

The accumulated weight of all these factors justifies the APS in taking a strong public stance against sexual activity between psychologists and their clients, particularly because of allegations that professions (including psychology) have in the past protected errant professionals (Quadrio, 1994).

The 2007 Code is the first APS Code that makes it unethical for psychologists to accept as clients people with whom they have engaged in sexual activity (standard C.4.3(d)). The major reason for this prohibition is that the earlier sexual relationship may impair the judgement of the psychologists. This provision differs from the other provisions in standard C.4.3 in that it regulates who psychologists can accept as clients, and not with whom they can engage in sexual activity. It should, nevertheless, be pointed out that all ethical standards are relative, not absolute, and that there may be circumstances where psychologists would be justified to attend to a person with whom they have previously engaged in sexual activity. For instance, psychologists would be justified to attend to a former sexual partner who is acutely suicidal if that is the only reasonable course of action at the time. However, psychologists who find themselves in such situations should attempt to refer the client to another appropriate practitioner once they have dealt with the emergency.

In contrast to standard C.4.3(d) the proscription of sexual relationships between psychologists and existing clients has been in the APS Code since 1986. The Code of Professional Conduct (Australian Psychological Society, 1986) provided:

> *B.6. Psychologists may not exploit their professional relationships with clients, supervisees, students, employees, or research participants sexually or otherwise.*
>
> *B.7. Personal sexual relationships between psychologists and clients are unethical. When a therapeutic procedure entails some level of physical sexual intimacy with a client, documented informed consent must be obtained from the client or the client's legal guardian prior to the introduction of that procedure. Sexual intercourse between psychologists and clients is unethical.*

The Group had no hesitation in retaining this prohibition in the 2007 Code, but reformulated it and expanded it. Standard C.4.3(a) provides that psychologists should not "engage in sexual activity with a client or anybody who is closely related to one of their clients". The rationale for extending the prohibition is the same as that for the standard C.4.3(d), namely, that there is a potential for the sexual relationship with a person closely related to the client to impair the professional judgement of the psychologist.

Psychologists generally support the prohibition of sexual activity with clients because they consider such behaviour as constituting an unacceptable multiple relationship (Atkins & Stein, 1993). However, national surveys in the USA found that about one third of psychologists (Akamatsu, 1988; Pope, Keith-Spiegel, & Tabachnick, 1987) and psychiatrists (Herman, Gartrell, Olartes, Feldstein, & Localio, 1987) who responded in the different studies thought that *post-termination sex* between psychologists and their former clients may be acceptable. In fact, only 30 per cent of the therapists employed by a specific department of psychiatry in the USA believed that marrying a client after proper termination of long-term therapy was unethical. Later studies in the USA confirm that substantial numbers of psychologists do not view sexual activity with former clients as harmful and that sexual boundary violations occur between them and former clients (Lamb & Catanzaro, 1998; Lamb et al., 2003; Shavit & Bucky, 2004). The lack of consensus regarding the ethical appropriateness of post-termination sexual activity with former clients (Malmquist & Notman, 2001) is understandable because the ethical basis for a prohibition of sex with former clients is weaker than in the case of current clients. Firstly, if an intervention was successful, clients should be able to make decisions independently from their former psychologists after completion of therapy, unless they are permanently incapable of giving informed consent or extremely vulnerable people, such as people with severely debilitating mental disorders or disabilities. Most clients of psychologists do not fall in these categories. There are, secondly, many examples of situations where the proscription of sexual activity between psychologists and former clients will be unrealistic, unfair and on the face of it disrespectful of their autonomy and human rights. Few people would, for example, consider it wrong for a psychologist to marry a client who she assessed twenty years before as a careers counsellor at a university.

Some authors, nevertheless, argue for the placement of a total ban on post-termination sexual relations, particularly in the case of therapists (see, e.g., Lazarus, 1992; Moleski & Kiselica, 2005). This argument is based on the belief that therapy is fundamentally interminable (Firestein, 1969). This *once a client, always a client* belief is particularly strong amongst psychoanalytically trained psychologists, but even other psychologists retain knowledge about former clients that maintains the risk of exploitation even after the end of the professional relationship. A further argument is that much of the therapy gains that clients make in therapy may be undone during later sexual relationships, especially if these relationships do not work out. However, the major concern is that if post-termination sex is not banned, unscrupulous psychologists will merely terminate the psychologist-client relationship to engage in sexual relationships with clients. The effect of this could be that vulnerable clients may be harmed twice: by the premature termination of the service and the later sexual behaviour.

Ethical codes in the mental health area therefore have standards aimed at regulating the sexual activity between psychologists and their former clients. However, the drafters of the codes differ in their approaches to finding compromise positions that take into account the human rights and autonomy of clients and psychologists, but at the same time protect clients' from potential harm and exploitation.

The ethical codes of, for instance, the Royal Australian and New Zealand College of Psychiatrists (1998) and the American Association of Sexuality Educators, Counselors and Therapists (AASECT, 2004) proscribe sexual activity with clients for perpetuity. However, it is more common to proscribe sexual activity with clients for a specific period. In Australia the then Victoria Psychological Council (VPC) decided in 1991 that sexual relationships between psychologists and former clients within one year after termination of the professional relationship was unethical. However, this was not a formal ruling, as the VPC found that the sexual activity in the relevant case actually commenced before termination of the professional relationship. In 1997 the APS for the first time dealt with sexual relationships between psychologists and their former clients by incorporating the following provisions in its Code of Ethics (Australian Psychological Society, 1997):

> *B.10. No member may engage in a sexual relationship with a former client when less than two years have expired since the ending or termination of the professional relationship.*
>
> *B.11. In circumstances where more than two years have elapsed since the ending or termination of the professional relationship between the member and former client, in determining whether a sexual relationship between the member and former client is unethical, the following matters will be taken into consideration: a) the length of the professional relationship; b) the nature of the professional relationship;*

c) the client's mental state at the time he or she commenced the sexual relationship with the member; d) the circumstances in which the professional relationship ended or was terminated; and e) the duration of time that has expired since the ending of the professional relationship. Additionally, any other salient matters may be taken into consideration when evaluating the conduct of a member who has engaged in a sexual relationship with a former client.

The American Psychological Association's (2002) comparable provision, standard 10.08 (b) of the Ethical Principles of Psychologists and Code of Conduct is narrower in that it refers to therapeutic relationships only. It provides that:

Psychologists do not engage in sexual intimacies with former clients/patients even after a two-year interval except in the most unusual circumstances. Psychologists who engage in such activity after the two years following cessation or termination of therapy and of having no sexual contact with the former client/patient bear the burden of demonstrating that there has been no exploitation, in light of all relevant factors, including (1) the amount of time that has passed since therapy terminated; (2) the nature, duration, and intensity of the therapy; (3) the circumstances of termination; (4) the client's/patient's personal history; (5) the client's/patient's current mental status; (6) the likelihood of adverse impact on the client/patient; and (7) any statements or actions made by the therapist during the course of therapy suggesting or inviting the possibility of a posttermination sexual or romantic relationship with the client/patient.

Provisions that stipulate a period of time, whether it is a year, two years or more, are arbitrary because there are some former clients who may remain vulnerable for the rest of their lives whilst others may not be vulnerable at all. Another concern is that these provisions create a situation that former clients can exploit when their relationships with their former psychologists deteriorate. The APA's provision also places a very onerous burden of proof on psychologists charged of having engaged in sexual activity with former clients after two years. It, for instance, requires psychologists to prove the negative, namely to demonstrate that there had not been any exploitation as a consequence of the prior professional relationship. This is virtually impossible, especially if the former client does not cooperate.

In contrast to these attempts of the APS and APA to regulate the sexual activity between psychologists and clients and former clients in detail, the authors of the Canadian Code provide that psychologist should not "encourage or engage in sexual intimacy with therapy clients … for that period of time following therapy during which the power relationship reasonably could be expected to influence the client's personal decision-making" (standard II.27 of Canadian Psychological Association, 2000). Whilst this provision places the responsibility of deciding about sexual relationships on psychologists it does guide their decision-making. However, it also creates a high degree of uncertainty.

The Group recognised that provisions that proscribe sexual relationships between psychologists and former clients violate their autonomy and right of free association. The Group decided that there was no justification for an absolute ban on post-terminal sexual activity between psychologists and clients. It decided, nevertheless, that the magnitude of potential harm to former clients was such that it justified the retention of a mandatory period of abstinence in the 2007 Code. Standard C.4.3(b) provides that psychologists:

> *Do not engage in sexual activity with a former client, or anybody who is closely related to one of their former clients, within two years after terminating the professional relationship with the former client.*

The Group decided to specify a specific period of time because it would bring clarity. Psychologists and clients know in advance how long they need to wait should they want to engage in sexual activity and this may discourage psychologists from terminating the professional relationship to engage in a sexual relationship (Appelbaum & Jorgenson, 1991). It further eliminates the virtually impossible task that tribunals and courts otherwise have to determine retrospectively whether former clients' ability to make autonomous decisions were compromised when they agreed to sexual activity with their psychologists. The fixed period finally allows both psychologists and their clients a cooling off period during which they can reflect on their mutual attraction without any undue pressure from the other. Whilst transference may never dissipate in some cases, there is anecdotal evidence that it diminishes over time (Firestein, 1969).

There was an intense debate in the Group regarding the duration of the waiting period. The members recognised that any period they decided upon would be arbitrary because what would be an appropriate time for one psychologist-client pair in one situation could be inappropriate for them in another situation, or for another psychologist-client pair in the same situation. Some members of the Group were swayed by Appelbaum and Jorgenson's (1991) argument in favour of a one year period. These two authors rely on their own substantial experience of working with clients who complain of sexual activity between them and their psychiatrists and the observations of the staff of the Minneapolis Walk-In Counseling Center, to argue that more than 99% of cases of practitioner-client sex activity start within one year of the termination (Gartrell, Herman, Olarte, Feldstein, & Localio, 1986). However, the majority of the Group felt that as part of the educative function of the Code it should give a strong message to psychologists that sexual activity between psychologists and former clients are undesirable except in exceptional circumstances. The views of the majority prevailed and the period of two years stipulated in the 1997 Code was retained.

The Group decided to place the responsibility on psychologists to decide whether it will be appropriate for them to engage in sexual activity with former clients after two years, but does prescribe a process that psychologists should follow. Standard C.4.3(c) provides that psychologists:

> *who wish to engage in sexual activity with former clients after a period of two years from the termination of the service, first explore with a senior psychologist the possibility that the former client may be vulnerable and at risk of exploitation, and encourage the former client to seek independent counselling on the matter ...*

It would be prima face unethical if psychologists fail to follow this procedure, but following the process in a superficial manner will not protect them if a disciplinary tribunal find on the facts that they had exploited their former clients. Nor will it prevent former clients from suing psychologists in a civil court if they can prove that they have been harmed by the wrongful behaviour of psychologists.

The Group discussed restricting standard C.4.3 to therapy clients as is the case in the American and Canadian Codes, but decided against it. The rationale for this is that therapeutic relationships are not the only professional relationships where clients may be vulnerable and potentially subject to exploitation. For example, organisational psychologists who do psychological assessments of job applicants may be in positions of power that they could exploit.

The Group decided to use the phrase *sexual activity* to make the ambit of the construct broad, however, as the authors of many other codes, it deliberately did not define the phrase in the 2007 Code because any definition is bound to have loopholes. Guidance as what sexual activity means in this context can be found in standard N of principle 3 of the AASECT Code which provides that therapists should:

> *not engage, attempt to engage or offer to engage a consumer in sexual behavior whether the consumer consents to such behavior or not. Sexual misconduct includes kissing, sexual intercourse and/or the touching by either the member or the consumer of the other's breasts or genitals. .... Sexual misconduct is also sexual solicitation, physical advances, or verbal or nonverbal conduct that is sexual in nature, that occurs in connection with the member's activity or roles as a counselor or therapist, and that either (1) is unwelcome, is offensive, or creates a hostile workplace or educational environment, and the member knows or is told this or (2) is sufficiently severe or intense to be abusive to a reasonable person in the context. Sexual misconduct can consist of a single intense or severe act, or of multiple persistent or pervasive acts.*

Standard C.4.3 does not include experiences of sexual attraction by psychologists because ethical standards describe behaviour, not experiences. Sexual attraction between psychologists and their clients is common and normal (Fisher, 2004; Pope, Tabachnick, & Keith-Spiegel, 1987). However, the self disclosure of such feelings by psychologists is generally not advisable because it may constitute verbal conduct that is sexual in nature. Such disclosures also frequently lead to sexual behaviour that is unethical (Fisher, 2004; Rodolfa et al., 1994). In fact, the findings of retrospective studies suggest that most cases of sexual activity between practitioners and clients started with self disclosure by psychologists of their attraction to their clients (Somer & Saadon, 1999). Vinson (1987) argues that for some clients psychologists' description of their sexual reaction to clients may in itself be traumatic.

Standard C.4.3(a) does not make sex therapy impossible. The heading of standard C.4 ("non-exploitation") firstly restricts the interpretation of the phrase to exploitive behaviour. Sex therapy by competent psychologists with clients under circumstances where it is indicated and where proper consent had been obtained (see standard A.3 in general, and A.3.5 in particular) will therefore not fall foul of standard C.4.3 (a). As with all therapy the most ethical sex therapy is that which has an evidence base; brings about the desired effect in the briefest time and at the smallest cost (AASECT, 2004; Lowery & Lowery, 1975) and does not offend public morality. Having sex with a client is never acceptable sex therapy, and even referring clients to a surrogate (Fox & Szego, 2003) is questionable.

Psychologists who do sex therapy must display the utmost respect for their clients in their communication with clients and in choosing the setting where the therapy takes place (General principle 1). They must also keep in mind that the risk of misunderstandings is high when they do sex therapy because sexual behaviour is such an emotionally charged and value-laden aspect of human functioning. To compound the risk, some clients experience sexual problems because of their backgrounds and personalities, and these factors may also make them vulnerable to exploitation and prone to developing strong feelings of affection for their psychologists. For the protection of both their clients and themselves, sex therapists must ensure that clients do not misunderstand their motives or are offended by their behaviour by defining boundaries very conservatively and maintaining them strictly (Koocher & Keith-Spiegel, 1998).

In conclusion, the provision governing sexual activity between psychologists and clients in the 2007 Code are unique in that they represent an interference with the right of autonomy of both psychologists and their clients to choose who they want to have relationships with and further ignore the basic human right of freedom of association that all humans are believed to have (United Nations, 1948). The 2007 Code furthermore prohibits only one of many forms of multiple relationships (see Hammond, Chapter 11), and relationships which may not involve less problems than many relationships generally sanctioned in our society (Appelbaum & Jorgenson, 1991). The likelihood of sexual relationships between psychologists and their clients is also relatively low. However, the strict governing of sexual activity between psychologists and their clients is justified, because when they occur the consequences for clients can be severe (Aviv et al., 2006). The provisions that regulate psychologist-client relationships also have an important educational function given that sexual activity is amongst the most common causes of complaints and civil actions against mental health providers (Norris, Gutheil, & Strasburger, 2003). The causes of sexual activity may be predatory behaviour, but they are often precipitated by *psychologist factors* such as life crises and transitions and idealisation of clients; and *client factors* such as dependency and seeking of love and acceptance.

A clear understanding by psychologists of professional boundaries and adherence to those boundaries provides a safeguard for both the client and the psychologist. Ongoing supervision by an experienced psychologist provides an additional mechanism to ensure that professional boundaries are not transgressed.

References

Akamatsu, T. J. (1988). Intimate relationships with former clients: national survey of attitudes and behaviors among practitioners. *Professional Psychology: Research & Practice, 19*, 454–8.

Allan, A. (2008). *An international perspective of law and ethics in psychology*. Somerset West, South Africa: Inter-ed.

American Association of Sexuality Educators, Counselors and Therapists (AASECT). (2004). Code of Ethics [Electronic Version]. Retrieved 17 May 2008 from www.aasect.org/PDFs/Code%20of%20Ethics%20Rev%20Sept%202004.pdf.

American Psychological Association (APA). (2002). *Ethical principles of psychologists and code of conduct*. Washington DC: American Psychological Association.

Appelbaum, P. S., & Gutheil, T. G. (1991). *Clinical handbook of psychiatry and the law* (2nd ed.). Baltimore: Williams & Wilkins.

Appelbaum, P. S., & Jorgenson, L. (1991). Psychotherapist-patient sexual contact after termination of treatment: An analysis and a proposal. *American Journal of Psychiatry, 148*, 1466–73.

Atkins, E. L., & Stein, R. (1993). When the boundary is crossed: A protocol for attorneys and mental health professionals. *American Journal of Forensic Psychology, 11*, 3–21.

Australian Psychological Society. (1986). *Code of professional conduct*. Melbourne, Australia.

Australian Psychological Society. (1997). *Code of ethics*. Melbourne, Australia.

Aviv, A., Levine, J., Shelef, A., Speiser, N., & Elizur, A. (2006). Therapist-patient sexual relations: Results of a national survey in Israel. *The Israel Journal of Psychiatry and Related Sciences, 43,* 119–25.

Ben-Ari, A., & Somer, E. (2004). The aftermath of therapist-client sex: Exploited women struggle with the consequences. *Clinical Psychology and Psychotherapy, 11,* 126–36.

Borruso, M. T. (1991). Sexual abuse by psychotherapists: The call for a uniform criminal statue. *American Journal of Medicine and Law, 17,* 289–311.

Canadian Psychological Association. (2000). Code of ethics for psychologists (3rd ed). Retrieved 25 September 2000 from www.cpa.ca/ethics.html.

Firestein, S. K. (1969). Problems of termination in the analysis of adults. *Journal of the American Psychoanalytical Association, 17,* 222–37.

Fisher, C. D. (2004). Ethical issues in therapy: Therapist self-disclosure of sexual feelings. *Ethics & Behavior, 14,* 105–21.

Fox, A., & Szego, J. (2003, 5 June). Sex and the substitute. *The Age,* 4–5.

Gartrell, N., Herman, J., Olarte, S., Feldstein, M., & Localio, R. (1986). Psychiatrist-patient sexual contact: Results of a national survey, I: Prevalence. *American Journal of Psychiatry, 143,* 1126–31.

Haspel, K. C., Jorgenson, L. M., Wincze, J. P., & Parsons, J. P. (1997). Legislative interventions regarding therapist sexual misconduct: An overview. *Professional Psychology: Research and Practice, 28,* 63–72.

Herman, J. L., Gartrell, N., Olartes, S., Feldstein, M., & Localio, R. (1987). Psychiatrist-patient sexual contact: Results of a national survey, II: Psychiatrists' attitudes. *American Journal of Psychiatry, 144,* 164–9.

Koocher, G. P., & Keith-Spiegel, P. (1998). *Ethics in Psychology* (2nd ed.). New York: Oxford University Press.

Lakin, M. (1988). *Ethical issues in the psychotherapies.* New York: Oxford University Press.

Lamb, D. H., & Catanzaro, S. J. (1998). Sexual and nonsexual boundary violations involving psychologists, clients, supervisees, and students: Implications for professional practice. *Professional Psychology: Research and Practice, 29,* 498–503.

Lamb, D. H., Catanzaro, S. J., & Moorman, A. S. (2003). Psychologists reflect on their sexual relationships with clients, supervisees, and students: Occurrence, impact, rationales, and collegial intervention. *Professional Psychology: Research and Practice, 34,* 102–107.

Lazarus, J. A. (1992). Editorial: Sex with former patients almost always unethical. *American Journal of Psychiatry, 149,* 855–7.

Lowery, T. S., & Lowery, T. P. (1975). Ethical considerations in sex therapy. *Journal of Marriage and Family Counseling, 1,* 229–36.

Malmquist, C. P., & Notman, M. T. (2001). Psychiatrist-patient boundary issues following treatment termination. *American Journal of Psychiatry, 158,* 1010–8.

Masters, W. H., & Johnson, V. E. (1976). Principles of new sex therapy. *American Journal of Psychiatry 32,* 593–602.

Moleski, S. M., & Kiselica, M. S. (2005). Dual relationships: A continuum ranging from the destructive to the therapeutic. *Journal of Counseling and Development, 83,* 3–11.

Nachmani, I., & Somer, E. (2007). Women sexually victimized in psychotherapy speak out: The dynamics and outcome of therapist-client sex. *Women and Therapy, 30,* 1–17.

Norris, D. M., Gutheil, T. G., & Strasburger, L. H. (2003). This couldn't happen to me: Boundary problems and sexual misconduct in the psychotherapy relationship. *Psychiatric Services 54,* 517–22.

Pope, K. S., & Bouhoutsos, J. (1986). *Sexual intimacy between therapists and patients.* New York: Praeger.

Pope, K. S., Keith-Spiegel, P., & Tabachnick, B. G. (1987). Sexual attraction to clients: The human therapist and the (sometimes) inhuman training system. *American Psychologist, 41,* 147–158.

Pope, K. S., Tabachnick, B. G., & Keith-Spiegel, P. (1987). Ethics of practice: The beliefs and behaviors of psychologists as therapists. *American Psychologist, 42,* 993–1006.

Quadrio, C. (1994). Sexual abuse involving therapists, clergy and judiciary: Closed ranks, collusions and conspiracies of silence. *Psychiatry, Psychology and Law, 1,* 189–98.

Re Hall. (2003). PRBD (Vic) 5.

Re Psychologist. (1997). South Australian Psychological Board 4.

Re Psychologist. (2001). South Australian Psychological Board 5.

Re Walsh. (2005). PRBD (Vic) 2.

Rodolfa, E., Hall, T., Holms, V., Davena, A., Komatz, D., Antunez, M., et al. (1994). The management of sexual feelings in therapy. *Professional Psychology: Research and Practice, 25,* 168–72.

Royal Australian and New Zealand College of Psychiatrists. (1998). *Code of ethics.*

Shavit, N., & Bucky, S. (2004). Sexual contact between psychologists and their former therapy patients: Psychoanalytic perspectives and professional implications. *American Journal of Psychoanalysis, 64,* 229–48.

Simon, R. I. (1994a). Transference in therapist–patient sex: The illusion of patient improvement and consent, Part I. *Psychiatric Annals, 24,* 509–15.

Simon, R. I. (1994b). Transference in therapist–patient sex: The illusion of patient improvement and consent, Part II. *Psychiatric Annals, 24,* 561–5.

Somer, E., & Saadon, M. (1999). Therapist-client sex: Clients' retrospective reports. *Professional Psychology: Research and Practice, 30,* 504–9.

Steere, J. (1984). *Ethics in clinical psychology.* Cape Town: Oxford University Press.

United Nations. (1948). *Universal declaration of human rights.* New York: Author.

Vinson, J. S. (1987). Use of complaint procedures in cases of therapist-sexual contact. *Professional Psychology: Research and Practice, 18,* 159–64.

Webb, W. L. (1986). The doctor-patient covenant and the threat of exploitation. *American Journal of Psychiatry, 143,* 1149–50.

Chapter 13
Looking Forward

Anthony W. Love and Alfred Allan

In the opening chapter, Alfred Allan outlined the history preceding the latest version of the Australian Psychological Society's (APS) Code of Ethics. He showed that its development, from its origins in 1949 to its current manifestation, has involved more than merely reworking ethical precepts inherited from the time of Hippocrates (Pellegrino, 1993). The history has been marked by multiple forces (intellectual, economic, social and political) that have shaped professional psychological practice (Darvall, 1993). Since its inception, the Code has been a living, evolving document, reflecting the aspirations and ideals of an emerging profession as it has struggled to construct its identity and contest its position in relation to other professions, societal standards, and competing demands of many different stakeholders.

It is worth reflecting on some of the social and political trends that have shaped the Code's development and imagine their possible impact on future Code revisions. This type of exercise is always tentative because it is difficult to predict what will happen in future or even fully understand the implications of current developments. The reflections in this chapter are therefore to a large degree based on our interpretations of the trends we observe and anecdotal evidence. Nevertheless, while this exercise is purely speculative, it allows us to think creatively and imaginatively about the future that might lie ahead for the profession of psychology and implications this might have for ethical practice (Koocher, 2007).

One trend has been the growth of psychology as a profession, both in terms of its practitioner numbers and its relative standing in the community (Morrissey & Reddy, 2006). A few short decades ago, there was a relatively small number of practising psychologists in Australia. That number has grown exponentially, and each year there are hundreds of new entrants to the profession. Currently membership of the APS stands at around 17,000, including subscribers and affiliates, while the number of registered psychologists across all Australian States and Territories is approximately 25,000 (Grenyer, 2009). Psychologists have relatively little difficulty finding employment. According to the Australian Government's Job Outlook website (http://jobsearch.gov.au), at the end of 2008, the prospects for psychologists remain "good" and employment growth is expected to be "strong". The number of psychology positions increases each year, it seems, as the unmet demand apparently manages to stay ahead of the expanding supply (Productivity Commission, 2005). There are few careers offering greater opportunities than what psychology provides new entrants to the profession.

Growth in a profession can engender conflicting forces. On the one hand, it can promote cohesion. For example, unity can bring increased political clout. Psychologists, in our view, will no doubt wield increasing influence over future government decisions in relation to health and welfare. The challenge will be to ensure that self-interest is not allowed to dominate the political discourse as this influence is exercised. See, for example, General Principle B: Propriety, of the 2007 Code, which states, "… The welfare of clients and the public and the standing of the profession, take precedence over a psychologist's self-interest." (p. 18).

Growth can also foster disunity. As the number of constituents grows, the task of ensuring that their interests are represented effectively becomes ever more difficult. The profession can expect to see further contesting of the identity psychology projects, as different subgroups within the profession question if that identity will best represent their professional activities or their world views. Similar challenges exist in relation to the Code's applicability for teaching, supervision and research practice. In principle, the Code has to work for all psychologists and be sufficiently inclusive of all professional practice contexts to be relevant. Whether this delicate balance has been achieved with the 2007 Code remains a point of self-reflection. It also remains an open question for the APS to consider with future revisions, as it grapples with the challenge of balancing the competing demands of its constituent members.

The growth in psychologist numbers has been accompanied by greater community acceptance and appreciation of the profession. Earlier stereotypical views of psychologists held in the broad community were not particularly appealing (Schultz, 2005). They involved a narrow understanding of the work psychologists performed, usually involving images of neurotic clients searching for answers to their problems. Consulting a psychologist professionally was often accompanied by fears of stigma and social ridicule (Sweet, Rozensky, & Tovian, 1991). According to these stereotypes, psychologists saw people who were "not right in the head" or "crazy" and they used arcane methods to uncover people's deep dark secrets. This traditional impression of psychologists as shrinks is not unique to majority culture Australians, as Davidson (1992) found. Aboriginal Australian respondents in Davidson's study also construed psychologists as clinicians who practised primarily in hospitals and dealt with a range of mental illnesses.

Improved levels of general education (psychology is now among the most popular science-based subjects in late high school) and public information campaigns about mental health (e.g., www.beyondblue.org.au) have ensured better information about psychological functioning, and broader knowledge of the effects of factors such as stress and trauma. Moreover, the wider availability of a range of psychological services has helped in the demythologizing of the profession and destigmatizing of the role of psychology client. It is difficult to imagine that this trend will decline or be reversed in the near future. Nevertheless, the profession cannot afford to take its reputation for granted. It must continue to demonstrate its effectiveness and its relevance to the community, while ensuring practitioners stay abreast of changing standards and expectations.

Changes in norms, attitudes and values in society have also led to a repositioning of professions (MacDonald, 1995). Historically, there were relatively few professions and the number of practitioners in each was strictly limited. Social status and rank accompanied this relative scarcity of professions and trained professionals and members were usually considered pillars of the local community. Those who consulted professionals were invariably deferential, as they understood the unwritten social compact that accompanied such consultation. This was no mere contractual exchange of goods and services; professionals held the lives of others – spiritual, financial or physical – in their hands. Clients were dependent on professionals for advice, assistance or treatment, and so expressed their dependency in what were considered to be socially appropriate ways. They were less likely to question the medical directives of physicians or the spiritual pronouncements of their religious figures, because the actions of professionals were informed by superior expertise in arcane fields and trust was typically an implicit quality of the relationship. Deference from clients, superior social ranking and special privileges were part of the rewards of lengthy, specialized study into the mysteries of one's chosen profession (Levine, 1995).

With increasing standards of education during the twentieth century, social barriers privileging professions began to break down. More people had access to the specialized knowledge of each profession, as it was held less tightly by the initiated few and became publically available to all who were interested in learning. For example, a person might complete a degree in medicine but never become a medical practitioner, but choose instead to pursue a career in research. Even so, as university courses in the traditional professions developed, the number of people joining the professions increased equally rapidly (Groenewegen, 2006).

Rising education levels not only worked to widen professions' specialist knowledge, but also encouraged ideas that challenged the specialized niche and social privileges that professions had sought to create and maintain for themselves. Respect for human rights, and wider appreciation of principles such as autonomy, gained currency (Shuster, 1997). The infamous Tuskegee experiments are a clear example. In the 1930s, scientists deliberately chose not to treat African-American citizens living in the United States of America (USA) who were suffering from syphilis, so they could study the natural course of the condition. This outrage, which persisted in concealment for many decades, could only have been contemplated in a social system where the children of slaves were still considered second-class citizens without rights or unworthy of equal treatment (Jones, 1981). Its disclosure in the 1970s was met with condemnation and led to mandatory requirements for greater ethical accountability in science. Growing belief in and demand for greater equality and more just societies ensured that such abominations became harder to initiate and conceal. The growth of information media, including mass circulation newspapers, radio and television, assisted this transformation. The credibility gap between ideal and actual behaviour will no doubt continue to affect psychological practice and encourage community demands for greater accountability.

Direct effects of these demands can be observed in legislative changes that have had bearing on the 2007 Code's development. Some of these changes have been documented in earlier chapters. For example, the impact of Privacy Law changes in Australia, at both national and state levels, has left a lasting impression. Psychologists must now be much more mindful of the need to obtain informed consent to the collection, use and disclosure of clients' personal information. Similarly, the 2007 Code has incorporated changes in other areas of law, including legislation in relation to freedom of information, whistle-blower protection, mandatory reporting of child abuse, and public sector ethics. It has been affected by policy development in many other areas, too. For example, the National Health and Medical Research Council's *National Statement on Ethical Conduct in Research Involving Humans* has had extensive and far-reaching impact on the conduct of psychological research. The 2007 Code requires that Society members comply with the current Statement (see B.14.1 of the 2007 Code).

The initial expansion in Australia of psychology as a profession largely took place within what can be described as welfare state or public service models of health care provision. That is, governments, both federal and state, responded to the needs of the community and its growing demand for psychological professional services by funding programs or positions within hospitals, community health services, or other not-for-profit organizations providing broad welfare services to those in need. Thus, most psychologists were in positions as salaried professionals, a term that differentiates them from members of the profession who are non-salaried, or private, practitioners. Such differences include perceived, or real, conflicts between professional ethics and organizational policies and procedures, debates over who the client of the salaried professional might be, and problems associated with confidentiality concerns. The growth in third party payers has further complicated this distinction, as many practitioners have discovered. The demands of third party payers such as health insurers and Medicare can be more limiting and create more potential for ethical dilemmas than those imposed by employers. For example, a third party payer might insist that clients be given formal psychiatric diagnoses in order to determine appropriate fee reimbursement, but this demand might be antithetical to the psychologist's theoretical paradigm, raising dilemmas for professional conduct.

The differences also typically include advantages enjoyed by many in salaried positions which are not always shared by their non-salaried colleagues (Gerpott & Domsch, 2006). For example, membership of larger organizations might provide opportunities in terms of continuing professional development, enhanced career prospects, and access to profession-specific supervision of practice. Those in private practice might not have immediate access to such advantages but instead have to provide for themselves. These costs are growing, as demands of membership of the APS and the new national registration system tighten and become more rigorous. For example, the Australian Health Workforce Ministerial Council has determined that there will be additional requirements as part of the national registration system, to be introduced in 2010. To ensure annual renewal of their registration, registrants will have to demonstrate that they have participated in a continuing professional development program approved by their national board. These imposts might be deemed some of the hidden costs of private practice, an area that is growing rapidly, which need to be considered carefully by those contemplating practising in this field (Hunt, 2005).

Probably the biggest single impact on the practice of psychology in Australia in recent years has been the introduction of public funding for the provision of some private psychological services. This initiative on the part of the federal government has had the impact, intended or otherwise, of increasing the number of psychologists in private practice, either full-time or part-time, often in conjunction with continuing salaried professional positions. As a corollary, anecdotal evidence suggests that it has also meant the depletion of senior psychologist numbers in the public sector, as experienced practitioners have been drawn to the possibility of establishing or expanding their private practice. In turn, this apparently has affected the number of placement opportunities for provisionally registered and less experienced psychologists; prospects for effective supervision have diminished and opportunities for peer mentoring have declined.

Despite the hidden costs of private practice, the rise in the proportion of non-salaried professional psychologists is likely to continue in future years. Governments appear to be drawn increasingly to the concept of public-private social partnerships. It perhaps also appeals to a new generation of psychologists that appears more comfortable than earlier generations with the concept of private practice. This trend will bring with it increasingly difficult and complex ethical challenges for psychologists. Practising in relative isolation, with fewer opportunities for peer support, consultations and professional supervision, is generally acknowledged to increase the risk of psychologists engaging in ethically questionable practices. The challenge for professional ethics committees, such as that of the APS, will be to ensure that they work with practitioners proactively to reduce risk and manage exposure to risk. For example, it might be necessary to increase education about the challenges of working as sole private practitioners, particularly for those who are moving into this area for the first time (Prinstein & Patterson, 2003). It might also require increased attention to patient or consumer education, to ensure that they are fully informed about their rights and about ways in which they can protect themselves from harm or reduce risk exposure (Corey, Corey, & Callanan, 2003).

The dilemma for the APS will be how to publicize and undertake these worthy initiatives without at the same time affecting the perceptions, both of the public and of members, of the ethical risks involved in consulting privately as professional psychologists. An important point not to be forgotten when focusing on what could potentially go wrong is that the vast majority of psychologists practice in ethically unimpeachable ways, holding in highest esteem the values of autonomy and beneficence, and respecting the rights of their clients unflinchingly.

The approach of the APS to these emerging trends has two aspects. The Guidelines, which form the connective tissue between the more abstract Code and benchmarks for best practice, are each reviewed on a regular rotating basis, or more frequently should circumstances require it. These documents address specific topics, such as *managing professional boundaries and multiple relationships*. They expand upon and explain in greater depth the more general statements made in the Code. For example, in the above-mentioned Guideline, the concept of *professional boundary* is defined and explicated, and references to further reading on that topic are provided. Points to consider when engaging in ethical decision-making are enumerated and further elucidated. In this case, one example addressed is the potential boundary dilemmas surrounding practice in small communities. Whenever a specific document has been updated, members are informed and encouraged to educate themselves about the current guidelines for practice in that given area. For instance, technological developments are likely to influence how psychologists provide their services in the future (see, e.g., Fuller & Stokes, 2009). This is a rapidly evolving area of practice and beginning to raise many implications for professional conduct that are entirely novel. For example, it is feasible that a client might live in another country entirely yet be receiving counselling from an Australian psychologist who is registered to practise in Australia but not in the client's country. Almost by definition, this issue has never been addressed by the APS Ethics Committee, as no case has ever appeared before it. Hence, there are few precedents to guide best practice in this area. Whilst the ethical principles of the 2007 Code appear to be sufficient to deal with current developments in this regard, this situation may change as psychologists embrace further innovations to make their services more effective and available to a broader part of the population who may currently not be served adequately (Allan, 2008).

The second aspect relates to the process described in this book: The Code itself can be updated and revised. Over time, small pressures for change accumulate, or else a seismic shift in the professional landscape occurs, requiring a major review of the Code. Changes in legislation, for example, can be a catalyst for major change. Hypothetically, a radical review of social welfare laws and their regulation might precipitate a major review of the 2007 Code. If psychologists were to be granted privileges in relation to prescribing medications for limited psychiatric conditions, then a review of the 2007 Code might be warranted. More typically, however, there is a gradual accretion of changes in the social and political zeitgeist that suggests it is time for an overhaul of the Code. Changing attitudes to refugee groups, for example, or new emphases on principles such as autonomy, can usually be documented over a period of time, representing salient changes in the social landscape. Similarly, international trends and initiatives might be monitored to inform decision-making about Code revisions. With the passage of time, say every decade or so, it can become obvious that the current Code is no longer reflecting the prevailing values and attitudes of the profession, the expectations of society, or international standards of practice. As discrepancies grow, the need for revision can become more insistent and it might then be time to undertake a review as extensive as that documented in this volume.

Concluding Remarks

This chapter has considered some of the forces that are likely to shape the evolution of the APS 2007 Code over the coming decades. The list is not exhaustive, by any means, and while a crystal-ball exercise of this sort has much to recommend it, the conclusions drawn should not lull us into a false sense of security. A major shortcoming of ethics codes is that they tend to be reactive; they relate largely to ethical issues and dilemmas that have arisen in the past and have been considered by the profession until a balance or consensus of views emerges on how to behave professionally in given contexts. However, new dilemmas arise constantly, as society changes and values shift. These are the points of vulnerability for a profession such as psychology. The profession need to remain vigilant, sensitive to the needs of our clients and self-reflexive about our own motivations and actions if we are to spot trends early. Psychologists must then devote the necessary time and energy to developing thoughtful positions on emerging dilemmas. Only then can a profession remain confident that its ethical standards will continue to evolve and ensure that it is equipped to meet the as yet unidentified challenges that lie ahead.

References

Allan, A. (2008). *An international perspective of law and ethics in psychology*. Somerset West, South Africa: Inter-ed.

Corey, G., Corey, M. S., & Callanan, P. (2003). *Issues and ethics in the helping professions* (6th ed.). Pacific Grove, CA: Brooks/Cole.

Darvall, L. (1993). *Medicine, law and social change: how bioethics, feminism and rights movements are affecting decision-making*. Aldershot, UK: Ashgate Publishing.

Davidson, G. (1992). Toward an applied Aboriginal psychology. *South Pacific Journal of Psychology, 5*, 1–20.

Fuller, T., & Stokes, D. (2009). Review of internet-based psychological services and products. *InPsych, 31*(2), 32–3.

Gerpott, T. J., & Domsch, M. (2006). The concept of professionalism and the management of salaried technical professionals: A cross-national perspective. *Human Resource Management, 24*(2), 207–26.

Grenyer, B. (2009). What a National Psychology Board will mean for current registrants, and what it might contribute to Australian psychology. *InPsych, 31*(1), 15.

Groenewegen, P. P. (2006). Trust and the sociology of the professions. *European Journal of Public Health, 16*(1), 3–6.

Hunt, H. A. (2005). *Essentials of private practice: Streamlining costs, procedures, and policies for less stress*. New York: W.W. Norton and Co.

Jones, J. (1981). *Bad blood: The Tuskegee syphilis experiment: A tragedy of race and medicine*. NY: The Free Press.

Koocher, G. P. (2007). Twenty-first century ethical challenges for psychology. *American Psychologist, 62*, 375–84.

Levine, D. N. (1995). *Visions of the Sociological Tradition*. Chicago, IL: University of Chicago Press.

MacDonald, K. M. (1995). *The sociology of the professions*. London: Sage Publications.

Morrissey, S., & Reddy, P. (Eds). (2006). *Ethics and professional practice for psychologists.* Melbourne, Australia: Thomson Social Science Press.

Pellegrino, E. (1993). The metamorphosis of medical ethics. *Journal of the American Medical Association, 269,* 1158.

Prinstein, M. J., & Patterson, M. D. (2003). *The portable mentor: Expert guide to a successful career in psychology.* New York: Springer.

Productivity Commission. (2005). Australia's health workforce: Research report [Electronic Version]. Retrieved 19 January 2006 from www.pc.gov.au/projects/study/healthworkforce/docs/finalreport.

Schultz, H. T. (2005). Hollywood's portrayal of psychologists and psychiatrists: Gender and professional training differences. In E. Cole & J. H. Daniel (Eds.), *Featuring females: Feminist analyses of media* (pp. 101–12). Washington, D.C.: American Psychological Association.

Shuster, E. (1997). Fifty years later: The significance of the Nuremburg Code. *New England Journal of Medicine, 337*(20), 1436–40.

Sweet, J. J., Rozensky, R. H, & Tovian, S. M. (1991). *Handbook of clinical psychology in medical settings.* New York: Springer.

Appendix

Code of
Ethics

The
Australian
Psychological
Society Ltd

© The Australian Psychological Society Limited
ABN 23 000 543 788

PO Box 38, Flinders Lane
Victoria 8009, Australia

Ph: +61 3 8662 3300
Fax: +61 3 9663 6177

Email: contactus@psychology.org.au
Website: www.psychology.org.au

Contents

Contents

Preface

The Australian Psychological Society Limited (the Society) adopted this Code of Ethics (the Code) at its Forty-First Annual General Meeting held on 27 September 2007. This Code supersedes the Code of Ethics previously adopted at its Thirty-First Annual General Meeting held on 4 October 1997, and modified on 2 October 1999; on 29 September 2002; and on 4 October 2003.

The Code of Ethics is subject to periodic amendments, which will be communicated to members of the Society, and published on the Society website. Members must ensure that they are conversant with the current version of the Code. An electronic version of the Code is available at www.psychology.org.au.

This Code may be cited as the Code of Ethics (2007) and a specific ethical standard should be referred to as "standard A.2. of the Code of Ethics (2007)". Amended standards can be referred to as: standard A.2. of the Code of Ethics (2007) (as amended in …). In a reference list the Code can be referenced as:

Australian Psychological Society. (2007). *Code of ethics*. Melbourne, Vic: Author.

Ethical Guidelines that accompany the *Code of Ethics* will be produced, amended and rescinded from time to time, and members are advised to ensure their versions of the Guidelines are current.

Psychologists seeking clarification or advice on the matters contained herein should write to the:
Executive Director
The Australian Psychological Society Limited
PO Box 38
Flinders Lane
Victoria 8009
AUSTRALIA

Preamble

The Australian Psychological Society Code of Ethics articulates and promotes ethical principles, and sets specific standards to guide both psychologists and members of the public to a clear understanding and expectation of what is considered ethical professional conduct by psychologists.

It is important that the codes of professional associations should be reviewed regularly to ensure that they remain relevant and functional in the face of the evolution of the relevant association and changes in its environment. Accordingly, since its inception in 1949, the Code of Ethics (which was at times called the Code of Professional Conduct) of the Australian Psychological Society has been reviewed in 1960, 1968, 1986, and 1997. In undertaking the current review, the Society has attempted to reflect established ethical principles in the practice of the profession within the context of the current regulatory environment.

The current Code has been developed through a process of ongoing reflection within the Society about the ethical responsibilities of psychologists and a formal review of the 1997 Code with reference to comparable national and international professional codes of ethics.

The Code is built on three general ethical principles. They are:
   A. Respect for the rights and dignity of people and peoples
   B. Propriety
   C. Integrity.

The general principle, Respect for the rights and dignity of people and peoples, combines the principles of respect for the dignity and respect for the rights of people and peoples, including the right to autonomy and justice.

The general principle, Propriety, incorporates the principles of beneficence, non-maleficence (including competence) and responsibility to clients, the profession and society.

The general principle, Integrity, reflects the need for psychologists to have good character and acknowledges the high level of trust intrinsic to their professional relationships, and impact of their conduct on the reputation of the profession.

The Code expresses psychologists' responsibilities to their clients, to the community and society at large, and to the profession, as well as colleagues and members of other professions with whom they interact.

Each general principle is accompanied by an explanatory statement that helps psychologists and others understand how the principle is enacted in the form of specific standards of professional conduct.

The ethical standards (standards) derived from each general principle provide the minimum expectations with regard to psychologists' professional conduct, and conduct in their capacity as Members of the Society. Professional conduct that does not meet these standards is unethical and is subject to review in accordance with the Rules and Procedures of the Ethics Committee and the Ethics Appeals Committee contained in the Standing Orders of the Board of Directors of the Society. These standards are not exhaustive. Where specific conduct is not identified by the standards, the general principles will apply.

The Code is complemented by a series of Ethical Guidelines (the Guidelines). The purpose of the Guidelines is to clarify and amplify the application of the general principles and specific standards contained in the Code, and to facilitate their interpretation in contemporary areas of professional practice. The Guidelines are subsidiary to the relevant sections of the Code, and must be read and interpreted in conjunction with the Code. Psychologists who have acted inconsistently with the Guidelines may be required to demonstrate that their behaviour was not unethical.

Psychologists respect and act in accordance with the laws of the jurisdictions in which they practise. The Code should be interpreted with reference to these laws. The Code should also be interpreted with reference to, but not necessarily in deference to, any organisational rules and procedures to which psychologists may be subject.

Preamble

Code of Ethics

Definitions*

For the purposes of this Code, unless the context indicates otherwise:

Associated party means any person or organisation other than *clients* with whom *psychologists* interact in the course of rendering a *psychological service*. This includes, but is not limited to:

(a)   *clients'* relatives, friends, employees, employers, carers and guardians;
(b)   other professionals or experts;
(c)   representatives from communities or organisations.

Client means a party or parties to a *psychological service* involving teaching, supervision, research, and professional practice in psychology. *Clients* may be individuals, couples, dyads, families, groups of people, organisations, communities, facilitators, sponsors, or those commissioning or paying for the professional activity.

Code means this APS Code of Ethics (2007) as amended from time to time, and includes the definitions and interpretation, the application of the *Code*, all general principles, and the ethical standards.

Conduct means any act or omission by *psychologists*:

(a)   that others may reasonably consider to be a *psychological service*;
(b)   outside their practice of psychology which casts doubt on their competence and ability to practise as *psychologists*;
(c)   outside their practice of psychology which harms public trust in the discipline or the profession of psychology;
(d)   in their capacity as *Members* of the *Society*;
as applicable in the circumstances.

* Defined terms are designated in the *Code* by appearing in italics.

Guidelines mean the Ethical Guidelines adopted by the Board of Directors of the *Society* from time to time that clarify and amplify the application of the Code of Ethics. The Guidelines are subsidiary to the *Code*, and must be read and interpreted in conjunction with the *Code*. In the case of any apparent inconsistency between the *Code* and the *Guidelines*, provisions of the *Code* prevail. A *psychologist* acting inconsistently with the *Guidelines* may be required to demonstrate that his or her *conduct* was not unethical.

Jurisdiction means the Commonwealth of Australia or the state or territory in which a *psychologist* is rendering a *psychological service*.

Legal rights mean those rights protected under laws and statutes of the Commonwealth of Australia, or of the state or territory in which a *psychologist* is rendering a *psychological service*.

Member means a Member, of any grade, of the *Society*.

Moral rights incorporate universal human rights as defined by the United Nations Universal Declaration of Human Rights that might or might not be fully protected by existing laws.

Multiple relationships occur when a *psychologist*, rendering a *psychological service* to a *client*, also is or has been:
(a) in a non-*professional relationship* with the same *client*;
(b) in a different *professional relationship* with the same *client*;
(c) in a non-*professional relationship* with an *associated party*; or
(d) a recipient of a service provided by the same *client*.

Peoples are defined as distinct human groups with their own social structures who are linked by a common identity, common customs, and collective interests.

Professional relationship or role is the relationship between a *psychologist* and a *client* which involves the delivery of a *psychological service*.

Definitions

Code of
Ethics | 9

Psychological service means any service provided by a *psychologist* to a *client* including but not limited to professional activities, psychological activities, professional practice, teaching, supervision, research practice, professional services, and psychological procedures.

Psychologist means any *Member* irrespective of his or her psychologist registration status.

Society means The Australian Psychological Society Limited.

Interpretation

In this *Code* unless the contrary intention appears:

(a)   words in the singular include the plural and words in the plural include the singular;

(b)   where any word or phrase is given a defined meaning, any other form of that word or phrase has a corresponding meaning;

(c)   headings are for convenience only and do not affect interpretation of the *Code*.

Application of the Code

This *Code* applies to the *conduct* of *psychologists* as defined above. Membership of the *Society*, irrespective of a *Member's* grade of membership or registration status, commits *Members* to comply with the ethical standards of the *Code* and the rules and procedures used to enforce them.

Members are reminded that there are legislative requirements that apply to the use of the professional title, "psychologist", and that where applicable, they must abide by such requirements.

Members are also reminded that lack of awareness or misunderstanding of an ethical standard is not itself a defence to an allegation of unethical *conduct*.

General Principle A: Respect for the rights and dignity of people and peoples

Psychologists regard people as intrinsically valuable and respect their rights, including the right to autonomy and justice. *Psychologists* engage in *conduct* which promotes equity and the protection of people's human rights, *legal rights*, and *moral rights*. They respect the dignity of all people and *peoples*.

Explanatory Statement

Psychologists demonstrate their respect for people by acknowledging their *legal rights* and *moral rights*, their dignity and right to participate in decisions affecting their lives. They recognise the importance of people's privacy and confidentiality, and physical and personal integrity, and recognise the power they hold over people when practising as *psychologists*. They have a high regard for the diversity and uniqueness of people and their right to linguistically and culturally appropriate services. *Psychologists* acknowledge people's right to be treated fairly without discrimination or favouritism, and they endeavour to ensure that all people have reasonable and fair access to *psychological services* and share in the benefits that the practice of psychology can offer.

Ethical Standards

A.1. Justice

A.1.1. *Psychologists* avoid discriminating unfairly against people on the basis of age, religion, sexuality, ethnicity, gender, disability, or any other basis proscribed by law.

A.1.2. *Psychologists* demonstrate an understanding of the consequences for people of unfair discrimination and stereotyping related to their age, religion, sexuality, ethnicity, gender, or disability.

A.1.3. *Psychologists* assist their clients to address unfair discrimination or prejudice that is directed against the clients.

General
Principle A

Code of
Ethics | **11**

A.2. Respect

A.2.1. In the course of their *conduct, psychologists*:
   (a) communicate respect for other people through their actions and language;
   (b) do not behave in a manner that, having regard to the context, may reasonably be perceived as coercive or demeaning;
   (c) respect the *legal rights* and *moral rights* of others; and
   (d) do not denigrate the character of people by engaging in *conduct* that demeans them as persons, or defames, or harasses them.

A.2.2. *Psychologists* act with due regard for the needs, special competencies and obligations of their colleagues in psychology and other professions.

A.2.3. When *psychologists* have cause to disagree with a colleague in psychology or another profession on professional issues they refrain from making intemperate criticism.

A.2.4. When *psychologists* in the course of their professional activities are required to review or comment on the qualifications, competencies or work of a colleague in psychology or another profession, they do this in an objective and respectful manner.

A.2.5. *Psychologists* who review grant or research proposals or material submitted for publication, respect the confidentiality and proprietary rights of those who made the submission.

General
Principle A

A.3. Informed consent

A.3.1. *Psychologists* fully inform *clients* regarding the *psychological services* they intend to provide, unless an explicit exception has been agreed upon in advance, or it is not reasonably possible to obtain informed consent.

A.3.2. *Psychologists* provide information using plain language.

A.3.3. *Psychologists* ensure consent is informed by:
    (a) explaining the nature and purpose of the procedures they intend using;
    (b) clarifying the reasonably foreseeable risks, adverse effects, and possible disadvantages of the procedures they intend using;
    (c) explaining how information will be collected and recorded;
    (d) explaining how, where, and for how long, information will be stored, and who will have access to the stored information;
    (e) advising *clients* that they may participate, may decline to participate, or may withdraw from methods or procedures proposed to them;
    (f) explaining to *clients* what the reasonably foreseeable consequences would be if they decline to participate or withdraw from the proposed procedures;
    (g) clarifying the frequency, expected duration, financial and administrative basis of any *psychological services* that will be provided;
    (h) explaining confidentiality and limits to confidentiality (see standard A.5.);
    (i) making clear, where necessary, the conditions under which the *psychological services* may be terminated; and
    (j) providing any other relevant information.

General Principle A

A.3.4. *Psychologists* obtain consent from *clients* to provide a
psychological service unless consent is not required because:
(a) rendering the service without consent is permitted by law; or
(b) a National Health and Medical Research Council (NHMRC)
or other appropriate ethics committee has waived the
requirement in respect of research.

A.3.5. *Psychologists* obtain and document informed consent from *clients*
or their legal guardians prior to using psychological procedures that
entail physical contact with *clients*.

A.3.6. *Psychologists* who work with *clients* whose capacity to give
consent is, or may be, impaired or limited, obtain the consent
of people with legal authority to act on behalf of the *client*, and
attempt to obtain the *client's* consent as far as practically possible.

A.3.7. *Psychologists* who work with *clients* whose consent is not required
by law still comply, as far as practically possible, with the processes
described in A.3.1., A.3.2., and A.3.3.

A.4.   Privacy

Psychologists avoid undue invasion of privacy in the collection of
information. This includes, but is not limited to:
(a) collecting only information relevant to the service being
provided; and
(b) not requiring supervisees or trainees to disclose their personal
information, unless self-disclosure is a normal expectation of
a given training procedure and informed consent has been
obtained from participants prior to training.

A.5. Confidentiality

A.5.1. *Psychologists* safeguard the confidentiality of information obtained during their provision of *psychological services*. Considering their legal and organisational requirements, *psychologists*:
- (a) make provisions for maintaining confidentiality in the collection, recording, accessing, storage, dissemination, and disposal of information; and
- (b) take reasonable steps to protect the confidentiality of information after they leave a specific work setting, or cease to provide *psychological services*.

A.5.2. *Psychologists* disclose confidential information obtained in the course of their provision of *psychological services* only under any one or more of the following circumstances:
- (a) with the consent of the relevant *client* or a person with legal authority to act on behalf of the *client*;
- (b) where there is a legal obligation to do so;
- (c) if there is an immediate and specified risk of harm to an identifiable person or persons that can be averted only by disclosing information; or
- (d) when consulting colleagues, or in the course of supervision or professional training, provided the *psychologist*:
  - (i) conceals the identity of *clients* and *associated parties* involved; or
  - (ii) obtains the *client's* consent, and gives prior notice to the recipients of the information that they are required to preserve the *client's* privacy, and obtains an undertaking from the recipients of the information that they will preserve the *client's* privacy.

A.5.3. *Psychologists* inform *clients* at the outset of the *professional relationship*, and as regularly thereafter as is reasonably necessary, of the:
- (a) limits to confidentiality; and
- (b) foreseeable uses of the information generated in the course of the relationship.

General
Principle A

A.5.4. When a standard of this *Code* allows *psychologists* to disclose information obtained in the course of the provision of *psychological services*, they disclose only that information which is necessary to achieve the purpose of the disclosure, and then only to people required to have that information.

A.5.5. *Psychologists* use information collected about a *client* for a purpose other than the primary purpose of collection only:
   (a)   with the consent of that *client*;
   (b)   if the information is de-identified and used in the course of duly approved research; or
   (c)   when the use is required or authorised by or under law.

A.6.   Release of information to clients

Psychologists, with consideration of legislative exceptions and their organisational requirements, do not refuse any reasonable request from *clients*, or former *clients*, to access *client* information, for which the *psychologists* have professional responsibility.

A.7.   Collection of client information from associated parties

A.7.1. Prior to collecting information regarding a *client* from an *associated party*, *psychologists* obtain the consent of the *client* or, where applicable, a person who is authorised by law to represent the *client*.

A.7.2. *Psychologists* who work with *clients* whose capacity to give informed consent is, or may be, impaired or limited, obtain the informed consent of people with legal authority to act on behalf of the *client*, and attempt to obtain the *client's* consent as far as practically possible.

A.7.3. *Psychologists* who work with *clients* whose informed consent is not required by law nevertheless attempt to comply, as far as practically possible, with the processes described in standards A.7.1., A.7.2., and A.7.4.

A.7.4. *Psychologists* ensure that a *client's* consent for obtaining information from an *associated party* is informed by:

(a) identifying the sources from which they intend collecting information;

(b) explaining the nature and purpose of the information they intend collecting;

(c) stating how the information will be collected;

(d) indicating how, where, and for how long, information will be stored, and who will have access to the stored information;

(e) advising *clients* that they may decline the request to collect information from an *associated party*, or withdraw such consent;

(f) explaining to *clients* what the reasonably foreseeable consequences would be if they decline to give consent;

(g) explaining the *associated party's* right to confidentiality and limits thereof; and

(h) providing any other relevant information.

A.7.5. Prior to collecting information about a *client* from an *associated party*, psychologists obtain the *associated party's* consent to collect information from them by, as appropriate to the circumstances:

(a) providing the *associated party* with demonstrable evidence that the *client* had given consent for the collection of such information;

(b) explaining the nature and purpose of the information they intend collecting;

(c) stating how the information will be collected;

(d) indicating how, where, and for how long, information will be stored, and who will have access to the stored information;

(e) advising them that they may withdraw their consent at any time;

(f) explaining to them what the reasonably foreseeable consequences would be if they withdraw their consent;

(g) explaining the *associated party's* right to confidentiality and limits thereof; and

(h) providing any other relevant information.

General
Principle A

General Principle B: Propriety

Psychologists ensure that they are competent to deliver the *psychological services* they provide. They provide *psychological services* to benefit, and not to harm. *Psychologists* seek to protect the interests of the people and *peoples* with whom they work. The welfare of *clients* and the public, and the standing of the profession, take precedence over a *psychologist's* self-interest.

Explanatory Statement

Psychologists practise within the limits of their competence and know and understand the legal, professional, ethical and, where applicable, organisational rules that regulate the *psychological services* they provide. They undertake continuing professional development and take steps to ensure that they remain competent to practise, and strive to be aware of the possible effect of their own physical and mental health on their ability to practise competently. *Psychologists* anticipate the foreseeable consequences of their professional decisions, provide services that are beneficial to people and do not harm them. *Psychologists* take responsibility for their professional decisions.

Ethical Standards

B.1.   Competence

B.1.1.   *Psychologists* bring and maintain appropriate skills and learning to their areas of professional practice.

B.1.2.   *Psychologists* only provide *psychological services* within the boundaries of their professional competence. This includes, but is not restricted to:
(a)   working within the limits of their education, training, supervised experience and appropriate professional experience;
(b)   basing their service on the established knowledge of the discipline and profession of psychology;
(c)   adhering to the *Code* and the *Guidelines*;

    (d)   complying with the law of the *jurisdiction* in which they provide *psychological services*; and

    (e)   ensuring that their emotional, mental, and physical state does not impair their ability to provide a competent *psychological service*.

B.1.3.   To maintain appropriate levels of professional competence, *psychologists* seek professional supervision or consultation as required.

B.1.4.   *Psychologists* continuously monitor their professional functioning. If they become aware of problems that may impair their ability to provide competent *psychological services*, they take appropriate measures to address the problem by:

    (a)   obtaining professional advice about whether they should limit, suspend or terminate the provision of *psychological services*;

    (b)   taking action in accordance with the psychologists' registration legislation of the *jurisdiction* in which they practise, and the Constitution of the *Society*; and

    (c)   refraining, if necessary, from undertaking that *psychological service*.

B.2.   Record keeping

B.2.1.   *Psychologists* make and keep adequate records.

B.2.2.   *Psychologists* keep records for a minimum of seven years since last *client* contact unless legal or their organisational requirements specify otherwise.

B.2.3.   In the case of records collected while the *client* was less than 18 years old, *psychologists* retain the records at least until the *client* attains the age of 25 years.

General
Principle B

B.2.4. *Psychologists*, with consideration of the legislation and organisational rules to which they are subject, do not refuse any reasonable request from *clients*, or former *clients*, to amend inaccurate information for which they have professional responsibility.

B.3.   Professional responsibility

Psychologists provide *psychological services* in a responsible manner. Having regard to the nature of the *psychological services* they are providing, *psychologists*:

(a)   act with the care and skill expected of a competent psychologist;

(b)   take responsibility for the reasonably foreseeable consequences of their *conduct*;

(c)   take reasonable steps to prevent harm occurring as a result of their *conduct*;

(d)   provide a *psychological service* only for the period when those services are necessary to the *client*;

(e)   are personally responsible for the professional decisions they make;

(f)   take reasonable steps to ensure that their services and products are used appropriately and responsibly;

(g)   are aware of, and take steps to establish and maintain proper professional boundaries with *clients* and colleagues; and

(h)   regularly review the contractual arrangements with *clients* and, where circumstances change, make relevant modifications as necessary with the informed consent of the *client*.

B.4.   Provision of psychological services at the request of a third party

Psychologists who agree to provide *psychological services* to an individual, group of people, system, community or organisation at the request of a third party, at the outset explain to all parties concerned:

General
Principle B

(a) the nature of the relationship with each of them;
(b) the *psychologist's* role (such as, but not limited to, case manager, consultant, counsellor, expert witness, facilitator, forensic assessor, supervisor, teacher/educator, therapist);
(c) the probable uses of the information obtained;
(d) the limits to confidentiality; and
(e) the financial arrangements relating to the provision of the service where relevant.

B.5. Provision of psychological services to multiple clients

Psychologists who agree to provide *psychological services* to multiple *clients*:
(a) explain to each *client* the limits to confidentiality in advance;
(b) give *clients* an opportunity to consider the limitations of the situation;
(c) obtain *clients'* explicit acceptance of these limitations; and
(d) ensure as far as possible, that no *client* is coerced to accept these limitations.

B.6. Delegation of professional tasks

Psychologists who delegate tasks to assistants, employees, junior colleagues or supervisees that involve the provision of *psychological services*:
(a) take reasonable steps to ensure that delegates are aware of the provisions of this *Code* relevant to the delegated professional task;
(b) take reasonable steps to ensure that the delegate is not in a *multiple relationship* that may impair the delegate's judgement;
(c) take reasonable steps to ensure that the delegate's conduct does not place *clients* or other parties to the *psychological service* at risk of harm, or does not lead to the exploitation of *clients* or other parties to the *psychological service*;
(d) take reasonable steps to ensure that the delegates are competent to undertake the tasks assigned to them; and
(e) oversee delegates to ensure that they perform tasks competently.

General
Principle B

B.7.   Use of interpreters

Psychologists who use interpreters:
(a)   take reasonable steps to ensure that the interpreters are competent to work as interpreters in the relevant context;
(b)   take reasonable steps to ensure that the interpreter is not in a *multiple relationship* with the *client* that may impair the interpreter's judgement;
(c)   take reasonable steps to ensure that the interpreter will keep confidential the existence and content of the *psychological service*;
(d)   take reasonable steps to ensure that the interpreter is aware of any other relevant provisions of this *Code*; and
(e)   obtain informed consent from the *client* to use the selected interpreter.

B.8.   Collaborating with others for the benefit of clients

B.8.1.   To benefit, enhance and promote the interests of *clients*, and subject to standard A.5. (Confidentiality), *psychologists* cooperate with other professionals when it is professionally appropriate and necessary in order to provide effective and efficient *psychological services* for their *clients*.

B.8.2.   To benefit, enhance and promote the interests of *clients*, and subject to standard A.5. (Confidentiality), *psychologists* offer practical assistance to *clients* who would like a second opinion.

B.9.   Accepting clients of other professionals

If a person seeks a *psychological service* from a *psychologist* whilst already receiving a similar service from another professional, then the *psychologist* will:
(a)   consider all the reasonably foreseeable implications of becoming involved;
(b)   take into account the welfare of the person; and
(c)   act with caution and sensitivity towards all parties concerned.

General
Principle B

B.10. Suspension of psychological services

B.10.1. *Psychologists* make suitable arrangements for other appropriate professionals to be available to meet the emergency needs of their *clients* during periods of the *psychologists'* foreseeable absence.

B.10.2. Where necessary and with the *client's* consent, a *psychologist* makes specific arrangements for other appropriate professionals to consult with the *client* during periods of the *psychologist's* foreseeable absence.

B.11. Termination of psychological services

B.11.1. *Psychologists* terminate their *psychological services* with a *client*, if it is reasonably clear that the *client* is not benefiting from their services.

B.11.2. When *psychologists* terminate a *professional relationship* with a *client*, they shall have due regard for the psychological processes inherent in the services being provided, and the psychological wellbeing of the *client*.

B.11.3. *Psychologists* make reasonable arrangements for the continuity of service provision when they are no longer able to deliver the *psychological service*.

B.11.4. *Psychologists* make reasonable arrangements for the continuity of service provision for *clients* whose financial position does not allow them to continue with the *psychological service*.

B.11.5. When confronted with evidence of a problem or a situation with which they are not competent to deal, or when a *client* is not benefiting from their *psychological services*, *psychologists*:
   (a)   provide *clients* with an explanation of the need for the termination;
   (b)   take reasonable steps to safeguard the *client's* ongoing welfare; and
   (c)   offer to help the *client* locate alternative sources of assistance.

General Principle B

B.11.6. *Psychologists* whose employment, health or other factors necessitate early termination of relationships with *clients*:
- (a)   provide *clients* with an explanation of the need for the termination;
- (b)   take all reasonable steps to safeguard *clients'* ongoing welfare; and
- (c)   offer to help *clients* locate alternative sources of assistance.

B.12.   Conflicting demands

B.12.1. Where the demands of an organisation require *psychologists* to violate the general principles, values or standards set out in this *Code*, *psychologists*:
- (a)   clarify the nature of the conflict between the demands and these principles and standards;
- (b)   inform all parties of their ethical responsibilities as *psychologists*;
- (c)   seek a constructive resolution of the conflict that upholds the principles of the *Code*; and
- (d)   consult a senior psychologist.

B.12.2. *Psychologists* who work in a team or other context in which they do not have sole decision-making authority continue to act in a way consistent with this *Code*, and in the event of any conflict of interest deal with the conflict in a manner set out in B.12.1.

B.13.   Psychological assessments

B.13.1. *Psychologists* use established scientific procedures and observe relevant psychometric standards when they develop and standardise psychological tests and other assessment techniques.

B.13.2. *Psychologists* specify the purposes and uses of their assessment techniques and clearly indicate the limits of the assessment techniques' applicability.

General Principle B

B.13.3. *Psychologists* ensure that they choose, administer and interpret assessment procedures appropriately and accurately.

B.13.4. *Psychologists* use valid procedures and research findings when scoring and interpreting psychological assessment data.

B.13.5. *Psychologists* report assessment results appropriately and accurately in language that the recipient can understand.

B.13.6. *Psychologists* do not compromise the effective use of psychological assessment methods or techniques, nor render them open to misuse, by publishing or otherwise disclosing their contents to persons unauthorised or unqualified to receive such information.

B.14.   Research

B.14.1. *Psychologists* comply with codes, statements, guidelines and other directives developed either jointly or independently by the National Health and Medical Research Council (NHMRC), the Australian Research Council, or Universities Australia regarding research with humans and animals applicable at the time *psychologists* conduct their research.

B.14.2. After research results are published or become publicly available, *psychologists* make the data on which their conclusions are based available to other competent professionals who seek to verify the substantive claims through reanalysis, provided that:
(a)   the data will be used only for the purpose stated in the approved research proposal; and
(b)   the identity of the participants is removed.

B.14.3. *Psychologists* accurately report the data they have gathered and the results of their research, and state clearly if any data on which the publication is based have been published previously.

General
Principle B

Code of
Ethics |

General Principle C: Integrity

Psychologists recognise that their knowledge of the discipline of psychology, their professional standing, and the information they gather place them in a position of power and trust. They exercise their power appropriately and honour this position of trust. *Psychologists* keep faith with the nature and intentions of their *professional relationships*. *Psychologists* act with probity and honesty in their *conduct*.

Explanatory Statement

Psychologists recognise that their position of trust requires them to be honest and objective in their professional dealings. They are committed to the best interests of their *clients*, the profession and their colleagues. *Psychologists* are aware of their own biases, limits to their objectivity, and the importance of maintaining proper boundaries with *clients*. They identify and avoid potential conflicts of interest. They refrain from exploiting *clients* and *associated parties*.

Ethical Standards

C.1.   Reputable behaviour

C.1.1.   *Psychologists* avoid engaging in disreputable *conduct* that reflects on their ability to practise as a psychologist.

C.1.2.   *Psychologists* avoid engaging in disreputable *conduct* that reflects negatively on the profession or discipline of psychology.

C.2.   Communication

C.2.1.   *Psychologists* communicate honestly in the context of their psychological work.

C.2.2.   *Psychologists* take reasonable steps to correct any misrepresentation made by them or about them in their professional capacity within a reasonable time after becoming aware of the misrepresentation.

General Principle C

C.2.3. Statements made by *psychologists* in announcing or advertising the availability of *psychological services*, products, or publications, must not contain:

(a) any statement which is false, fraudulent, misleading or deceptive or likely to mislead or deceive;

(b) testimonials or endorsements that are solicited in exchange for remuneration or have the potential to exploit *clients*;

(c) any statement claiming or implying superiority for the *psychologist* over any or all other psychologists;

(d) any statement intended or likely to create false or unjustified expectations of favourable results;

(e) any statement intended or likely to appeal to a *client's* fears, anxieties or emotions concerning the possible results of failure to obtain the offered services;

(f) any claim unjustifiably stating or implying that the *psychologist* uses exclusive or superior apparatus, methods or materials; and

(g) any statement which is vulgar, sensational or otherwise such as would bring, or tend to bring, the *psychologist* or the profession of psychology into disrepute.

C.2.4. When announcing or advertising the availability of *psychological services* or at any time when representing themselves as a psychologist, *psychologists* use accurate postnominals, including the postnominals used to represent their grade of membership with the *Society*.

C.2.5. *Psychologists* take reasonable steps to correct any misconceptions held by a *client* about the *psychologist's* professional competencies.

General
Principle C

C.3.   Conflict of interest

C.3.1. *Psychologists* refrain from engaging in *multiple relationships* that may:
   (a)   impair their competence, effectiveness, objectivity, or ability to render a *psychological service*;
   (b)   harm *clients* or other parties to a *psychological service*; or
   (c)   lead to the exploitation of *clients* or other parties to a *psychological service*.

C.3.2. *Psychologists* who are at risk of violating standard C.3.1., consult with a senior psychologist to attempt to find an appropriate resolution that is in the best interests of the parties to the *psychological service*.

C.3.3. When entering into a *multiple relationship* is unavoidable due to over-riding ethical considerations, organisational requirements, or by law, *psychologists* at the outset of the *professional relationship*, and thereafter when it is reasonably necessary, adhere to the provisions of standard A.3. (Informed consent).

C.3.4. *Psychologists* declare to *clients* any vested interests they have in the *psychological services* they deliver, including all relevant funding, licensing and royalty interests.

C.4.   Non-exploitation

C.4.1. *Psychologists* do not exploit people with whom they have or had a *professional relationship*.

C.4.2. *Psychologists* do not exploit their relationships with their assistants, employees, colleagues or supervisees.

C.4.3. *Psychologists*:

    (a)   do not engage in sexual activity with a *client* or anybody who is closely related to one of their *clients*;

    (b)   do not engage in sexual activity with a former *client*, or anybody who is closely related to one of their former *clients*, within two years after terminating the *professional relationship* with the former *client*;

    (c)   who wish to engage in sexual activity with former *clients* after a period of two years from the termination of the service, first explore with a senior psychologist the possibility that the former *client* may be vulnerable and at risk of exploitation, and encourage the former *client* to seek independent counselling on the matter; and

    (d)   do not accept as a *client* a person with whom they have engaged in sexual activity.

C.5.   Authorship

C.5.1. *Psychologists* discuss authorship with research collaborators, research assistants and students as early as feasible and through the research and publication process as is necessary.

C.5.2. *Psychologists* assign authorship in a manner that reflects the work performed and that the contribution made is a fair reflection of the work people have actually performed or of what they have contributed.

C.5.3. *Psychologists* usually list the student as principal author on any multiple-authored article that is substantially based on the student's dissertation or thesis.

C.5.4. *Psychologists* obtain the consent of people before identifying them as contributors to the published or presented material.

C.6.   Financial arrangements

C.6.1. *Psychologists* are honest in their financial dealings.

General
Principle C

Code of
Ethics | 29

C.6.2.   *Psychologists* make proper financial arrangements with *clients* and, where relevant, third party payers. They:

     (a)   make advance financial arrangements that safeguard the best interests of, and are clearly understood, by all parties to the *psychological service*; and

     (b)   avoid financial arrangements which may adversely influence the *psychological services* provided, whether at the time of provision of those services or subsequently.

C.6.3.   *Psychologists* do not receive any remuneration, or give any remuneration for referring *clients* to, or accepting referrals from, other professionals for professional services.

C.7.   Ethics investigations and concerns

C.7.1.   *Psychologists* cooperate with ethics investigations and proceedings instituted by the *Society* as well as statutory bodies that are charged by legislation with the responsibility to investigate complaints against psychologists.

C.7.2.   *Psychologists* who reasonably suspect that another *psychologist* is acting in a manner inconsistent with the ethical principles and standards presented in this *Code*:

     (a)   where appropriate, draw the attention of the *psychologist* whose *conduct* is in question directly, or indirectly through a senior psychologist, to the actions that are thought to be in breach of the *Code* and cite the section of the *Code* which may have been breached;

     (b)   encourage people directly affected by such behaviour to report the *conduct* to a relevant regulatory body or the Ethics Committee of the *Society*; or

     (c)   report the *conduct* to a relevant regulatory body or the Ethics Committee of the *Society*.

C.7.3.   *Psychologists* do not lodge, or endorse the lodging, of trivial, vexatious or unsubstantiated ethical complaints against colleagues.

General
Principle C

Appendix

Current Ethical Guidelines
(as at September 2007)

Guidelines for the provision of psychological services for and the conduct of psychological research with Aboriginal and Torres Strait Islander people of Australia – revised May 2003

Guidelines for the use of aversive procedures – July 2000

Guidelines on confidentiality (including when working with minors) – July 1999

Guidelines on co-ordinated disaster response, pro bono, or voluntary psychological services – July 2003

Guidelines regarding financial dealings and fair trading – July 2002

Guidelines for working with people who pose a high risk of harm to others – February 2005

Guidelines on the teaching and use of hypnosis, and related practices – revised December 2005

Guidelines for providing psychological services and products on the internet – March 2004

Guidelines for psychological practice with lesbian, gay and bisexual clients – October 2000

Guidelines for psychological services involving multiple clients and associated parties – December 2006

Guidelines for the provision of psychological services for and the conduct of psychological research with, older adults – September 2005

Guidelines for managing professional boundaries and multiple relationships – August 1999

Guidelines on the prohibition of sexual relationships with clients – revised March 2007

Guidelines for the use of psychological tests – July 1998

Guidelines relating to procedures/assessments that involve psychologist-client physical contact – revised May 2006

Guidelines on record keeping – June 2004

Guidelines relating to recovered memories – revised May 2000

Guidelines on reporting child abuse and neglect, and criminal activity – modified December 2003

Guidelines for psychological practice in rural and remote settings – August 2004

Guidelines relating to suicidal clients – revised November 2004

Guidelines on supervision – July 2003

Guidelines for psychological practice with women – revised May 2003

Index